Jesse Jackson's 1984 Presidential Campaign

Jesse Jackson's 1984 Presidential Campaign

Challenge and Change in American Politics

Edited by
Lucius J. Barker
and
Ronald W. Walters

University of Illinois Press
Urbana and Chicago

© 1989 by the Board of Trustees of the University of Illinois
Manufactured in the United States of America
C 5 4 3 2 1

This book is printed on acid-free paper.

Library of Congress Cataloging-in-Publication Data

Jesse Jackson's 1984 presidential campaign : challenge and change in
   American politics / edited by Lucius J. Barker and Ronald W.
   Walters.
       p. cm.
    ISBN 0-252-01537-1 (cloth : alk. paper). ISBN 0-252-06014-8 (paper : alk.
paper)
     1. Presidents—United States—Election—1984.   2. Jackson, Jesse,
1941–   .   3. United States—Politics and government—1981-   .   4. Afro-
Americans—Politics and government.   I. Barker, Lucius Jefferson,
1928–   .   II. Walters, Ronald W.
E879.J47 1989
324.973′0927—dc 19   88-5097
                                                                 CIP

Contents

Preface

Jesse Jackson's candidacy for the 1984 Democratic presidential nomination remains one of the most dramatic developments in modern American political history. Jackson was the first Black American whose candidacy for a major party nomination had to be taken seriously by all concerned. Moreover, as conceptualized and developed, Jackson's campaign offered broad challenges that portended pervasive and fundamental changes in American politics and society. This volume attempts to capture the essential nature and meaning of the Jackson campaign and to assess its broader impact and implications. Although geared primarily for an audience of professional scholars, the volume should hold great interest for the general reading public as well.

The Jackson candidacy developed into more than just an ordinary campaign for a major-party presidential nomination. His drive for the nomination was just one phase of a much larger mobilization which, in many ways, revives and expands the civil rights movements of the 1950s and 1960s. Indeed, Jackson's drive, which went all the way to the San Francisco nominating convention of the Democratic party, may be more aptly characterized as a "campaign-movement." The central objectives of this campaign-movement encapsulate Jackson's overall goal to bring about the *full* inclusion of those who have been traditionally "locked out" of society and whose participation and influence in the American political system have long been minimized and restricted.

The "locked-out," as Jackson used the term, includes such groups as blacks, Hispanics, women, the poor, senior citizens, and the small family farmer. The apparent strategy of Jackson's campaign-movement was to forge these groups into an effective political organization referred to as a Rainbow Coalition. With this new political constituency, based largely on the politics of the Black community as its driving force, Jackson hoped to develop policy objectives that would allow the Rainbow Coalition to more aggressively seek and realize such public benefits as jobs, peace, and justice, thus creating the proper socioeconomic environment within which all Americans might develop to their full potential.

These are indeed laudable goals. However, they are certainly not the kind that can be achieved in a *single* presidential nomination or election campaign. Rather, this vision presupposed that the Rainbow Coalition would become the governing coalition of a new presidency, an ambitious view which merely adds to the campaign's uniqueness. But whatever its intentions, too many formidable, seemingly intractable barriers made it difficult, if not impossible, for the campaign to successfully achieve its objectives. These barriers include certain aspects of the very nature and organization of the American political system, forces and influences that shape public opinion and political attitudes, and the current sociopolitical status of women and minority groups and the political relationships among them and between them and authoritative institutions.

These factors would impinge upon any effort to broadly redistribute power and influence in American society, but the effort to achieve the Jackson campaign objectives was made further difficult by its complexity. The usual problems with campaign organization, funding, and technique were compounded by a staff largely inexperienced in managing meager resources in the midst of tremendous campaign demands. One of the most significant of these, not made on the other campaigns, was the need for Jackson's staff to run both a campaign and a popular mobilization. By any standard, these were formidable and difficult challenges. But the Jackson campaign apparently saw them as just the kind of problems that had to be confronted and overcome if the locked-out were to be fully included in the sociopolitical order. It was this edge of protest demonstration politics which gave a distinctive force to the 1984 Jackson campaign and which stimulated much of the controversy that ensued.

This volume offers original contributions that examine the Jackson campaign from a number of perspectives. It brings together a group of social scientists, some of whose research and analyses have been richly informed by their active role as participant observers in the Jackson campaign. Obviously, only time and history will tell the extent to which such contributors succumbed to the pitfalls or profited from the benefits of participant observation as a mode of research. Nevertheless, by inviting such contributions, the editors express their confidence that the resulting analyses were enhanced by the insight derived from actual engagement with the issues addressed.

Through the attempt of each writer to assess the meaning and implications of the Jackson campaign, this volume contributes to an historical record from which other scholars and the lay public might profit as they continue to study and evaluate this campaign and other such political phenomena of the black and other minority communities. Hopefully, this work will help place the Jackson campaign within the large context of American politics, thus filling a rather considerable void in the available studies on the political behavior of minorities in American presidential politics. This may improve our understanding of the dynamics responsible for shaping the process of presidential selection by factoring into our analyses a critical variable that is often ignored.

Insofar as possible, the volume is organized chronologically to follow the development of the 1984 campaign. In Part 1 the introductory chapters (1 and 2) discuss the contextual background from which the Jackson candidacy developed. Barker suggests that the campaign was conditioned by such broad factors as the persistent socioeconomic inequalities between blacks and whites, the enhancement of this inequality by the Reagan administration, the disenchantment of blacks with the Democratic party and its symbolic importance in the dynamics of black politics, and the impact of Jackson's personality on his candidacy. Using a "political process" model of social movements developed by Doug McAdam, Walters attempts to mine the sources of the black community's mobilization from which the campaign emerged in 1983 into a campaign-movement.

Part 2 (chapters 3, 4, and 5) sets the campaign against the varieties of American political culture, including the political expectations of the white majority, the cultural style of blacks, and the political development of Hispanics. Thus, Crotty examines the conflict in black-white political orientations as reflected in the attempt of blacks to expand their political boundaries by the adoption of a candidate and issues inconsistent with the views of the white majority and the Democratic party's nomination campaign rules. Smith and McCormick interpret the Jackson campaign style of decision-making within the context of certain features of Afro-American culture, as illustrated by their case study of Jackson's decision to seek the release of Navy Lt. Robert Goodman. Gutierrez discusses the status of the black-Hispanic coalition within the Democratic party, the extent to which the Jackson campaign provided a unique opportunity for the expansion of the coalition, and the factors which limited the achievement of this goal.

Part 3 (chapter 6) is more narrowly concerned with analyses of the Jackson voter. Preston examines the "new black voter," who emerged as early as the mayoral campaigns of Harold Washington of Chicago and Wilson Goode of Philadelphia in 1983, and discovers severe weaknesses in the age and gender composition of the Jackson vote during the primary election process.

Part 4 (chapters 7 and 8) addresses the role of the Jackson campaign in the platform and convention politics of the Democratic party. Moreland-Young discusses the conflict which developed during the platform committee deliberations and the politics behind the resulting profile of issues eventually presented to the convention. Newby demonstrates how the difference between the Jackson delegates and Mondale's black delegates was more than a distinction between political novices (the "naive and unwashed") and political sophisticates.

Part 5 (chapters 9, 10, and 11) focuses on the local and national impact of the campaign. The contribution by Thornton, a comprehensive case study of the Jackson campaign in Maryland, describes the impact of a statewide Rainbow Coalition and its confrontation with the established political machine on a wide range of bargainable political issues. The article by Zipp tests the notion that a national outgrowth of the Jackson campaign's performance in the primary election was a backlash among white voters and finds that there was some evidence of a different kind of backlash phenomenon based on the demographic concentration of blacks in the electorate. Linda Williams and Lorenzo Morris assess the overall Jackson effort in the combined context of the primaries and the 1984 election. The chapter examines how and why Jackson chose to mobilize historically dispossessed groups, his success in this effort, the constraints he faced, and the implications of the 1984 attempt for the future of the Rainbow Coalition.

In a volume of this kind, in which a number of contributors focus on a single attractive subject such as Jesse Jackson, there is bound to be some overlap in information and analysis. Obviously, as editors we sought to eliminate as much unnecessary duplication as possible. However, we also realized early on that overlap in a project of this nature was not only inevitable but, in some instances, desirable, suggesting additional research propositions from possible contrasts and comparisons. Overall, our hope is that this collection of informed perspectives of the Jackson campaign will both spark the kind of creative dialogue that might better inform traditionally established areas of study and research and facilitate the growth and standing of black politics as a newly developing area of intellectual endeavor.

PART I

The Context

Jesse Jackson's Candidacy in Political-Social Perspective: A Contextual Analysis

1

Lucius J. Barker

The pervasive influence of the president in American politics and society insures that the quadrennial contest for that office will command the attention and interest of the nation and the entire world. Even so, however, Jesse Jackson's candidacy for the Democratic presidential nomination stirred much more than the high interest usually shown in those who contest for a major party nomination. His decision to run in the Democratic contest made him the first black presidential candidate in history whose efforts had to be taken seriously by those concerned. Indeed, as we approached the 1984 presidential election, the black vote appeared potentially crucial, perhaps even determinative, in that election. Obviously, then, there was much concern as well as uncertainty over how Jackson's candidacy would affect the black vote and how it might generally affect the presidential election.

This concern and uncertainty sparked an unusual amount of interest in Jackson's candidacy. Jackson certainly held the potential to materially affect the outcome of the Democratic nomination and the presidential election itself. At a minimum his candidacy portended to hold an especial appeal to Black Americans, both symbolically and substantively. Indeed, over time blacks have come to represent one of the largest and most unified voting blocs in the Democratic party and in American politics generally. Jackson held the opportunity to alter and even forge new directions and patterns of influence in our politics and public policy. Thus, the thrust and scope of his candidacy were deep and far-reaching. This essay attempts to explain why this was so.

Specifically, this essay discusses several contextual factors which seem to have given rise and impetus to the Jackson candidacy and examines what these factors reveal about the nature and dynamics of black politics, party politics, and American politics generally. These factors include: (1) the persistence of the many glaring socioeconomic inequities that still exist between blacks and whites; (2) the attitudes and actions of the Reagan administration toward blacks and minorities which renewed the concern and attention of these groups to their condition; (3) increasing concern and disenchantment of blacks with policies and practices of the Democratic party; (4) the importance of symbols and symbolic forms in American politics; (5) the nature and structure of black politics and the black community; and (6) the impact of Jackson's personality, style, and mission on the development of his candidacy.

Socio-Economic Inequities between Blacks and Whites

Despite notable progress of the past twenty or thirty years, many glaring socioeconomic inequities remain between blacks and whites. Some scholars and others suggest that factors other than race—i.e., class—now account mainly for these differences.[1] And indeed in some measure they do. But while we might hope that race will disappear as a major explanatory factor, that time does not appear to be near. Both concrete data and casual observation vividly reveal the continuing socioeconomic gaps that exist between blacks and whites. And these gaps exist along a number of dimensions.

Inequities in employment are especially disturbing. Proportionately, more than twice as many blacks as whites are unemployed, and black unemployment rates show few signs of abating, even when one controls for education. Indeed, only among those with eight years of schooling or less is white unemployment roughly comparable (although some 4 points lower) to that of blacks (see table 1). Among blacks with one year of high school or more, unemployment tends to decrease as the level of educational attainment increases, but the rate remains twice the white unemployment rate from four years of high school through four years or more of college (see table 1). In terms of age the situation is even more disturbing. Almost one half (48.8 percent) of black youths (16–19 years) are unemployed as compared to about 20% of white youths. And among those 20 years or older, blacks are more than twice (17.3%) as likely to be unemployed than whites (7.5 percent).[2]

Additionally, while median family income has risen for both whites and blacks, the most revealing aspect of this rise is that black median family income remains almost approximately one-half as much as that of white families (see fig. 1). Moreover, an overwhelming majority of black families (about 71%) make below $25,000 as compared to less than one-half of white families (about 47 percent) (see table 2). More than half of white families make above $25,000; more than 30 percent make above $35,000. Only about 13 percent of black families make $35,000 or more. Indeed more than one-third of all black families (about 35%) have incomes below $10,000, while only 13% of white families have such meager incomes. This approximates the racial distribution of population below the poverty level (see fig. 2). In absolute numbers there are more poor whites than blacks. However, in terms of population proportions,

Table 1. Unemployment rates by educational attainment, race, and Hispanic origin, 1962–84

Year, race, and Hispanic origin	Total[a]			Elementary less than 5 years[b]			Elementary 5 to 8 years			High school 1 to 3 years			High school 4 years			College 1 to 3 years			College 4 years or more		
	H	B	W	H	B	W	H	B	W	H	B	W	H	B	W	H	B	W	H	B	W
1962		12.1	5.2		12.6	8.0		—	—		15.3	7.2		12.4	4.6		—	—		—	—
1964		10.0	5.0		7.8	9.3		—	—		12.5	6.4		10.0	4.3		—	—		—	—
1965		8.5	4.3		7.8	7.4		—	—		13.5	6.4		8.2	3.7		—	—		—	—
1966		7.0	3.3		5.5	6.1		6.6	4.5		9.7	4.5		7.0	2.8		6.3	2.8		1.9	1.0
1967		7.3	3.2		6.3	4.4		6.9	4.2		10.6	4.6		6.5	2.9		5.8	2.5		1.9	.8
1968		6.5	3.0		4.9	5.4		5.7	4.0		9.8	4.6		6.7	2.7		3.9	2.5		1.6	1.0
1969		5.7	2.8		2.7	3.2		5.0	3.6		7.6	4.4		6.4	2.6		4.8	2.3		1.2	.9
1970		6.7	3.9		5.7	5.3		5.3	4.7		9.5	5.7		7.2	3.6		6.1	3.7		1.4	1.5
1971		8.8	5.5		5.2	7.2		8.4	6.6		11.8	8.1		8.8	5.1		9.0	5.4		3.3	2.2
1972		10.4	5.6		6.6	5.9		9.4	6.5		15.5	9.2		9.6	5.1		9.7	4.5		2.8	2.5
1973	7.2	8.9	4.7	6.6	3.6	4.7	6.7	7.5	6.1	10.2	13.6	8.0	6.0	8.8	4.1	5.7	8.8	3.6	5.0	2.3	2.1
1974	8.1	9.3	4.8	6.5	3.9	5.4	9.0	8.5	5.7	12.2	14.7	8.7	7.1	8.9	4.3	5.0	6.9	3.9	4.8	3.4	1.8
1975	12.8	14.7	8.5	16.5	8.6	15.2	14.2	15.8	10.9	18.4	22.0	14.0	10.5	15.2	8.4	7.9	10.1	6.6	3.6	3.9	2.8
1976	11.4	13.1	7.4	9.4	8.2	8.6	12.3	10.4	10.0	15.5	19.0	12.6	11.6	14.3	7.5	8.2	12.5	5.7	4.4	3.0	2.8
1977[c]	11.4	14.7	7.2	10.9	2.2	8.7	11.9	12.0	9.9	17.2	20.0	12.7	10.0	14.4	6.8	8.2	12.5	5.5	5.0	5.0	3.2
1978	9.5	13.2	5.8	10.5	8.2	7.6	10.0	8.9	8.3	14.0	21.6	10.7	7.4	12.7	5.5	7.3	10.4	4.1	7.3	4.7	2.3
1979	8.7	12.6	5.4	8.2	9.1	7.5	7.0	10.3	7.4	14.6	19.6	10.9	8.2	12.6	5.0	6.5	8.8	3.8	3.6	4.2	2.1
1980	9.2	13.4	6.0	9.2	8.5	8.7	12.8	11.6	9.8	14.3	20.5	11.6	7.1	13.1	5.9	5.9	10.8	4.4	3.7	4.4	1.9
1981	11.2	15.9	7.0	11.1	1.7	10.0	14.4	13.2	11.7	17.0	24.7	13.5	9.7	16.4	7.2	6.3	11.8	4.4	2.8	4.0	2.3
1982	13.4	18.9	8.6	16.2	23.4	15.2	15.4	16.1	13.2	21.8	24.1	17.0	11.4	20.7	9.1	7.1	15.8	5.8	4.9	8.3	2.9
1983	16.3	21.0	9.7	20.6	21.8	15.1	18.6	16.2	16.1	23.9	29.5	19.0	14.4	22.8	10.3	10.9	17.3	7.0	6.8	8.5	3.4
1984	11.6	17.2	7.2	17.8	15.7	12.9	12.9	16.7	12.2	18.4	27.3	15.2	9.6	18.3	7.4	7.2	12.0	5.1	3.5	6.3	2.6

Source: BLS, Handbook of Labor Statistics, 1985, pp. 169–171, Bulletin 2217
Note: Surveys of educational attainment were not conducted in 1963
[a]Data for 1972 forward refer to persons 16 years and over, 18 years and over for period years
[b]Includes persons reporting no school years completed
[c]Prior to 1977, data refer to black and other workers

thousands of dollars

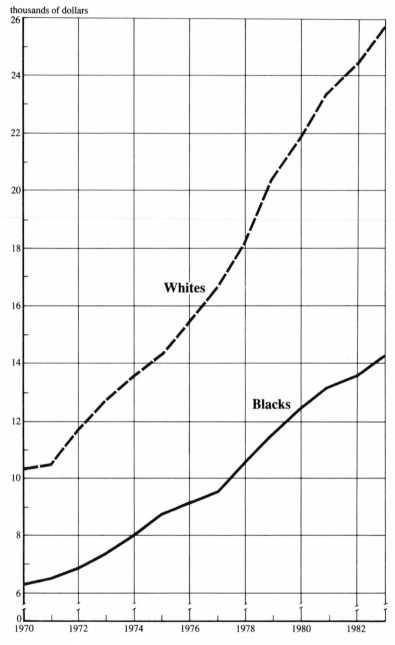

Figure 1. Median family income, 1970–83 by total income and race

Table 2. Family income, 1970–83

Total Money Income		Percent of population by race													
		1970	1971	1972	1973	1974	1975	1976	1977	1978	1979	1980	1981	1982	1983
Under $2,500	White	5.6	5.0	4.2	3.4	3.0	2.7	2.4	2.2	2.0	1.7	1.6	1.7	1.9	1.8
	Black	16.4	15.0	13.8	12.4	10.2	8.7	7.2	7.4	6.6	6.2	5.3	5.2	5.4	5.6
$2,500 to $4,999	White	11.4	11.2	10.2	9.1	7.6	7.5	6.0	5.4	4.5	3.8	3.3	2.8	2.7	2.6
	Black	22.2	23.5	23.0	21.6	20.5	19.7	18.9	16.6	15.8	13.3	11.3	11.5	11.6	10.6
$5,000 to $7,499	White	14.4	13.8	12.5	11.2	10.5	10.0	9.1	8.3	7.2	5.7	5.3	4.7	4.4	4.1
	Black	20.4	19.1	17.6	17.6	16.4	14.9	15.4	15.6	12.2	12.9	13.4	12.2	11.7	11.4
$7,500 to $9,999	White	17.0	15.6	14.0	12.3	11.4	10.5	9.6	8.7	7.7	6.6	6.0	5.6	4.9	4.7
	Black	14.6	14.6	13.8	13.7	13.5	12.8	12.0	12.6	11.6	11.1	10.4	9.4	9.1	9.0
$10,000 to $12,499	White	16.4	16.3	15.1	14.1	13.0	11.3	10.2	9.1	8.4	8.1	7.1	6.7	6.2	5.9
	Black	10.7	10.7	10.3	11.3	10.5	11.8	9.5	10.0	9.5	10.3	9.1	9.5	9.3	8.0
$12,500 to $14,999	White	11.5	11.8	12.0	12.2	11.8	11.3	10.2	9.4	8.2	7.3	6.8	6.4	5.9	5.4
	Black	6.2	6.5	7.2	7.8	9.1	8.8	9.4	8.0	8.2	7.4	7.7	7.0	6.4	6.7
$15,000 to $19,999	White	13.8	15.1	17.5	19.8	18.9	19.5	19.8	18.4	17.3	15.4	14.1	12.6	12.3	11.9
	Black	6.9	7.6	9.4	9.9	10.7	12.3	13.5	12.8	13.9	12.3	12.8	12.4	11.2	11.8
$20,000 to $24,999	White	4.9	5.4	6.7	7.8	10.9	12.2	13.6	14.6	15.2	14.9	14.2	13.0	12.6	11.8
	Black	1.7	1.8	2.7	3.1	6.0	6.0	7.4	8.2	8.9	9.7	10.2	9.6	10.7	9.7
$25,000 to $34,999	White	3.2	3.7	5.2	6.6	8.6	10.1	12.5	15.4	18.4	20.0	20.8	21.1	20.3	20.3
	Black	.7	.8	1.4	2.1	2.4	4.4	5.3	6.8	10.5	11.3	11.8	13.0	14.1	14.0
$35,000 to $49,999	White	1.2	1.4	1.8	2.3	2.9	3.4	4.4	5.7	7.2	10.9	13.6	15.7	16.9	17.9
	Black	.2	.2	.5	.4	.5	.5	1.2	1.7	2.4	4.6	6.3	8.0	7.8	9.2
$50,000 and over	White	.6	.7	.9	1.1	1.3	1.5	2.1	2.8	4.0	5.6	7.2	9.7	11.9	13.6
	Black	.1	.1	.2	.1	.1	.1	.3	.5	.6	.9	1.7	2.1	2.6	4.0
Median income (dollars)	White	10,236	10,672	11,549	12,595	13,408	14,268	15,537	16,740	18,368	20,439	21,904	23,517	24,603	25,757
	Black	6,279	6,440	6,864	7,269	8,006	8,779	9,242	9,563	10,879	11,574	12,674	13,266	13,598	14,506
Mean income (dollars)	White	11,495	11,997	13,106	14,163	15,252	16,111	17,525	18,997	20,860	23,232	24,939	26,934	28,603	29,875
	Black	7,442	7,695	8,346	8,807	9,647	10,401	11,276	11,962	13,409	14,508	15,806	16,696	17,259	18,317

Source: U.S. Deparment of Commerce, Bureau of the Census, Current Population Reports, Series P-60, No. 145, p. 8.

percent of population

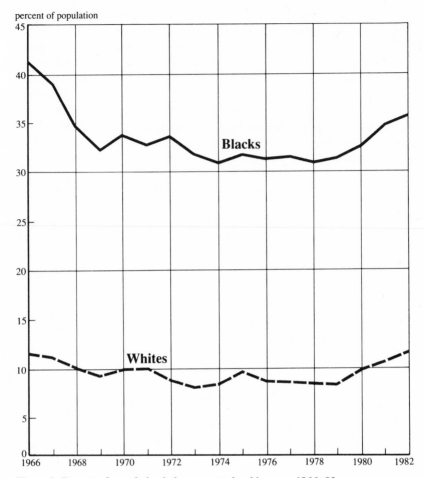

Figure 2. Percent of population below poverty level by race: 1966–83

blacks as a group suffer from poverty far more than whites. After a drop in the 1970s, the poverty rate for blacks began to climb again in the 1980s, a situation exacerbated by the 1982 recession. Thus, in 1983–84 the overall socioeconomic condition that characterized the everyday lives of most blacks and other minorities was not at all promising.[3] Unemployment rates were generally more than twice as high as for whites, with almost one half of black youth unable to find work. By the time of Jackson's campaign more than one third of all blacks (about 35%) were in poverty in contrast to about 13% of the white population.

To be sure, blacks have made some notable progress in a few areas, such as education, where blacks seem to be closing the schooling gap. But generally, in terms of both employment and income, blacks tend not to fare as well as whites even when educational qualifications are comparable or higher, and even these signs of progress were being blunted and frustrated. Attitudes and actions of the Reagan administration have created a climate that restricts rather than increases access to educational opportunities and erodes the nation's commitment to uphold the principles and pursue the policies necessary to achieve equality for all.[4] Thus, as we approached the 1984 presidential elections, black leaders in particular were openly searching for ways to cope with gross socioeconomic inequities that continued to disproportionately plague blacks as a group.

Attitudes and Actions of the Reagan Administration

The attitudes and actions of the Reagan administration toward blacks, women, minorities, the poor, and other disaffected groups were also part of the political-social context out of which the Jackson candidacy developed. It was this factor, perhaps more than anything else, that dramatized the singularly crucial role and influence of the president in the formulation and implementation of public policy. Specifically, the Reagan administration illuminated vividly how the actions of a president can directly affect our everyday lives. Budget cuts and budget allocations indicated clearly that the interests of blacks, women, minorities, and the poor were not among the priority interests of the Reagan administration.[5] This was exemplified in the administration's stance toward certain social benefit programs, legal aid services, and the implementation and enforcement of civil rights laws in general.

Certainly, the effect of these attitudes and actions of the Reagan Administration was reflected in the continuing high rates of unemployment—rates that had persisted and even increased since 1980. And though unemployment under Reagan has affected persons from many groups and classes, its most devastating impact has been on those who have been traditionally relegated to the lower strata of our political-social order—e.g., blacks.

Potentially even more damaging for groups such as blacks were the attitudes and actions of the Reagan administration toward those fundamental civil rights policies which constitute the very foundation upon which our modern civil rights law is based.[6] The new legal regime ushered in by the 1954 *Brown* decision and subsequent civil rights legislation in the 1960s fashioned a national commitment to the attainment of liberty, equality, and justice for all, specifically renewing long-broken constitutional commitments to blacks, women, and minorities.[7] The new legal regime also supported the view that the federal government "should play a major role in vindicating civil rights" and in fulfilling this commitment.[8]

Despite variations in levels of support, until the Reagan administration these premises had provided the operational framework for both Democratic and Republican administrations.[9] Leadership of the president and his chief administrative officials—such as the attorney general—has long been considered appropriate and crucial to the implementation and enforcement of civil rights law. Civil rights interests had viewed the president and federal officials as friends, albeit sometimes not too "friendly," certainly not as adversaries. But by 1983 the Reagan administration had changed all this.

In contrast to the more recent practice of presidential leadership and support, the Reagan administration, most visibly through the assistant attorney general in charge of civil rights (H. Bradford Reynolds), had acted to impede and frustrate the structure and spirit of legal change envisioned by *Brown* and subsequent civil rights legislation. Especially damaging were actions by the Reagan administration that struck at the very heart of civil rights law. For example, consider the administration's attempt in 1982 to have the Internal Revenue Service terminate its long-standing policy that denies tax-exempt status to schools that enforce a policy of racial segregation and discrimination. The basic argument was that Congress had not authorized such policy and that only Congress, and not the IRS, possessed such authority. But the argument was flatly rejected by the Supreme Court in *Bob Jones University v. United States*. Chief Justice Warren Burger, who spoke for seven of the eight-member majority, focused particularly on the policy implications of the tax-exemption benefit. Burger stated unequivocally that racial discrimination policies and practices are contrary to "fundamental national policy" and concluded that when the IRS withholds exemption benefits from those whose policies and practices are contrary to this "fundamental national policy" its actions are consistent with that policy goal.[10]

Consider another 1982 effort of the Reagan administration to erode the national commitment established in *Brown* and its progeny. For the first time since busing was established as a desegregation remedy in the 1971 *Swann* case, the administration attempted to push its strong anti-busing stance. The Department of Justice (DOJ) petitioned lower federal courts to halt busing plans already in operation in Nashville, Tennessee, and East Baton Rouge Parish, Louisiana.[11] However, not only did the lower courts deny such petitions, but the Supreme Court itself rebuffed the DOJ's attempt to use the Nashville case as the vehicle through which to reexamine the overall *Swann* ruling.[12]

In addition, consider administration efforts to scuttle the Voting Rights Act when the Congress debated extension of that law in 1982.[13] This administration posture in regard to the Voting Rights Act was especially disturbing since it is through the electoral process that groups—such as blacks—ordinarily have expected to protect their interests.

Consider still further the open, visible, and unprecedented attempts by the Reagan administration to reshape and remold the Civil Rights Commission, long viewed since its establishment in 1957 as the primary symbol of civil rights presence in the country.[14] Initially the president sought to remove, without cause, three "unfriendly" commissioners and replace them with three "friendly" ones. And though the president did not have his way altogether, he largely succeeded in restructuring the commission to reflect the policies of his administration.

This generally unsympathetic and insensitive posture of the Reagan administration toward civil rights was perhaps most vividly exemplified in a news conference in which the president himself equivocated and vacillated in his answer to a query concerning an allegation that Martin Luther King was a "Communist or Communist sympathizer."[15] His response was anything but reassuring and could well have left doubts as to whether King had Communist affiliations. And the president's subsequent attempt to clarify his response added even more confusion. His "explanatory" phone call to Mrs. King tended to exacerbate the matter and highlight once again the president's own insensitivity (and perhaps lack of knowledge) about the goals and aspirations of the civil rights movement. It is rather ironic that this incident obscured the determinative role and significance of the president's eventual support for the King holiday legislation.[16] It also minimized whatever political benefits might have accrued to Reagan for this support, without which the King holiday legislation would almost certainly not have passed.

When viewed in broad perspective, President Reagan and his policies have proven perhaps the most effective stimuli and catalysts that the "cause" has had since the civil rights movement. Simultaneously, however, for the very first time since the 1954 *Brown* breakthrough, this posture of the Reagan administration has cast the federal government as a hostile adversary rather than a compliant sympathizer or active supporter. Perhaps most disturbing of all, by 1983 blacks and civil rights interests saw increasing signs of congruence between Reagan's initiatives and seemingly indifferent, uncaring, or even hostile currents of leadership and public attitudes with respect to the interests of blacks and minorities.[17] These developments served as timely warnings of the awesome influence and role of the president in American politics and undoubtedly provided both substantive and symbolic incentives for those considering the idea of a black presidential candidacy.

Increasing Disenchantment with the Democratic Party

Another spur to a black presidential candidacy was the increasing disenchantment of blacks with policies and practices of the Democratic party. While Republicans were openly hostile and had all but written off black interests, Democrats too were becoming increasingly more inattentive and uncaring of their interests and concerns. "There is a growing sense today," wrote Rep-

Table 3. Black and white voting patterns, 1952–84

Year	Race	% Democratic	% Republican	% Other
1952	Black	80	20	—
	White	40	60	—
1956	Black	64	36	—
	White	39	61	—
1960	Black	71	29	—
	White	48	52	—
1964	Black	100[a]	0	—
	White	65	35	—
1968	Black	97	3	—
	White	36	52	12
1972	Black	87	13	—
	White	30	70	—
1976	Black	94	5	—
	White	50	48	—
1980	Black	93	6	1[b]
	White	33	57	1 (9[b])
1984	Black	84	9	2
	White	36	63	1

Source: Survey Research Center, University of Michigan (Presidential Elections from 1952–1976).
[a]The 100% voting of blacks for the Democratic party probably results from the small size of sample. Certainly a few blacks voted for Goldwater as probably a very few voted for Wallace in 1968. Furthermore, the reported 100% Democratic support is consistent with a bias to report having supported the winner—a well-known artifact in re-call data.
[b]Anderson Vote.

resentative John Conyers (D. Mich.) in July 1983, "that the Tweedle Dee and Tweedle Dum politics practiced by both Democrats and Republicans has ceased to furnish the answers to the real problems of jobs, justice, and peace that afflicts so many citizens." Conyers explained well the increasing strength behind the "unannounced and unfunded" presidential campaign of Jesse Jackson: "The momentum that is building behind the idea [of a black presidential candidacy] is no freak occurrence or accident. There are good reasons for this remarkable achievement that have a history behind them—a growing voter registration drive among minority citizens, black and Hispanic; the emergence of an alternative political platform within the Democratic party and a growing alienation with mainstream politics, whether practiced by Democrats or Republicans, that of late has become politicized and credible." [18] In general, then, there was indeed growing concern among black leaders with respect to attitudes and actions of both major parties: Republicans had written blacks off, and Democrats were taking them for granted. Blacks were especially concerned that Democrats were not according them the benefits and respect which their loyalty and strong support would seem to warrant. Over the years blacks have been one of the largest and most loyal constituent groups in the party and have consistently given overwhelming support to Democratic candidates (see table 3).

More specifically, black leaders were especially disturbed with the position and actions taken by party leaders and white Democratic voters generally in the 1983 Chicago mayoral campaign of Harold Washington. For one thing, both former Vice President Walter Mondale and Senator Edward Kennedy—the two most prominent national Democratic party leaders—chose to become involved in Chicago politics and to endorse, respectively, Washington's white opponents in the Democratic primary, Jane Byrne and Richard M. Daley. And even though national party leaders united to support Washington in the general election, Chicago white Democrats did not similarly respond and instead backed the Republican nominee in great numbers. In the end, however, Harold Washington prevailed in a narrow victory and became the first black mayor of Chicago. But the drama and excitement of the Chicago election had become a national story, and blacks across the nation expressed concern and disgust with the position and actions taken by party leaders and voters in the primary and general election. The 1983 Chicago mayoral election thus came to symbolize all too well the lack of respect and support shown by white party leaders and voters toward black candidates and black interests.

The Chicago experience had national reverberations. Quite clearly it lent impetus to meetings among black leaders to chart a national political strategy for the up-coming 1984 elections and more generally, as Jesse Jackson put it, to renegotiate the fundamental relationship between blacks and the Democratic party. Jackson was especially determined that "no longer can blacks allow Democrats to take them and their votes for granted." In commenting on the matter in April 1983, Jackson said that "power and responsibility must be shared fully, or the delicate balance of the traditional Democratic coalition will be destroyed." "This is clear to most blacks," said Jackson, "but some Democrats seem not to have gotten the message." Jackson thus thought it would be a good idea for a black to run for the Democratic nomination since it would "force Democrats now (and Republicans later) to have a greater appreciation of the black vote and its potential positive contribution to party politics and the nation." "The idea of running a black for president is a hot topic among black leaders and is exciting the black masses across the country," said Jackson, "because so many of them are unhappy with current arrangements, . . . with white Democrats telling blacks what is best for them, while reminding blacks that they have nowhere to go outside the Democratic party." Then Jackson drove the point home and summarized his views on why there should be a black presidential candidate: "Why run? Blacks have their backs against the wall. They are increasingly distressed by the erosion of past gains and the rapidly deteriorating conditions within black and poor communities. As black leaders have attempted to remedy these problems through the Democratic party—of which black voters have been the most loyal and disciplined followers—too often have they been ignored and treated with disrespect. Mounting a serious presidential candidacy is one way of insisting that black leaders play significant roles and help to shape policy and programs for the party." [19] Another factor in the political-social context which stimulated a black presidential candidacy was simply that there was not an attractive candidate among those who had decided to run for the Democratic nomination. To be sure, Mondale's civil rights record and his long identification with liberal causes made it quite likely that he would receive a large vote from women, blacks, and minority groups. However, despite this acceptable, even strong, record, Mondale did not project well; he did not exude the enthusiasm, appeal, and charisma that would attract people to him and stir them to work for his candidacy. This situation obviously led blacks and others to look for "something more," for "someone else." By late June 1983 one NAACP official aptly described the Democratic field of candidates up to that time. "The Democrats," he said, "have fielded six of the most undramatic, noncharismatic white men that they could find to run for President of the United States." "If there had been a Kennedy-type running," he concluded, "Jesse [Jackson] would not be getting that amount of publicity." [20]

And perhaps most important, Jackson was able to attract this publicity and keep the idea alive despite some rather discouraging signals. For example, by late spring and early summer 1983 it was becoming increasingly clear that a number of prominent black leaders were either opposed or cool to the idea of a black presidential candidacy and, more concretely, to a possible Jackson candidacy. Moreover, by this time some of these leaders had decided—primarily as a matter of pragmatic politics—to support Mondale as the candidate most sympathetic to minority interests and most able to defeat President Reagan. There was the additional fear that a black presidential candidacy could stir increased white "racial" voting, possibly leading to the defeat of other black candidates at state and local levels. But despite these and other obstacles, there was just no stopping a black presidential candidacy. And one of the chief reasons was simply that there was no Democratic candidate who was attractive and charismatic and whose issue positions were sufficiently congruent with those to whom a black presidential candidacy would appeal. Thus Jackson adroitly sought to fill the perceived void in the Democratic field of candidates.

The Symbolic Side of American Politics

To appreciate more fully the context out of which Jackson's candidacy developed, we must examine more closely the importance of symbolism in

American politics. As Murray Edelman brilliantly documents, there is indeed a close nexus between symbolic politics and the actual allocation of substantive resources and benefits.[21] Symbols may be fought over without much effect on who gets what substantive benefits, and symbolic politics may sometimes be a substitute for debate over "real" issues. Often, however, politics involves both symbols and substance, and it may be seriously misleading to try to separate them.[22]

Certainly this vital linkage could not have escaped those who pondered the idea of a black presidential candidacy. There was widespread agreement among black leaders that effective yet dramatic strategies were needed to demonstrate anew the deep and widespread concern that black Americans still felt about the serious problems they faced. As a result, black leaders (and others) saw a dire need to reaffirm and refuel their own unity and their determination to fulfill the goals and objectives of Martin Luther King and the civil rights movement.[23] They saw the continued need for a focused, persistent prodding of the nation in order to put into practice the constitutional-legal principles emanating from that movement.

How best to express and act on these concerns was the basic problem facing black leaders. Viewed in this context, a black presidential candidacy ranked high among the strategy options that could dramatically symbolize and highlight these concerns. It did not rank so high, however—indeed it provoked disagreement among black leaders—as a strategy appropriate to deal with the very concrete problems that faced blacks at this time. Nonetheless, it was the powerful symbolism of a black presidential candidacy which did much to keep the idea alive, notwithstanding practical arguments used against it. And in the end, it was this potent symbolism, plus the inextricable linkage between symbols and substance, which made it difficult to impede the momentum of a black presidential candidacy.

Symbols do much to shape peoples' minds, guide their behavior, and structure the political environment. People love, hate, fight, and even die for symbols. Even so, the symbolic side of politics remains one of the most underestimated, or at least underanalyzed, areas of our political life. Our political system is replete with symbols and symbolic forms. These include institutions, structures, myths, beliefs, values, rituals, and language that hold the political-social order together. For example, as Edelman puts it, the "themes a society emphasizes and reemphasizes about its government may not accurately describe its politics, but they do at least tell us what men want to believe about themselves and their state." [24] To be sure, we like to emphasize that every person is treated equally under the law and that the law itself reflects the will of the people, the ends of justice, and equity for all regardless of race, sex, etc. Such beliefs not only serve as a description of common goals and aspirations but also help to promote ties among diverse groups and to maintain social order.

We should not forget that what people want to believe about their country and, critically, about themselves is very important to the ways in which they define themselves and their country.

These themes and forms serve and promote symbolic needs, but at the same time they serve and promote material interests. Candidates for political office function in a similar fashion. They may offer different cues to the electorate, evoke different feelings and emotions, invoke or reflect different symbols and symbolic forms, and represent different interests or some of the same interests differently. For example, Mondale's candidacy clearly represented established interests and reassured those interests that prevailing patterns of influence in the Democratic party would continue. On the other hand, it was equally clear that a black presidential candidacy—i.e., Jackson's—would reflect the concerns of potential and aspiring groups and thus signal established interests in the party and the country generally that their positions of influence would be challenged. In short, "a black presidential bid—even in the primaries—calls for a level and kind of political mobilization among black Americans that has not heretofore been experienced in American politics. Hence, it does create a measure of uncertainty for presidential politics and black politics generally which many established leaders—black and white—are wont to avoid." [25]

Thus, as it developed, the strategy of a black presidential candidacy threatened some very fundamental aspects of our basic social and belief structure (symbols, mechanism, processes, myths, etc.) which undergird much of our politics and public policies. It would certainly focus attention on the structures and processes by which influence and benefits are distributed. A serious black presidential candidacy would concretely challenge all Americans to consider "what they fear, what they regard as possible, and even who they are." [26] It is not that leaders and elites mold or shape myths to serve their ends, although they might sometimes attempt to do so. Rather, in their "social role taking" leaders affect and are affected by popular myths and expectations.

At base then, a black presidential candidacy could force us to revitalize, reshape, or at least rethink certain myths and belief structures which in turn influence social role taking. Such a candidacy held the capacity to disrupt the rather general discussion (and perhaps even general agreement) among Democratic candidates on fundamental issues. A potential Jackson candidacy, combining a high measure of symbolic excitement with substance, might well arouse, not dull, the critical faculties of his listeners. It would tend to condense and articulate much of what is left unspoken and unexamined in American political life. As such, it portended to be an uncomfortable exercise for many of us—an excercise which many, both black and white, wanted to avoid.

Jackson's speech formally announcing his candidacy and his objectives vividly illustrates many of these observations. [27] "I seek the presidency," he said, "to serve notice at a level where I can help restore a moral tone, a redemptive spirit, and a sensitivity to the poor and the disposessed of the nation." He said he wanted to offer the nation "a clear choice," not the vague and centrist politics so strongly supported by the cherished myth and belief that the "middle way is the best way." He talked about the bitter and divisive racism that still remains and how this must be dealt with directly by the Democratic party and its candidates. This, of course, runs afoul of myths and beliefs that have long supported racism and sexism and whose legacies still serve important interests in the Democratic party. It also runs afoul of attempts to accommodate diverse interests within the party by avoiding controversial issues. He talked about promoting self respect and dignity for those whom he would bring into his Rainbow Coalition and said that these things were "non-negotiable." This assertion also runs contrary to the strong belief in compromise and moderation that undergirds American politics.

Jackson's candidacy was considerably more "symbolic" than Mondale's. But this was no more than an accurate reflection of the current political-social status of blacks as compared to whites. Blacks receive more of the "symbols" than substance of politics, while whites have both in relative abundance. The very purpose of Jackson's campaign was to change this situation. Through his charisma and oratorical skills, Jackson stood to provide the sort of symbolic focus and appeal that could stir the interest and attention of those who have been outside the political process or who have remained relatively politically inactive. Getting attention in political campaigns is indispensable. A Jackson candidacy could provide a symbolic focus that would activate people who then would proceed to vote *their* substantive interests. Symbols thus may provide the way to reach people who are typically not motivated. In short, it was this linkage of symbols to substance, coupled with the fact that blacks constitute more than one-fifth of the total Democratic vote in presidential elections, that gave an importance and potency to Jackson's candidacy which it would not otherwise have had.

Ironically, one might conclude that it is the gross disparities and incongruities between the symbolic side of politics (rituals, myths, goals) and the actual allocation of substantive benefits and rewards that perhaps did the most to spur Jackson's candidacy. His candidacy posed threats and challenges at several levels and to many people, black and white. In particular it posed a threat to those who have prospered in, have become accustomed to, or otherwise accommodated themselves to the practice of "practical" politics within prevailing conceptions and perceptions of our symbolic value structure. Jackson's candidacy threatened all of this, but it was also spurred by it.

Nature of Black Politics and the Black Community

The evolution of Jackson's candidacy may also tell us something about the nature and structure of black politics and the black community. Politics in the "black nation," as Matthew Holden calls it,[28] was from the beginning shaped mainly by questions of relations with the external world of white America. The internal politics, structure, and functions of black institutions and groups similarly reflect these relationships with white America in terms of how best to maintain and promote the interests of the black community. This preoccupation with external relations has been necessitated, of course, by the very strict legal and practical separation imposed upon blacks by the white majority. The formation and functions of early black organized interest groups, such as the NAACP and the Urban League, reflected this concern and in many ways still does.

Of course, a major dividing line was the 1954 *Brown* decision and subsequent policy breakthroughs which legally mandated a new set of relationships between blacks and whites. It is instructive to note that even the forging of this new relationship—consummated through the civil rights movement—was at times beset by internal disputes among blacks over strategies. For example, the success of the historic 1963 March on Washington depended largely on whether unity could be achieved among various civil rights groups. However, achieving such unity and cooperation was not easy. A situation which occurred just prior to the march makes the point.

Ordinarily, . . . one would have expected the June 13, 1963, murder of Medgar Evers, Field Director of the Mississippi NAACP, to serve as a rallying point among the various groups. But such was not the case. Groups suspected each other of trying to "use" an emotional situation to demonstrate and promote particular causes. Frictions inevitably developed. Perhaps because of this and other "irritating incidents" largely caused by "local eager beavers," Roy Wilkins, Executive Secretary of the NAACP, openly criticized CORE, SNCC, and SCLC for taking "the publicity while the NAACP provides the manpower and pays the bill." "The only organization that can handle a long sustained fight," said Wilkins, "is the NAACP. We are not here today, gone tomorrow." However, a few days later Wilkins called for cooperation among the various groups, noting that such collaboration was especially important at the "present time" because of civil rights legislation pending in Congress. "Intelligent work in the Capitol lobbies," said Wilkins "could be more important than mass marches on Washington or sit-downs or sit-ins in the halls of Congress." SNCC and CORE leaders disclaimed any divisions and did not, at the time at least, join the argument, but Martin Luther King did. King said:

We all acknowledge that the NAACP is the oldest, the best established, it has done a marvelous job for many years and has worked rigorously, But we feel we also have a role to play in supplementing what the NAACP has done. Unity is necessary. Uniformity is not. The highway that leads to the city of freedom is not a one-lane highway. New organizations such as SCLC are not substitutes for the NAACP, but they can be wonderful supplements.

King's remarks seemingly sounded a note upon which there could be unity and cooperation among the various groups. The commonality of their goal overcame, for the time being at least, group differences in strategy and tactics and led to cooperative ventures.[29]

In many ways the controversy over a black presidential candidacy strategy reflects well the situation just described. The positions of Wilkins in 1963 and Benjamin Hooks in 1983 were strikingly similar. Hooks put the NAACP on record as opposing the black presidential strategy, saying it could interfere with the main goal of defeating an incumbent president (Reagan) whom Hooks thought had been detrimental to civil rights progress.[30] The Urban League also opposed the idea.[31] In short, both the NAACP and the Urban League tended to shun these more direct action and confrontational methods—i.e., the 1963 march and black presidential strategy—in dealing with whites. In general, both organizations prefer negotiations and persuasion rather than direct action and confrontation. (Under John Jacob, however, there is some indication that the Urban League is taking a more aggressive posture.[32])

The same might be said of many established political and civic leaders who, just as the NAACP, have invested much time and effort in forging relationships and access which could serve to gain benefits for their constituents. A black presidential candidacy not only threatened these relationships and access points but, because of its minimal chances of success, might require development of alternative relationships and access. Conversely, those who supported the idea, even including a few established Black leaders, did not seem to be as concerned about upsetting whatever relationships and access they had, which, of course, could have already been minimal. They appeared more daring, more willing to take risks to achieve their objectives. Jackson himself, of course, was a leader of this group. But he was not part of the black political elite and, initially at least, did not seem too concerned about their lack of support. Rather, he seemed willing and content to work the "grass roots" and to rely heavily on black churches.

Put differently, a potential Jackson candidacy posed risks not only for his opponents but for his supporters as well. Take, for example, his goals of political mobilization—recruitment and registration of new voters, increasing voter turnout, and the arousal of political interest generally. Such activity, of course, is of interest to most politicians, but it is of especial interest to black politicians. Whether they say so publicly or not, they realize that race still looms as an important variable in voting. Black candidates, whether running for office in black-majority or white-majority contexts, continue to need almost united black support to offset the relatively small white support for black candidates, regardless of their qualifications.[33]

However, as Schattschneider reminded us long ago, not all interests and groups stand to benefit equally from voter registration and political mobilization campaigns.[34] The infusion and activation of new and old voters could bring new and potential candidates for public office, and while black voters tend to vote for black candidates, it is by no means clear or certain that new or re-activated black voters will vote for a black incumbent over a black challenger. Given the civic virtues surrounding such activity, established politicians of any color can ill-afford to oppose, at least openly, attempts to increase political participation. But depending on particular contexts, they well might attempt to manage or control this kind of activity. This is only natural and may very well be consistent with the interests of the office-holder and the particular groups he represents.

However, the Jackson campaign as projected, given its very explicit objectives, meant at least that black political leaders would have to deal with more politically active black constituents, even if this activity is limited only to voting. Undoubtedly, this infusion of new black voters and aroused black political interest could affect the nature and structure of black politics and black political leadership; the extent of the effect would depend on the success of the potential Jackson challenge.

The potential Jackson candidacy related to black politics and the black leadership structure in other ways. Despite appearances of heterogeneity, the black community remains highly homogenous. There is a very strong congruence among blacks, in contrast to whites, in their positions on public policy matters. Public opinion data support this observation, leading scholars to conclude that

> blacks are becoming more liberal than the population at large, not only on issues like school integration, but also on foreign policy and the size of the government. In fact, in each of five issue areas (economic welfare, size of government, black welfare, school integration, and foreign policy) blacks have enlarged their distance from the general population between the 1950's and the 1970's. Indeed, "no other group in American society is as distinctively liberal as American blacks."
>
> The degree of liberal attitude consistency (for blacks) across such a diverse set of issues is greater than for any other group." The implication of this may be that the increased salience of race on the political agenda has provided an organizing principle for American blacks, guiding choices not only on racial issues, but on other issues as well. The end product has been a group of people with very tightly organized, highly consistent issue beliefs.[35]

In short, there is an unusually strong measure of cohesion and unity among blacks on policy issues; this undercuts the view of those who suggest that the growing diversity among blacks renders attempts to define common goals and objectives a useless endeavor. This simply cannot be supported by the data. And this evidence was given life by the enthusiastic response Jackson received during "trial heats" of his 1983 pre-campaign. Among blacks and many others, Jackson found widespread support for his views on eliminating poverty and unemployment and achieving decent housing, a quality integrated public school system, a more inclusive and positive foreign policy in the

Middle East and toward the Third World, and for his general position that the national government must take the lead in forging and implementing these policy changes.

Another factor in the black community that influenced the political-social context that gave rise to Jesse Jackson's candidacy was the uncertain status and declining influence of major civil rights organizations, which precluded them from playing the kind of role that groups in American politics must perform if they are to effectively promote and safeguard their interests. Indeed, by 1983 black civil rights organizations, in the main, had come upon hard times. They operated in an environment in which the matter of defining goals, objectives, and strategies—in short, their very reason for being—was much more difficult than in earlier days of the civil rights movement. Previously, the barriers to be overcome were much more obvious, visible, and repulsive. But by 1983 these earlier barriers had fallen, and such progress had been widely reported and extolled by the media and other sources as having met major black policy objectives.

One result of this was to make it more difficult for civil rights organizations to continue to capture the attention, monies, and other resources needed to function effectively. Further, this record of visible accomplishments made it easier for civil rights opponents to frustrate and dilute further progress by pointing to these visible symbols of accomplishment. As a result, civil rights leaders and their organizations had to define and redefine goals and objectives in a context in which the nature of the problems had indeed become more complex. Coupled with this, civil rights organizations are still confronted with a political system that is purposefully structured so that those who oppose particular changes or policies hold distinct structural advantages by which to slow, stop, or otherwise frustrate such policies. Problems in the 1970s and 1980s, especially during the Reagan administration, over implementation of earlier civil rights laws such as the Voting Rights Act provide good illustrations.

Overall, then, the nature of the situation facing civil rights leaders in 1983 required levels of resources of a somewhat different kind and nature than those needed at earlier stages of the civil rights movement. In contrast to the 1960s, to operate effectively in the 1980s these organizations need policy analysts, public opinion experts, experienced lobbyists, and informational specialists and managers. Adding such personnel requires continuing high levels of financial support. Most important of all, organizations need high levels of support and visibility among the groups they purport to represent. In recent years, civil rights organizations clearly have not enjoyed the status or influence they held in earlier years. Hence they are correspondingly hampered in their efforts to deal with problems facing their memberships.

By 1983 the nature of black politics had also been influenced by the dramatic increases in the number of black elected officials.[36] In that year there were more than 5,600 such officials, by 1985, some 6,000 (see table 4). The infusion of this relatively new cadre of elected officials into black politics both reflected recent increases in black voter registration and turnout and accelerated black political development in those states and areas with sizeable black populations. These officials add a relatively new dimension to black politics and the black community, in which every black elected official is perceived as part of the black leadership structure.

Overall, however, the benefits expected to flow to the black community by the dramatic increase in the number of black elected officials have not been apparent. Blacks still hold *less than 1.5%* of all elective offices (see table 5). Even when blacks make dramatic gains at local levels—e.g., by election of big city mayors—meaningful progress toward achieving minority policy objectives has not been forthcoming. Interdependence of various levels of government, the structure and operation of local processes, and the presence of other factors constrain the influence of local officials, including black mayors, to bring about major changes needed to meet black policy objectives. To be sure, research findings show that the presence of black mayors has had some small but discernable impact on black municipal employment levels. Essentially, black mayors have made a difference in affirmative action hiring in urban bureaucracies. But, as one commentator points out, "after decades of black political activity and protest, legislative enactments, and judicial rulings, it is significant that an overwhelming majority of . . . cities (in the study) are nowhere near providing their black citizens with an equal share of available resources." Moreover, black penetration of municipal jobs tends to occur in professional (e.g., nurses, dieticians) rather than administrative positions (e.g., department heads, division and bureau chiefs) which "are considerably more likely to influence major policy choices than professionals." In short, "the presence of a black mayor . . . has not generated significant employment rewards for black constituents."[37] This obviously has led to frustration and restiveness among blacks and minorities, especially in view of the strong encouragement blacks received from their leaders and others to turn from "protests to politics." In the end this "politics of frustration" leads to the suggestion that something more needs to be done. And it was this "something more" thinking that spawned Jesse Jackson's candidacy.

Overall, the approaching 1984 election posed difficult challenges to black politics and black leadership generally. Problems facing black Americans were indeed enormous. Earlier progress toward achieving policy goals and objectives seemed to have been stalemated and was even retrogressing. Civil rights groups were experiencing trouble. The black church, though still an influential force in the black community, was not equipped by function, role, or resources to deal with the manifold problems that still plague the everyday lot of blacks and minorities. In addition, black elected officials, though a highly visible presence in black politics, were finding that the limitations and constraints of

Table 4. Change in number of black elected officials by category of office, 1970–85

Year	Total BEOs N	% Change	Federal N	% Change	State N	% Change	Substate regional N	% Change	County N	% Change	Municipal N	% Change	Judicial/law enforcement N	% Change	Education N	% Change
1970	1,469	—	10	—	169	—	—	—	92	—	623	—	213	—	362	—
1971	1,860	26.6	14	40.0	202	19.5	—	—	120	30.4	785	26.0	274	28.6	465	28.5
1972	2,264	21.7	14	0.0	210	4.0	—	—	176	46.7	932	18.7	263	−4.0	669	43.9
1973	2,621	15.8	16	14.3	240	14.3	—	—	211	19.9	1,053	13.0	334	27.0	767	14.6
1974	2,991	14.1	17	6.3	239	−0.4	—	—	242	14.7	1,360	29.2	340	1.8	793	3.4
1975	3,503	17.1	18	5.9	281	17.6	—	—	305	26.0	1,573	15.7	387	13.8	939	18.4
1976	3,979	13.6	18	0.0	281	0.0	30	—	355	16.4	1,889	20.1	412	6.5	994	5.9
1977	4,311	8.3	17	−5.6	299	6.4	33	10.0	381	7.3	2,083	10.3	447	8.5	1,051	5.7
1978	4,503	4.5	17	0.0	299	0.0	26	−21.2	410	7.6	2,159	3.6	454	1.6	1,138	8.3
1979	4,607	2.3	17	0.0	313	4.7	25	−3.8	398	−2.9	2,224	3.0	486	7.0	1,144	0.5
1980	4,912	6.6	17	0.0	323	3.2	25	0.0	451	13.3	2,356	5.9	526	8.2	1,214	6.1
1981	5,038	2.6	18	5.9	341	5.6	30	20.0	449	−0.4	2,384	1.2	549	4.4	1,267	4.4
1982	5,160	2.4	18	0.0	336	−1.5	35	16.7	465	3.6	2,477	3.9	563	2.6	1,266	−0.1
1983	5,606	8.6	21	16.7	379	12.8	29	−17.1	496	6.7	2,697	10.0	607	7.8	1,377	8.8
1984[a]	5,700	1.7	21	0.0	389	2.6	30	3.4	518	4.4	2,735	1.4	636	4.8	1,371	−0.4
1985	6,056	6.2	20	−4.8	396	1.8	32	6.7	611	18.0	2,898	6.0	661	4.0	1,438	4.9

Source: Joint Center for Political Studies, *Black Elected Officials: A National Roster*, 1985, p. 9.

[a] The 1984 figures reflect blacks who took office during the seven-month period between July 1, 1983, and January 30, 1984.

Table 5. Black elected officials as a percentage of all elected officials, by state, January 1985

State	Blacks as a percent of voting-age population	Elected Officials		
		Total	Black	% Black
Alabama	23.0	4,160	375	9.0
Alaska	3.0	1,365	3	0.2
Arizona	3.0	2,412	11	0.5
Arkansas	14.0	10,692	317	3.0
California	7.5	18,135	296	1.6
Colorado	3.4	7,801	15	0.2
Connecticut	6.2	7,920	68	0.9
Delaware	14.7	999	22	2.2
District of Columbia	66.6	370	252	68.1
Florida	10.8	4,902	167	3.4
Georgia	25.0	6,672	340	5.1
Hawaii	2.1	176	1	0.6
Idaho	*	4,183	0	0.0
Illinois	13.6	40,422	357	0.9
Indiana	7.1	11,029	68	0.6
Iowa	1.2	17,730	9	0.05
Kansas	4.9	17,070	29	0.2
Kentucky	6.7	7,013	55	0.8
Louisiana	26.6	4,720	475	10.1
Maine	*	5,885	1	0.02
Maryland	22.5	2,172	97	4.5
Massachusetts	3.7	11,605	32	0.3
Michigan	12.3	19,403	300	1.6
Minnesota	1.2	19,153	9	0.05
Mississippi	31.3	5,278	444	8.4
Missouri	9.6	17,802	156	0.9
Montana	*	4,335	0	0.0
Nebraska	2.7	15,747	4	0.03
Nevada	5.5	1,145	9	0.8
New Hampshire	*	5,991	0	0.0
New Jersey	11.7	9,431	200	2.1
New Mexico	1.7	2,052	5	0.2
New York	13.1	24,112	246	1.0
North Carolina	20.7	5,308	291	5.5
North Dakota	*	18,045	0	0.0
Ohio	9.6	19,913	196	1.0
Oklahoma	6.1	9,018	122	1.4
Oregon	1.2	7,880	11	0.1
Pennsylvania	8.2	28,928	138	0.5

Table 5. (*Continued*)

State	Blacks as a percent of voting-age population	Elected Officials		
		Total	Black	% Black
Rhode Island	2.4	1,107	8	0.7
South Carolina	27.7	3,233	310	9.6
South Dakota	*	9,191	0	0.0
Tennessee	14.4	7,256	138	2.0
Texas	11.0	24,757	260	1.1
Utah	*	2,363	1	0.04
Vermont	*	7,323	1	0.01
Virginia	17.9	3,053	116	3.8
Washington	2.5	7,467	16	0.2
West Virginia	3.0	2,899	20	0.7
Wisconsin	3.4	18,973	22	0.1
Wyoming	0.5	2,174	3	0.1
Total	10.8	490,770	6,016	1.2

*Less than 0.5 percent.

Note: The 40 BEOs in the Virgin Islands are not included in this table, because the Virgin Islands are not included in the 1977 Census of Governments.

Source: Joint Center for Political Studies, *Black Elected Officials: A National Roster*, 1985, pp. 10–11.

office make it very difficult to achieve expected goals and objectives. Black voters and leaders agreed that something must be done to deal with problems and to stem retrogressive mood, but they disagreed over what that something else should be and how it should be done.

Let us put the matter in sharper perspective. Survey data suggest a remarkable degree of consensus and unity in the black community with respect to policy interests and goals. This consensus and unity is held together by a strong attitudinal base, and black leaders, civil rights organizations, and others are, in their various ways, seeking to achieve these objectives. But unlike the unity revealed by survey data, in 1983 there was no unifying structure or focal point to rally these forces together. Since Martin Luther King, there has been no such force in the black community. Some, of course, suggest that the many points of black leadership and access that have developed since King's day now obviate the need for such a unifying force. A sign of maturing political development, they suggest, is that the black community no longer speaks with one voice but speaks with many voices from leaders who speak from various positions. Thus, a black presidential candidate could well rally the black leadership into a plan of action that would speak with a unity similar to that with which the black community continues to speak.

In addition, the idea of a black presidential candidacy touched at the heart of certain cultural attributes which undoubtedly affect black political attitudes and behavior. (For a more detailed discussion of these cultural traits, see chapter 4.) Matthew Holden describes these attributes with enviable sensitivity and clarity. They include a "hope for deliverance," "the wish for defiance," "Dionysian Individualism," a high value on "moralism," and "cynicism and fear." A black presidential candidate, especially one such as Jesse Jackson, clearly stood to benefit from and in turn refuel these deep cultural traits. For example, some undoubtedly saw Jackson as God's instrument of deliverance, helping black people overcome years of suffering and deprivation. Still others saw Jackson's candidacy as a symbol of defiance, a "wish" to defy the "white power structure" for its pervasive insults and humiliation of past and present by telling "the white man where to go and what to do and making him go and do it." Blacks see the "defiant hero" as one "asserting an elemental right in a situation where the legal order would almost certainly deny that right." This wish for defiance is buttressed by a belief in the black capacity to endure, no matter what, and that view is not bound by class differences: well-educated blacks, too, have invariably wanted to do something that was "more dramatically defiant."[38] The relation of these observations to Jackson's candidacy is obvious and requires little comment.

Similarly, "Dionysian Individualism" is also seen in the black presidential idea, an idea to which Jackson gave expression and which understandably struck a responsive chord in the black community. As a presidential candidate, Jackson would seem particularly well qualified to personify the concept of Dionysian Individualism. "The black culture," says Holden, "is a culture in which, relatively speaking, oratorical-debating competence is far more praiseworthy than technical bureaucratic skill or the investment of oneself in the tedium of organizational detail."[39] Thus, those who sought to diminish Jackson's credibility by criticizing what they perceived as his poor organizational or administrative habits did nothing to hurt Jackson among blacks. However, Jackson disappointed those who value another characteristic of "Dionysian individualism"—"the adoption of segmentation and secession as a means for the defense of honor, in those cases where honor cannot be reconciled with continuing in an existing organization." Soon after his announcement, Jackson was criticized by some black political scientists for renouncing in advance the idea that, if necessary, he would lead a secession from the party, perhaps through an independent movement.[40] Even at the 1984 Democratic National Convention, after Jackson's minority plans were thoroughly defeated, some Jackson delegates were ready to "secede" (walk out) had Jackson led them, and some were openly critical that he did not do so.

The black presidential strategy also stood to benefit from the strong attachment of the black community to *moralism,* to the view nourished by protestantism that "men ought to do *right.*" Blacks see themselves, in contrast to whites, as possessing a "greater sensitivity, a greater humaneness or (in one version) more soul." The idea "that 'the white man is dirty' and 'does not care about you,' " says Holden, "is so often advanced [among blacks] that it is quite striking." Blacks make high moralistic demands not only of whites but of their own leaders as well. Indeed, blacks expect their leaders to "approach perfection *in their heroism,* and the more nearly they do so the more their other failings can be excused." "But the absence of heroism," concludes Holden, "activates the bitter cynicism and the almost paranoid fear of being sold out." [41]

This raises the aspects of *cynicism and fear* in black culture, where experience suggests that in their "wish for defiance" and "hope for deliverance" blacks are simultaneously cynical of their prospects for success and fearful of trying. Most black leaders are unable or unwilling to demonstrate the sort of heroism needed to "go the uttermost distance commanded by the wish for defiance and deliverance." [42] Thus, Jackson's refusal to give full vent to heroism by walking out of the democratic convention may have brought him plaudits from party regulars and established black leaders, but that refusal made it much more difficult for him to maintain credibility in the black community. Jackson could ill afford to have blacks become cynical about his motives or, worse yet, perceive him as being afraid to stand up to the white power structure. Jackson's memorable one-hour, prime-time television speech to the Democratic National Convention may be viewed as one major way he sought to deal with this problem.

Indeed, the centerpiece of Jackson's entire campaign was an effort to overcome "clientage politics," particularly salient in presidential politics, wherein blacks traditionally rely on their powerful white patrons to protect and promote their interests. Jackson thought the time had come in presidential politics when blacks should represent and bargain for themselves *directly,* rather than remain clients or surrogates of white leaders who call the shots. But Holden is correct in recalling that "clientage" politics, though "uncomfortable and denounced in the symbol system," has been "a source of desired goods which people have been unable or unwilling to forego." [43] Obviously this may continue to pose problems for established, as well as aspiring, black leaders. Nonetheless, overcoming "clientage" politics, as Jackson's campaign vividly demonstrates, remains a viable and attractive notion in the black community.

Overall, the encouraging response and enthusiastic support Jackson received from blacks demonstrate well the congruence of the black presidential strategy with particular cultural traits in the black community. Jackson's candidacy thus held a sort of built-in appeal and attractiveness and profited greatly therefrom.

Impact of Personality, Style, and Mission

The nature of the political situation in 1983, in contrast to the civil rights movement, suggests that no single group is in a position to effect political change without a broad base of participative support from all affected groups. The plain truth is that black leaders (the "Black leadership family") simply do not command the resources or the authority to deal with the nature and scope of the problems that they or other minority groups face. Consequently, they cannot conclusively determine or influence what strategies or options should be used, including whether a black or anyone else should run for president. Rather, one of the most obvious and viable routes for these groups is coming together to maximize their political strength through electoral politics. This necessarily includes the very fundamental tasks of unearthing new voters and reactivating old ones—grassroots efforts aimed at the masses, not at leaders or the elite. One might reasonably assume that this could be facilitated greatly through some magnetic, energizing focal point that could attract attention and allow for a discussion of issues so as to illuminate the commonality of interests shared by these groups.

This was exactly what Jackson proposed to do. Through his Rainbow Coalition he aspired to rally the voices, of not only Blacks but also of women, Hispanics, and many others, including whites, who still constitute the largest number of poor, elderly, and unemployed. Jackson's plan sounded very reminiscent of Martin Luther King's attempt to expand the civil rights movement to include the nation's poor and those who were opposed to the Vietnam War. Similarly, it was clear that Jackson's "dream" and objectives posed untold problems for him and his supporters. Nonetheless they were altogether lofty, worthy, and noble goals—strongly consistent with the spirit and goals of the American Dream and the Constitution. His message struck a responsive chord among many blacks and similarly disaffected groups. His candidacy held potential as a unifying voice or structure that would serve a role similar to that performed during the civil rights movement by Martin Luther King.

Moreover, it would seem to be preferable to convey this message (discussion of issues) in a forum that would offer the best possible chance to meet the stated objectives. In American electoral politics, the contest for the presidency would certainly rank high as that forum. It is the one forum that is unmatched in American politics, commanding as it does the vast and sophisticated resources of the media and information industry, and the rapt attention of the entire nation and world. Here the concerns and objectives of disaffected groups could be put forth directly, by one of them, not by a surrogate. Moreover, such an effort would dramatize—more than any other single act—some of the deep fundamental human aspirations held by all persons regardless of race, color, sex, or station in life. These very human desires include the right of every individual to be accorded and to enjoy the same respect, dignity, and opportunity structures so that one has an equal chance to reach one's full potential, even if one does not succeed.

The situation just described seemed almost tailor-made for Jesse Jackson. His qualifications could reasonably impel, indeed "require," him to fill this role. Consider the causes he championed throughout his adult life, most recently through PUSH; his personal attributes and appeal; and—very important in modern political campaigning, especially presidential campaigns—his past success in gaining media attention. He seemed a particularly logical choice since he had almost single-handedly, and for a good while, kept the idea of a black presidential candidacy alive and before the public. Even more than this, during this time no other black or minority leader—elected or otherwise— came forth to offer his or her candidacy. The field was thus open for Jackson to offer himself for this role, and he did.

It seemed indeed rather ironic that most established black political leaders —those with the practical political experience of public office—were unable or unwilling to seize or support the opportunity so graphically presented by the political situation described above. As a result, some found themselves in the awkward position of criticizing the one person who, for whatever reasons (courage, ego-satisfaction, etc.) decided to undertake what loomed as one of the greatest political challenges that has ever been undertaken, perhaps even surpassing the challenge facing John F. Kennedy in 1960 when he sought to overcome the "religious" barrier and become the first Catholic elected president.

One commentator summarized well the effect of Jackson's entry on black Americans. "The only question facing Black voters at this point (and white Democratic voters as well) . . . is whether Jesse Jackson's candidacy will help or hinder the effort to defeat Ronald Reagan." And "the other question" continued this commentator, "—is Jackson the right man to represent their hopes—is simply irrelevant: for Jesse Jackson . . . has now become *the man*" (emphasis his).[44] The question of whether a black presidential candidacy would hurt or help the effort to defeat Ronald Reagan gave pause to a number of persons. A major concern for some was that a black candidate could jeopardize the existing fragile coalition of interests and groups that sustain the Democratic party and thus endanger the unity which some thought necessary to defeat Ronald Reagan. In short, there were risks to the Jackson candidacy. But once again we saw a demonstration of the truism that politics is about risks, and well-meaning people may well come to different conclusions in their assessments and calculations of the possible costs and benefits involved.

Obviously, of course, Jackson's entry shifted the nature of the debate over a black presidential candidacy. Attention now focused, not on some abstract idea or unknown candidate, but on the strengths and weaknesses of Jackson.

And his record of public service, mainly in civil rights work, did offer some informative clues. That record indicated that Jackson possesses sharp political instincts and has over the years demonstrated his sensitivity and concern for causes in such a way as to strike a responsive chord among blacks and many others. This, of course, has been facilitated greatly by Jackson's reputation as a powerful, articulate speaker (black Baptist preachers had better be!), one whose personality, style, and charisma make him stand out among the crowd. And, very importantly, the record shows that Jackson knows how to use these strengths in attracting media attention and coverage.

But Jackson's record also pointed up some weaknesses, some areas of concern. There was the charge, for example, that Jackson is a poor administrator, a poor manager, and does not follow through on projects he starts. Additional concern was expressed over the fact that he had never held elective public office and, consequently, lacked the political experience necessary to be president. But this concern was somewhat tempered by the fact that President Eisenhower had never held elective public office but had developed his leadership abilities and experience through public service in the military. Nonetheless, the lack of experience in elective public office haunted Jackson's candidacy and allowed critics to suggest that his very decision to run for the presidential office reflected this weakness.

Finally, there are those who suggest that Jackson possesses tremendous drive, courage, and self-confidence. Critics, however, see it as a drive for personal gain, to satisfy a not-so-subtle ego problem. The fact is that Jackson did persist in his presidential effort, despite strong criticism and dissuasion from friends and well-known, established black leaders. And this persistence reflected a measure of political wisdom and history: his willingness to fight against the odds—the establishment. The role of the underdog is not the worst role one can have in American politics.

But in terms of major party presidential politics, Jackson was not the usual underdog, he was rather unusual. Whatever his strengths or shortcomings, Jackson did not measure up to the "concept of availability" in one particular respect: he was black. "Availability," as one writer put it, "sums up the qualities the two major parties believe make a politically appealing and acceptable candidate."[45] Availability reflects "the distribution of power" in American politics as well as "widely held expectations (or beliefs) in the American electorate of what a president should be." Among these beliefs are that one must be successful in business or public life, happily married with an attractive family, a "reasonably" observant Protestant, and a *white male* in his 40s or 50s.

Obviously, these beliefs are subject to changing public attitudes. For example, John F. Kennedy was able to overcome the stigma against Roman Catholics by his nomination and election as president in 1960. And, of course, Geraldine Ferrarro's nomination for Democratic vice presidential candidate in 1984 undoubtedly contributes to erasing the barriers erected against women. Thus, as attitudes and behavior change, it is possible that the "availability" criteria will also change. But in 1983, when Jackson announced his candidacy, it was widely held that no black American, no matter how qualified, could *as a matter of practical politics* be nominated by either of the major parties. Thus, to say that Jackson was fighting against the odds was an understatement: he was attempting to overcome a deeply entrenched though slowly eroding white racism long practiced against blacks in all areas of American life and politics.

"What made Jesse run?" The various contextual factors discussed in this chapter might well explain the background which gave rise and potency to Jesse Jackson's candidacy. These factors include: (1) the persistence of many glaring socioeconomic inequities that still exist between blacks and whites; (2) the attitudes and actions of the Reagan administration toward blacks, women, and minorities—attitudes and actions which renewed the concern and attention of these groups about their general welfare; (3) increasing concern and disenchantment of blacks with policies and practices of the Democratic party; (4) the important role of symbols and symbolic forms in shaping American politics and society; (5) the nature and structure of black politics and the black community and their influence on Jackson's candidacy; and (6) the impact of Jackson's personality, style, and mission on the development of his candidacy.

Our discussion indicates that an assessment of these factors, especially in the aggregate, provided a rational, even compelling, basis upon which to launch a black presidential bid. The analysis firmly suggests that, in terms of its potential, the strategy of a black presidential candidacy was encompassing and powerful. It represented an enviable blend of idealism with realism, principles with practice, and symbols with substance. Moreover, it was altogether congruent with both certain deep cultural strains within the black community as well as with certain cherished ideals and principles of American politics and society.

Simply put, the potential benefits of a black presidential candidacy were too great and appealing to be overcome by the perceived costs and risks involved. Jackson thus entered the Democratic contest. His very candidacy reminded us anew of the important role of symbols and symbolic forms in shaping our politics and political behavior. It embodied in one attractive symbol—Jesse Jackson's candidacy—what's good and what's bad about our country. It dramatically portrayed much about the state of race relations in America—the progress that has been made and the problems that remain. Further, Jackson's candidacy could be viewed as an attempt to fill a leadership void left by Martin Luther King and to once again focus attention on the importance of finishing the work of King and the civil rights movement.

Jackson's candidacy provided still other opportunities. It allowed him to undertake the political education normally associated with election campaigns, raising questions about and offering perspectives on policy issues which might otherwise be muffled or ignored altogether and increasing political consciousness and activity among those groups he proposed to represent. In addition, Jackson's candidacy reflected the depth of anger and disillusionment felt by women, blacks, and minorities over the attitudes and actions of the Reagan administration. It also represented a growing concern and frustration with the Democratic party for taking the support of these groups for granted without their receiving commensurate benefits in return.

To be sure, as one of the three major Democratic contenders, Jackson represented the growing "dispossessed" sector of the party: women, blacks and minorities, small farmers, the poor, or as Jackson put it, the locked-out, filling an apparently increasing *representational void* being felt by "have-nots" and disaffected groups not only in the Democratic party but in our political system generally. Mondale tended to represent established interests, traditional liberals, the solid working class, unionized Democrats of the New Deal coalition. Gary Hart's candidacy appealed to the recently affluent, the YUPPIE types, the young urban upwardly mobile professionals. Thus each of the three major candidates represented one of the three major groupings (socioeconomic divisions?) within an increasingly fragile Democratic coalition.

Finally, and very importantly, Jackson's decision to run for the Democratic presidential nomination reaffirmed the determination of blacks and minorities to maximize and develop their political leverage, indicating the ultimate preference of these groups to use *politics* rather than *protests* to achieve their political objectives. And perhaps most appealing of all, Jackson's candidacy allowed him to do these things in a forum which commands the kind of interest and visibility that is unmatched in American politics and society. In short, the opportunities presented by a black presidential candidacy were much too powerful, challenging, attractive, and timely to let pass. The perceived benefits were high and far-reaching; the perceived costs were low and transient. It was out of this context that the Jackson candidacy developed.

NOTES

1. See William Wilson, *The Declining Significance of Race* (Chicago: University of Chicago Press, 1978).

2. BLS #2217, Table 27, p. 69 and pp. 71 ff.

3. See annual reports published by the National Urban League on *The State of Black America*, esp. reports of 1983, 1984, and 1985.

4. Drew Days, "Turning Back the Clock: The Reagan Administration and Civil Rights," *Harvard Civil Rights-Civil Liberties Law Review* 19 (1984): 309.

5. John Palmer and Isabel Sawhill, eds., *The Reagan Record: An Assessment of America's Changing Priorities* (Cambridge, Mass: Ballinger, 1984).

6. Days, "Turning Back the Clock."

7. *Brown v. Board of Education of Topeka*, 347 U.S. 483 (1954), and civil rights legislation of 1975, 1960, 1964, 1965, and 1968.

8. Days, "Turning Back the Clock."

9. Ibid.

10. *Bob Jones University v. United States*, 103 S. Ct. 2017, 1983.

11. See Lucius Barker and Twiley Barker, *Civil Liberties and the Constitution*, 5th ed. (Englewood Cliffs, NJ: Prentice Hall, 1986), p. 313.

12. *Metropolitan County Board of Education of Nashville v. Kelly*, 103 S. Ct. 834 (1983).

13. For an overview of this issue see "Voting Rights Act Extended, Strengthened," 1983 *Congressional Quarterly Almanac*, pp. 373–77.

14. For an overview and background of this controversy see "Civil Rights Commission Reconstituted," 1983 *Congressional Quarterly Almanac*, pp. 292–95.

15. See *New York Times*, October 20, 1983, B-10, c.1. Also see Anthony Lewis, "The Real Reagan," Ibid., October 24, 1983, A-19, c. 5.

16. Public Law 98-399, 98 Stat. 1473 (August 27, 1984).

17. Survey Research Center data (1980, 1984) suggest some inconclusiveness in this regard with respect to public attitudes. Take, for example, the matter of government "spending priorities." While many persons approve of government spending, the data show that sharp differences in support patterns emerge for particular types of programs. Specifically, there was broad support among the public to spend considerably *less* for programs "associated" with blacks, minorities, and the poor—e.g., food stamps, welfare—than for programs that are viewed as also "beneficial" to the "middle class"—public schools, social security, medicare, defense. On the other hand, the data also show that the number of persons who thought government should spend less on "improving the condition of blacks" had dropped seven points, from 29% in 1980 to 22% in 1984. Obviously, many interpretations may be given to such data. In general, however, the overall contextual thrust of the data *plus* majority congressional support for certain Reagan policy initiatives (budget cuts in social programs—e.g., food stamps) does suggest that there was basis in *perception* and in *fact* for the apprehension of blacks with respect to what they saw as an increasing congruence of attitudes and policy preferences between President Reagan and the American public. Also see Benjamin Ginsberg and Martin Shefter, "A Critical Realignment? The New Politics, The Reconstituted Right, and the 1984 Election," in *The Elections of 1984*, ed. Michael Nelson (Washington: Congressional Quarterly, 1985), pp. 1–25; and Scott Keeter, "Public Opinion in 1984," in *The Election of 1984*, ed. Gerald Pomper et al. (Chatham, N.J.: Chatham House, 1985), pp. 91–109.

18. *Washington Post*, July 21, 1983, A-23.

19. All quotes from Ibid., April 10, 1983, C-1.

20. *New York Times*, June 23, 1983, A-2. The NAACP official was Joe Madison, director of political action.

21. Murray Edelman, *The Symbolic Uses of Politics* (Urbana: University of Illinois Press, 1967; new ed., 1985).

22. For example, some black leaders, such as Mayor Coleman Young of Detroit, criticized Jackson's candidacy as being "merely symbolic."

23. For a review of the rise and decline of the civil rights movement, see Lucius Barker and Donald Jansiewicz, "Coalitions in the Civil Rights Movement," in *The Study of Coalition Behavior,* ed. Sven Groennings et al. (New York: Holt, Rinehart, Winston, 1970).

24. Edelman, *The Symbolic Uses of Politics.*

25. Lucius J. Barker, "Black Americans and the Politics of Inclusion," *PS* 16 (Summer, 1983): 500–507, see 504.

26. Edelman, *The Symbolic Uses of Politics,* p. 2.

27. See *New York Times,* November 4, 1983, A-13, cols. 1–4.

28. Mathew Holden, *The Politics of the Black Nation* (New York: Chandler, 1973).

29. Barker and Jansiewicz, "Coalitions in the Civil Rights Movement."

30. See comments of Benjamin Hooks, executive director of the NAACP, in opposition to black presidential candidacy, *New York Times,* June 22, 1983, A-21, C-2, and July 4, 1983, A-6.

31. See *New York Times,* June 22, 1983, A-21, C-2.

32. See, for example, Carlyle C. Douglas, "The Urban League Tries to Shake Its Soft-Spoken Image," *New York Times,* July 28, 1985, IV-5.

33. Marguerite Barnett, "The Strategic Debate over a Black Presidential Candidacy," *PS* 16 (Summer, 1983): 489–91.

34. E. E. Schnattschneider, *The Semi-Sovereign People.*

35. Norman Nie, Sidney Verba, and Joan Petrocik, *The Changing American Voter* (Cambridge: Harvard University Press, 1979), pp. 243–56 esp. at pp. 253–56. Also see Thomas Cavanagh, *Inside Black America: The Message of the Black Vote in the 1984 Election* (Washington, D.C.: Joint Center for Political Studies, 1986).

36. See generally annual volumes on *Black Elected Officials: A National Roster,* published by Joint Center for Political Studies beginning in 1970. Data for this discussion is taken from the 1985 volume.

37. See Kenneth R. Mladenka, "Comment on Eisinger: Black Employment in Municipal Jobs, *American Political Science Review* 76 (September, 1982): 645–47.

38. Holden, *The Politics of the Black Nation,* pp. 16–25.

39. Ibid., p. 21.

40. Papers delivered at a conference at Howard University, November 18, 1983.

41. Holden, *The Politics of the Black Nation,* pp. 21, 24.

42. Ibid.

43. Ibid., p. 25.

44. Comments made by Eddie Williams, Joint Center for Political Studies.

45. Materials in the section on "availability" are taken from Frank Sorauf, *Party Politics in America* (Boston: Little Brown, 1980), p. 300.

The Emergent Mobilization of the Black Community in the Jackson Campaign for President

2

Ronald W. Walters

In the aftermath of the campaign of the Rev. Jesse L. Jackson for president in 1984, the analyses that have begun to appear almost invariably focus on Jackson and his ideas, or upon the accomplishments of the campaign, without sufficient attention to the milieu out of which the campaign emerged. Such a serious omission only compounds the task of understanding the essential meaning of this campaign, which was a formidable event in the history of black political behavior. The campaign emerged out of the incipient mobilization of black people and thus served as a vehicle for the expression of their political aspirations as well as those of other minorities and progressive whites. In an effort to fill an analytical void and to provide the proper framework for more accurate formulations of the campaign's objectives, style, and accomplishments, I will emphasize the "emergent mobilization" stage of the campaign in 1983.

In addressing this topic, I will utilize the "political process" model developed by Doug McAdam to explain the phenomenon of insurgent social movements in the black community.[1] McAdam's model is a variant of the "resource mobilization" model derived from the traditional literature on social movements, yet he criticizes this literature as having relied too much upon psychosocial processes and upon an improper or ill-described definition of mobilization "resources." While agreeing substantially with McAdam, I also include the views of Shingles and Hagner and Pierce, to the extent that the most accurate description of the emergence of social movements does not *substitute* political factors for psychological ones but recognizes a basic linkage between the development of *political consciousness* and increased *political participation*.[2]

Thus, I support the existing theoretical notion that "status inconsistency" is a stimulant to the collective actions of a group, often fostering and enhancing the goal of achieving social change. But while McAdam's model also includes the intervening variable of political consciousness (which he calls "cognitive liberation"), he is even more comprehensive than other analysts in suggesting that social movements are initiated out of a dynamic relationship between this variable and those such as "broad socio-economic processes," "shifting political opportunities," and "indigenous organizational strength."[3] Therefore, if we interpret political participation to be related to the variable of "shifting political opportunities," then the connection between the variables "political consciousness" and "political opportunities" will provide a rough, though comprehensible, framework for a discussion of the dynamics responsible for the emergence of the Jackson campaign.

Broad Socioeconomic Processes

It has long been accepted that inequality in the social structure among significant groups has bred a consistent measure of discontent; those who have less status and resources envy those who have more. Such is the origin of the term *relative deprivation.*[4] Therefore it has appeared logical that the genesis of social movements would be enhanced by the sudden addition of new forces which would radically increase the inequality, prompting a parallel increase in levels of discontent and thus providing the basis for large-scale corrective mobilization. However, McAdam eschews this scenario, opting instead for the cumulative impact of social forces, such as industrialization, which take place over longer periods of time and produce larger, though often indirect, social effects (such as unemployment and displacement).[5]

The advent of the Reagan administration in 1980 was a broad social force of relatively immediate impact that fanned the sparks of already extant social inequalities and ignited a black corrective mobilization. Blacks were from the very beginning demonstrably opposed to a radically conservative president occupying the White House, and as the early years of Reagan's administration clearly showed that they would be one of the prime targets of the negative impact of his social, economic, and political policies, their opposition mounted. The raw material for the combustion of social movement was thereby created.

Indigenous Organizational Strength

McAdam supports other theorists of social movements in his view that "indigenous structures frequently provide the organizational base out of which social movements emerge" but adds that they "do not so much emerge out of established organizations as they represent a merger of such groups."[6] Between 1980 and 1983 the black anti-Reagan movement slowly matured, establishing a political consciousness (or collective opinion) about the administration, and leaders of various black organizations became preoccupied with selecting methods of opposing its initiatives.

This resulted in acrimonious attempts by the administration to supplant black leadership by more conservative organization leaders—a strategy that immediately generated strong reaction. For instance, at the July 1983 convention of the NAACP, Vice President George Bush was booed loudly while making an apparently unsuccessful defense of Reagan's policies.[7] In 1985 John Jacob, the new president of the National Urban League, attempting to strike a constructive posture, suggested how the Reagan administration's relations with black organization heads might improve:

> For starters, the President could lay down the law to his Administration's officials that they cool the rhetoric. Some top officials have made ill-tempered attacks on black leaders who reflect the opinions of their constituents. Others have been polarizing influences through their refusal to enforce civil rights laws.
>
> Another positive would be for the White House to open channels of communications with blacks. This is the first Administration in memory in which the President and his key advisors do not have regular contacts with representative black leadership.[8]

Many black leadership organizations were severely alienated from the Reagan administration, including political organizations such as the Congressional Black Caucus, which was unable to secure a meeting with the president during his entire first term. Moreover, leaders of the black church had become concerned about the conservative impact of white fundamentalist religious leaders through organizations such as the Moral Majority. These factors created an atmosphere of hostility, and the need for corrective action was clear to all kinds of organizations, both national and local. Thus the organizations necessary to provide a "sustaining resource" for social movement—some of the largest black organizations—were ready to mobilize support for an electoral movement directed against the Reagan administration.

Shifting Political Opportunities

McAdam implies that one of the sources of group alienation is exclusion from "routine decision making processes," and he utilizes Peter Eisinger's suggestion that protests—or challenges to the system—indicate that the initial changes have occurred within the political group itself. McAdam then explains, "The point is that *any* event or broad social process that serves to undermine the calculations and assumptions on which the political establishment is structured occasions a shift in political opportunities."[9]

Although McAdams mentions as examples of such "broad social processes" wars, industrialization, international political opportunities, unemployment, and demographic changes, his reference to an "event" might comfortably accommodate the fact that one of the routine "opportunities" for decision-making is in the national elections, where a structured opportunity to change the political system, however modestly, has been established. To the extent that elections present a routine opportunity for systemic change, at those times the system may be vulnerable—depending, of course, upon the openness of the process—to the effective mobilization of groups. Therefore, we will look at the various elections which occurred in the period of "emergent mobilization" to see whether we can detect activities that indicate opportunities to which blacks responded.

Political Socialization: Mayoral Campaigns of 1983

From the very inception of the Reagan presidential candidacy in 1980, blacks began to take advantage of a series of "shifting opportunities" to express themselves politically. In the 1980 election black turnout reversed a downward trend that had been occurring since 1964. Turnout stood at 48.7 percent in 1976 but was up 1.85 percent to 50.5 percent in 1980. This upward trend increased in the off-year congressional elections; between the 1978 and 1982 elections black registration jumped 5.8 percent.[10]

In 1983 three important mayoral elections, the first featuring former congressman Harold Washington, who won the office of mayor of the city of Chicago, provided positive proof that political resources were being developed in a substantial mobilization that occurred early in the year. Between 1980 and 1983 black opposition to Mayor Jane Byrne's administration in Chicago grew in reaction to a series of events perceived to be against black interests. For example, she hired a white chief of police when a black person was clearly in line for the job, refused to appoint the black leadership's choice for school superintendent, replaced two blacks on the Board of Education with two anti-integration whites, and reduced the number of blacks on the Housing Authority Board and in other city departments.[11] Racial alienation obviously motivated the black community to use the elections to oppose Byrne's policies. In fact, their mobilization had already begun with voter registration drives targeted to defeat the Republican governor, James Thompson, in 1982.[12]

The black community had many opportunities to oppose the Byrne administration, but two deserve a brief mention. First, Rev. Jesse Jackson's Operation PUSH organized a boycott to protest the lack of community economic benefit from Chicagofest, a series of festivals promoted by the Byrne administration. The protest was sustained by the CBUC (Chicago Black United Communities) and eventually developed the kind of coalition with latino and white groups necessary for expressing electoral power. Alkalimat and Gillis have observed that "out of the Fest boycott was generated the momentum leading to the mass voter registration drives in September and early October 1982, preceding the statewide November elections and the primary campaign. Politically, the Fest boycott expressed the basic coalition-building process that underpinned Washington's election victory."[13] Second, a group known as POWER (People Organized for Welfare and Economic Reform) pointedly mobilized at the neighborhood level against the impact of the Reagan welfare cuts and in an important way made targets simultaneously of Reagan, Thompson, and Byrne. In 1982 this coalition organized opposition to the Reagan-induced, Thompson-implemented austerity program which "fueled the spontaneous upsurge of protest and electoral participation in the summer and fall . . . and winter of 1982, the period immediately preceding the 1983 mayoral campaign." [14]

As a result of this activity a broader coalition was able to register over 200,000 voters, producing a black turnout of nearly 80 percent of a total registration of 650,000 and giving Washington a victory in the primary in a three-way race with 36 percent of the vote. The coalition manifested itself in the important contribution of 10 percent white and 11 percent Hispanic votes as well.[15] By the time of the highly-charged, racially-oriented general election in April, where the general turnout of 88 percent bested the old record, blacks had registered an additional 100,000 voters and turned out solidly to buttress Washington's victory, with over 20 percent of his support coming from white and Hispanic votes.[16] In an important debut to the exercise of political influence in Chicago, the Hispanics delivered 66 percent of their sizeable vote to Washington.[17]

The Washington campaign turned into an opportunity for wide-spread popular mobilization in the black community: in addition to the three important organizations mentioned above, black Ministers formed a "Committee of One Hundred"; black businesses such as Afro-Sheen funded radio commercials; black labor organizations provided disciplined cadres for various campaign tasks; and black professionals such as educators formed various committees for Washington.[18] Through skillful organizing tactics such as the use of media slogans, special events, and spontaneous appearances by Washington to increase his exposure in the community, the campaign mobilized the "man in the street" to register and to vote for Washington.

This campaign was critical because it exhibited the kind of "crusade," or movement, character which prompted a "spill-over" effect upon the generalized willingness of the black community beyond Chicago to similarly mobilize. Just as important, it provided an opportunity for Rev. Jackson to play a constructive role in that mobilization, which would be critical to his subsequent campaign in 1984. For instance, in surveys of local leadership popularity taken by various organizations between 1980 and 1982, Rev. Jackson's stature clearly improved; he moved from tenth place in 1980 into the top grouping by 1981 and 1982.[19]

This election also provided a preview of national Democratic party politics when prospective presidential candidates Walter Mondale and Ted Kennedy came to Chicago before the mayoral primary and endorsed Jane Byrne and Richard M. Daley respectively.[20] Only after Washington's victory in the primary did Democratic party leaders become his visible supporters, and even then somewhat reluctantly, because of the strong opposition of local white party leaders to Washington, as 350,000 white Democrats crossed over to vote for Republican candidate Bernard Epton. Washington counterbalanced this defection by seeking to involve resources outside of Chicago, concentrating on raising funds and endorsements from blacks and other Democratic party members in major cities such as New York, Washington, D.C., Detroit, and others. This further nationalized the campaign, including the electoral strategy and its racial implications. The initial lack of endorsements by major white Democratic party leaders sent strong symbolic signals to black leaders, becoming a negative stimulus to party unity, and though he subsequently became reconciled, Washington's counteraction helped to nationalize the sentiment for independent black electoral mobilization.

The mayoral race in Philadelphia confirmed the trend toward national political mobilization of the black electorate. In the primary black Democratic candidate Wilson Goode successfully challenged former mayor Frank Rizzo. The central difference between the two mayoral elections was that Philadelphia was not as overtly racially polarized as Chicago, as Goode's margin of victory came from 20 percent of the white vote.[21] Nevertheless, the city's 40-percent black population constituting one third of his base, turned out solidly to vote 97 percent for Goode in the primary, which he won by 50,000 votes. He went on to win the November general election easily against his Republican opponent.

It was a central irony of this race, however, that in an attempt to prevent racial tension and polarization Goode sought mightily to prevent comparisons to the Chicago campaign. But while comparisons were easily made by the press, the nationalization of the Chicago campaign was an opportunity which could not be overlooked by Goode's opponent, Rizzo. Rizzo sought to imply that Jesse Jackson was a partisan of PLO leader, Yasir Arafat, linking Jackson to Wilson Goode. Then, he attempted to associate Harold Washington with Chicago gangsters, linking Washington to Jesse Jackson and Wilson Goode. This happened so frequently that one magazine suggested, "The Chicago connection became part of Rizzo's standard pitch with reporters—so much so that it seemed he was running against Harold Washington, as well as Wilson Goode."[22] In reality, Rizzo was running against the tide of mobilization of the black community and its allies which was underway in Philadelphia— another powerful manifestation of the political mood and the potential attitude of blacks toward a black presidential candidacy.

Finally, the mayoral campaign of black activists and former state legislator Mel King in Boston in the fall of 1983 was important in "modeling" a formidable Rainbow Coalition in electoral politics in advance of the Jackson campaign. A multiracial, progressive coalition in electoral politics had been tried in many sections of the country, but the far West had been known for this type of politics, as in the campaigns of Congressman Ronald Dellums (D. Calif.) and Mayor Gus Newport in the Bay area of Oakland. So, following the example that the Hispanic voters in Chicago had set when they turned out substantially for Washington earlier in the year, King ran on a platform directed toward the "empowerment of Black and Latino people." [23] Equally important, King's formulation of the issues was people-centered and progressive in nature.[24] Yet the impact of this race upon Boston blacks was clearly different: in King's 1979 mayoral campaign the black community turned out half-heartedly, believing that he could not win, but in the primary election of September 1983 he gained 95 percent of this vote and a 79 percent turnout, also taking 66 percent of the Hispanic vote and 13.5 percent of the white vote.[25] Even though he placed second in the primary to qualify for the general election and eventually lost, his campaign contributed to the "readiness" of the New England region for the kind of campaign Jackson eventually mounted.

The more one focuses on the large structural opportunities for political mobilization of both the electoral and nonelectoral variety in this period, the clearer the pattern becomes. Over 200,000 people mobilized to come to Washington, D.C. for the second March on Washington, August 27, 1983; another 100,000 simultaneously attended the San Francisco observance; and both groups heard numerous exhortations by speakers to utilize their voting power as an instrument of social change. In fact, at the Washington, D.C. site Andrew Young and other speakers noted that the assembled coalition of concerned groups possessed the potential to defeat Ronald Reagan if he ran for re-election in 1984.[26] In his speech Jesse Jackson tested the campaign theme "our time has come" to a thundering ovation of approval.

Through these major political dynamics, apparently, the nationalization of the strategy of electoral mobilization was accomplished, because in January 1984 the Joint Center for Political Studies reported that a four-year slide in the rate of blacks winning office had been halted in 1983.[27] In that year the rate of increase in the number of black elected officials was 8.6 percent, up from 2.4 percent in 1982, slightly better than a similar level it had achieved as far back as 1977 (8.3 percent). This indicates that these "shifting" opportunities for mobilization were, in fact, duplicated numerous times in elections at the local level and that what was missing was a *collective* opportunity to make the full impact of the mobilization felt.

Cognitive Liberation

The process of "cognitive liberation" develops and transforms political consciousness sufficiently to provide the group with a rationale for collective social action.[28] McAdam utilizes several compelling terms to define the concept. Simply put, the process of cognitive liberation is achieved through the collective perceptions that

1. based on the correlation of a wide variety of events, by a group of individuals who share intense community interests, there is the attribution that the system (or situation) is unjust, thus creating "cognitive dissonance," or the incentive for challenging the legitimacy of the system;
2. inasmuch as the system (or situation) has lost its legitimacy, it is "subject to change," and that, in an assessment of the shifting opportunities, there is indeed discovered to exist the "structural potential" for change;
3. based upon an enhanced feeling of group political efficacy there is a consensus formed with regard to strategy, or "a reasonable basis for successful collective action."

Having discussed the factors in the political environment which produced cognitive dissonance in the black community and the evidence which contributed to the perception that the response of the Democratic party was subject to change, I must now consider the issue of consensus among black leaders with respect to the strategy of a black presidential candidacy as a "reasonable basis for successful action." I will briefly describe the process by which that consensus was approached, as a crucial aspect of the emergent mobilization. In doing so, I will seek to assess the degree of mobilization of electoral campaign-movement resources in the conflict over consensus among black leaders, among the wider black population, and, to some extent, in the public at large.

Black Leadership Consensus

Early in 1983 black leaders, disturbed that no prominent white Democrat had endorsed Harold Washington in his primary election campaign, became concerned at the prospect that the black vote would similarly be taken for granted in the 1984 Democratic presidential campaign. In order to counter this prospect, the idea of running a black presidential candidate was considered in a series of meetings, beginning in March of 1983 in Atlanta and ending in a June meeting in Chicago. The group was chaired by Rev. Joseph Lowery, of the National Black Leadership Forum, a consultative body of thirteen heads of major black political, civil rights, fraternal, labor, religious, and other civic organizations. Projecting the rationale for the meeting, Lowery said, "We are determined not to be ignored, the Democratic party knows we're serious." [29] Lowery then went on to suggest that the meeting was held in order to "equip" blacks to become "empowered" to help defeat Ronald Reagan in 1984, given Reagan's role in what these leaders perceived as the deep erosion in civil rights which had occurred. He continued: "We intend to increase registration among Black voters; insure full Black participation in the presidential selection process; develop a people's agenda we are pledged to support above any candidate or any party; and to advance the interests of Black people in any way, legal and ethical, at our command. Black Americans have every right to exercise every option available to us, including offering a presidential candidate of our own." [30] This important coalition of blacks, augmented by politicians such as Andrew Young, Julian Bond, and others to number about thirty, carefully debated the issue of a black candidacy apart from the question of the identity of the candidate. Nonetheless, the fact that the two issues were related kept the group from eventually reaching a unanimous position on either question. Even before the election of Harold Washington, the name of Rev. Jackson was being discussed in connection with a black candidacy, and this generated a controversy in which other names came forth, including some of the more prominent members of the Congressional Black Caucus such as Congressmen Walter Fauntroy (D. D.C.), Ronald Dellums (D. Calif.), John Conyers (D. Mich.), and Parren Mitchell (D. Md.). The list also included Georgia State Senator Julian Bond and mayors Andrew Young, Richard Hatcher, Tom Bradley, former mayor Maynard Jackson, and others.[31]

Some of this competitive name-dropping was generated by the intense opposition to Rev. Jesse Jackson, leading at least one observer to publicly suggest that it was better to have no black candidate at all than to have Jackson.[32] This opinion was not persuasive to black leaders, who met again on April 30 in Chicago and issued a statement saying: "We affirm the necessity of a candidacy for the presidency of the United States which focuses the nation's attention on the urgent needs of our cities as well as depressed rural areas, our poor and our ailing economy and we find no reason why competent, dedicated leaders should eliminate themselves because they happen to be Black." [33]

Although some hoped that the mantle of the leadership of this strategy should fall to them, none stepped forth to claim it. Therefore the strategy was decided ostensibly upon its merits, though when the final decision was made in June, there were only a few abstentions in an overwhelmingly positive vote among the twenty-four people in attendance at the Chicago meeting.[34] At the end of the vote, without committing himself to a candidacy, Rev. Jackson announced the formation of an exploratory committee headed by Mayor Richard Hatcher. Obviously, he wanted time to solidify the various elements of the black leadership—important mayors, members of the Congressional Black Caucus, and the civil rights community—in order that his effort might have the proper legitimacy among blacks. Despite rumors that he was already running, he said on June 30 that he was "not inclined to make a unilateral move" to mount a candidacy without the sanction of the group assembled in Chicago and hoped that it would form the steering committee of the campaign.[35] In the end, the meeting also agreed to form the "Black Coalition for 1984" as a vehicle to support a "Peoples Platform" containing a policy agenda of black and minority concerns.

There existed objective differences with the strategy, based either upon a lack of understanding of its intrinsic value or upon its violation of past habits of political behavior. For example, Andrew Young, Julian Bond, Richard Arrington and Coleman Young were political pragmatists who felt that the place of the black community was with the obvious front-runner, Walter Mondale, and that any black candidacy would be a losing proposition, only symbolically useful. In fact, John Jacobs feared that a black candidate might take votes away from a white candidate sympathetic to the needs of blacks, thereby electing a conservative Democrat to compete with Reagan.[36] However, none went as far as the NAACP Board of Directors, which adopted a resolution saying, in part, "We call on Black Americans in every state to take no steps, however symbolically attractive, which may have the effect of diluting the Black vote. Black Americans must sharply focus on a number one priority: the defeat of the Ronald Reagan system of government by casting every possible vote for the candidate who is most likely to achieve that goal."[37] This statement was buttressed by the view of Benjamin Hooks, NAACP head, who said: "I don't think Black folks are that unsophisticated. I don't think you've got to run a Black presidential candidate to convince people to register. If Mr. Reagan hasn't convinced us to register, nothing else will."[38] These obvious indications of disapproval, however unpersuasive they would eventually become, were at least couched in strategic language.

Many black leaders appeared to be wedded to the old strategy by which the black community entered presidential politics—supporting the front-running white Democratic candidate who appeared most sympathetic to black concerns. Yet even Jackson's detractors seemed to be searching for a new strategy of influence to achieve such goals as (1) increasing black voter registration, (2) forging a "progressive" electoral coalition, (3) articulating the issues of concern to blacks and other dispossessed groups, and (4) wielding influence at the Democratic convention in exchange for the nominee's adoption of an agenda favored by blacks and others.[39] Even though there was grudging acceptance of the fact that a black candidate might attract 200 to 400 delegates, there was no consensus concerning how successful such an effort might be as a bargaining strategy. Even the Joint Center for Political Studies, a black political research institute, appeared to be urging the cautious approach by emphasizing the potentially negative consequences of a black candidacy, warning that "a black candidacy could divide Black leaders and drain support from the Democratic nominee, especially in the South, a key battleground where the Black voting strength is greatest."[40]

Jackson's strong supporters, such as John Conyers (D. Mich.), believed that his candidacy was needed (but opposed) because it was to be based on a "coalition of the rejected," people such as blacks, youth, women, and nonwhite minorities, who were powerless and had been taken for granted by the Democratic establishment. Thus he linked the source of the difficulty some "mainstream" leaders were having not only to political strategy but to the *class interests* which were represented by the campaign.[41]

General Black Consensus

In light of the conflict over the candidacy, engendered by the powerful elements of personality and strategy, a consensus among black leaders appeared difficult to achieve in the spring of 1983. Although the debates raging within the conventions of the larger black organizations revealed a perceptible split in the middle class, by the summer there was much less division among the masses. The chant "Run Jesse run" began to follow Rev. Jackson wherever he spoke among black audiences, lending credence to the feelings of Congressman Charles Rangel (D. N.Y.) who said in early June, "Nobody can stop a black candidate now." [42] By the end of July the strategy was inescapably identified with Jackson. One politician at the March on Washington, listening to Jackson amid now-familiar chants of "Run Jesse run," observed, "He's got a train going." [43]

The emergence of popular approval for a black candidacy indicated, of course, that the eventual decision of leaders to support it was not made in a vacuum but yielded to the considerable sentiment already present in the black community at large. The dominant feature of the split within the community, therefore, had the appearance of a *class dynamic,* with a large sector of the middle class preferring one group of potential candidates and nearly everyone else overwhelmingly preferring Jesse Jackson. Indeed, *Ebony* magazine initiated a poll of its readers in July; the results released in its October issue revealed that 67 percent of the respondents approved of the idea of a black presidential candidacy, while 62 percent believed that Rev. Jesse Jackson should be the candidate.[44] Although this was a survey of a biased sample, still the *Ebony* readership was representative enough to provide a rough indication of the prevailing sentiment among a generically mainstream black audience.

By September Jackson himself was busily lobbying black leaders, but he was also involved in two critical mass-oriented projects which were to affect the resource base of his campaign. One was the partially successful attempt to develop his network of religious contacts. An important group of religious leaders met in Memphis and declared their support for his candidacy. This effort was led by AME Bishop H. H. Brookins of Los Angeles, also head of the PUSH board and a powerful minister with national and international contacts. Jackson said on this occasion that although he was seriously considering the race for the Democratic presidential nomination, he did not then have sufficient funds. His own Baptist denomination had been somewhat slow in coming to his support, but his appearance at the 6.8-million-member National Baptist Convention convocation in September helped these prospects immensely.[45]

Then, on the other side of the Baptist community, in September the Progressive National Baptists Convention announced a drive among its 1,500 member churches to initiate a massive voter registration campaign. While Rev. Benjamin Hooks, NAACP head, was attending the meeting and was highly receptive to this announcement, his enthusiasm was limited to its prospects for increasing voter registration, not to the potential of Rev. Jackson's bid. In any case, his comment on this occasion was that "the Black church is the most powerful institution in the Black community, and with this type of cooperative endeavor, we can reach the overall goal of two million new Black voters." [46]

Jackson himself had launched a "Southern Crusade" to register two million new voters. He felt that the key to a Democratic victory resided in the black vote becoming the balance of power in the South; thus it was necessary to mobilize the large unregistered Black population that in many states could offset Reagan's 1980 margin of victory. The crusade, which sponsored as many as forty rallies per week in the month of August, appeared to be a warm-up for the campaign as reflected in the enthusiasm of the people who chanted "Run Jesse run" at each of his stops. But the political dividend was both to register new voters and to unearth issues that would be prominent in his campaign, such as implementation of the Voting Rights Act of 1965 through the elimination of run-off elections or "second primaries." [47]

Public Opinion At Large

Public opinion would be more difficult to assess but in general consisted of the views of various opinion leaders in the press and national political life. The terms *fascinate* and *frighten* appear to aptly describe the reaction of many to Jackson's potential candidacy.[48] The press appeared most fascinated of all because the charismatic Jackson had been good copy in the past and because the prospect of a serious black candidate for president was something new in American politics. At the same time, the press expressed hostility and dismay as though it came as a galling thought that blacks should blemish the sanctity of that bastion of white male power—the presidency of the United States of America. One journalist suggested that the proposed strategy was an advantage for black leaders because, since they had been successful in civil rights, "It obscures the fact that they are not sure what they want . . . what to do next." [49] Also misconstruing the candidacy as one which would seek only black votes, another writer sarcastically went on to pronounce the strategy "a dead end, a cul-de-sac, a way to escape rather than confront persistent and difficult problems." [50]

One issue which temporarily united black leaders was the charge that Rev. Jackson was unqualified to run for president, to which most responded that he had every right to run, citing the qualifications listed in the Constitution. In fact, the balance of the journalistic appraisals devoted to Jackson's biographical background dwelled at length upon such issues as his illegitimate birth, his aggressiveness, his ties to Middle Eastern leaders and his meeting with Yasir Arafat, his financial problems with the PUSH-EXCELL program, his dealings with corporate leaders, his connection to Martin Luther King, Jr., and distance from the King family, as well as statements from other blacks about character traits such as his ego.[51] Few comparable exposés were written of his accomplishments in any field which would give the impression that he was of equal stature with other candidates. Instead, there was dismay that someone who had never held elective office should run for the highest elected office in the land. The press appeared to be fearful of Jackson because his delivery and his opinions were strong and his demeanor was demanding and unapologetic —often interpreted as arrogant. Blacks with such a press image had never received favorable treatment in the past.

Democratic leaders also appeared frightened by Jackson's potential candidacy. After Harold Washington had won the primary election in Chicago earlier in the year, Charles Manatt, chairman of the Democratic National Committee, noted that blacks would become aware of their political significance.[52] However, after the mayoral contest was over, he was criticized by blacks for suggesting that the Washington victory would "take the pressure off for a Black presidential candidacy."[53] Confirming Manatt's cautious view, a poll of 191 members of the Democratic National Committee in the summer revealed the consensus (81 percent) that Jackson's entry into the race would "hurt" the other candidates.[54]

By the middle of 1983 the cast of Democratic challengers had begun to settle into a grouping headed by Walter Mondale and including John Glenn, Reubin Askew, George McGovern, Gary Hart, Alan Cranston, and Ernest Hollings. Although Mondale and Hollings said they would welcome a Jackson candidacy, Mondale stood to lose a substantial share of the black vote to a black candidate, and his operatives quietly began to meet with Rev. Jackson in an attempt to "assist" him with the array of necessary decisions and resources involved.[55] Others suggested that they were attempting to dissuade him as well.

In this light the developing public opinion supportive of Jackson as a presidential candidate apparently assisted in legitimizing his potential candidacy. For example, a New York Times/CBS poll in June, giving Jackson a 7 percent approval rate among all Democratic voters, was startling because Jackson was unannounced and also because this placed him third behind Mondale and Glenn with the largest ratings of 34 percent and 32 percent respectively.[56] This result, together with a poll by David Garth showing Jackson with a 9 percent favorable rating, was substantial proof that he might not win but that he could attract a sizeable black vote in the primaries, thus severely complicating the prospects for Mondale or any other front-runner. As indicated, some thought that this was a scenario for the defeat of a liberal Democrat in the primaries and the eventual re-election of Reagan. It is interesting, then, that a significant percent of the approval rating for Jackson came from those who identified themselves as conservative Democrats, or many who would likely not vote for a Democrat but possibly for Reagan in the general election.

What replaced a general receptivity to Jackson was anxious anticipation and a feeling that the coming campaign would be unlike any other because of his presence. Thus divergent assessments by the black community and the public at large was guaranteed, since a major segment of the black community had undergone cognitive liberation, while the general public grappled with the problem of how to receive a Jackson candidacy based upon racial stereotypes and other potential challenges such a campaign would present. In the end the operative scenario was suggested by Hamilton Jordan, who said: "One option for national party leaders and the presidential candidacy is to accept the inevitability of a black candidate as a consequence of black political strength and frustration and hope that the campaign can be conducted in a way that reconciles the different interests of black America and the Democratic Party in time to defeat Ronald Reagan."[57] This formulation inevitably attracted wide concurrence within the party, even though many within both the party and the media continued to question the legitimacy and the propriety of the campaign. One hastens to add, however, that in this case Jordan appears to be suggesting that the factor which made the candidacy even minimally acceptable within party circles was not as much a matter of choice as the resignation that blacks had "no place to go."

I shall not go on to address the remaining factors in McAdam's model, inasmuch as they are useful in analyzing a fully developed movement, while our concern is with the Jackson campaign's emergence. Nevertheless, many of the central elements in this black political mobilization obviously did mature as factors responsible for maintaining the course of this "campaign-movement." One of the major factors I have attempted to illustrate is a conclusion also reached by McAdam in his study of black insurgence—that "elite groups did not so much stimulate black protest activity as seek to respond to it in ways that would minimize the threat it posed to their interests."[58] Since the blacks were beginning to respond to Reagan long before black leaders began to consider a black candidacy, the emergence of the Jackson campaign clearly confirmed the thesis that it responded to a popular mobilization already building. If, as illustrated, Rev. Jackson could say as late as September 1983 that he would wait yet another month to make an announcement concerning his intentions because of the lack of funds, it must have been the *potential* resources of individuals and powerful black organizations, magnified by the spontaneous popular mobilization then occurring, which made it possible for him to take what was an incredible leap of faith that the actual campaign resources would materialize. By the time of his announcement in November, he still possessed neither the finances nor the organization customary for a presidential nomination campaign, but he did possess three important resources that were in various stages of mobilization.

First, although the idea of a black candidacy was embroiled in a struggle for legitimacy for most of 1983, by November, through a combination of persuasion and the perception of the overwhelming popularity of the idea, a substantial group of black leaders had come to support Rev. Jackson's candidacy. Powerful detractors held out—the heads of the three leading civil rights organizations, the leader of the largest Black labor coalition, and the mayors of five of the largest cities in America (Los Angeles, Detroit, Atlanta, Philadelphia, and Birmingham). Yet the strategy was supported by half of the Congressional Black Caucus, a large contingent of mayors of smaller cities, many other black urban and state elected officials, some national black professional organizations, many local grassroots organizations, rank-and-file black labor, a wide network of religious institutions involving thousands of churches, and, as we have seen, most black individuals.[59] In addition, Rev. Jackson was adamant that it would not be only a black campaign, so an important collection of the leadership of white progressive, women, youth, gay, and other issue-oriented organizations, combined with some of the leaders of "third world" minorities such as native Americans, Hispanics, Arabs, Asians, and others, were attracted to the support of his campaign. Although this grouping became known as the "Rainbow Coalition," support had not materialized from the main-line leaders of these groups nor from any major white politician or establishment institutional leader.

Second, although a cadre of leaders was necessary for legitimacy, it did not always carry their *institutional* support for the campaign. So the heaviest burden of institutional support fell on the religious community, a natural base of Rev. Jackson. As suggested, the Baptist denominations would be critical, especially in the South where the Southern Crusade had found the situation quite promising. However, the institutional network of the secular black middle class also mobilized through social clubs, civic organizations, educational and professional associations.

The strategy attracted general popular support that was not necessarily nullified by the objection of some political, civil rights, and religious leaders. For just as the posture of individual leaders did not always guarantee institutional support, neither did the rejection of the campaign by individual leaders guarantee that individuals would not support it. There was, then, the inevitable conflict within civil rights organizations, labor unions, and other organizations and within the cities, where voters often supported the campaign but the mayors did not.

One of McAdam's major improvements in the study of social movements is the addition of the seminal perspective of the political process as the structural opportunity for movement mobilization. This confirms the implications of others that there is a constant tension between an aggrieved group and the political system as the target of mobilizing activity which often helps to shape the character of a responsive movement. This is not a novel insight, but whereas resource mobilization theorists have focused on the analysis of the *group* almost as an autonomous unit in the process of mobilization, McAdam's model forces a concern with the interactive process between the group and the political system, and *even with the often more influential structuring which the political system contributes to the process of mobilization.* This important insight helps us to answer the critical question of why, since blacks have been excluded from political participation and the nature of their protests have often been antisystemic, did this mobilization occur *within* the system of electoral politics.

Since this intriguing question involves a wider analysis of the campaign after 1983 and of the social environment within which it took place, I will not attempt to answer it here. Nevertheless, we may observe that the obvious objective of removing Reagan had to be addressed within the electoral arena— the institutionalized system of national leadership change. The 1983 mayoral elections also helped to nationalize elements of the strategy. Then the participation of the national black leadership elite and voters in complimentary political events such as the March on Washington played a key role in testing premises of the eventual electoral mobilization.

Some additional structuring of the emergence of the campaign occurred through other dynamics outside the black community. For example, the sources of "Rainbow" campaign mobilization behavior were similar to the mobilization of other progressive groups such as the Nuclear Freeze campaign, which utilized mass mobilization to initiate a successful national referendum in 1983. Part of their strategy of opposing Reagan's policies involving nuclear weapons aimed, therefore, at the electoral arena and the hope for a change in administrations. In the presidential election, however, the Nuclear Freeze campaign was torn between the politics of pragmatism, which demanded support of Walter Mondale, and the politics of principle, which found some of their numbers supporting Jesse Jackson, whose defense position was actually closest to official statements of the Nuclear Freeze campaign. Thus the full impact of the prior mobilization of this issue was not achieved in the elections of 1984. Furthermore, in many states in the nation the electoral system is somewhat more open and available to blacks as an instrument of mobilization, since the promulgation of Democratic party reforms requiring the implementation of approved Affirmative Action Plans in each state and the assault on legal barriers to participation by the Voting Rights Act of 1965 with the consequent evolution of local elected leadership.

The simplicity of the strategy of defeating Ronald Reagan also evidently facilitated a level of cohesion; it was a strategy with which most political actors and voters in the black community had identified. Although the ultrapragmatists and Jackson supporters were divided, they agreed that all methods should be attempted to increase black turnout in an effort to elect a Democratic president. Thus after the Democratic convention, there was a basis for unity of the black community that did result in a higher turnout rate than in the previous presidential election.

Besides these factors, which illustrate the growing cognitive liberation of most blacks with respect to the idea of a black presidential candidacy, the most important ingredient was the emergence of Rev. Jesse Jackson, who, as the most popular black leader of that period, also became the standard bearer for the idea and through his initiation of the campaign gave the Rainbow Community the strategy to express itself through a presidential campaign. Social science has not been able to adequately describe what happens in the germination process, when the readiness of a people for mobilization is ignited by the charisma of an individual leader whose force of personality and creation of an organizational apparatus works to facilitate the genesis of a movement. Yet campaigning as an objective activity obviously fits the familiar political behavior of the black community, where protest demonstrations of an infinite variety were used to achieve various social ends, so that the *style of mobilization* was easily transferrable to a movement addressing electoral objectives.

If we may assume that most of the Jackson supporters accepted the strategy of enhanced voter mobilization as the key to defeating Reagan, then we have another partial answer to a related question concerning why the campaign-movement emerged so strongly, even though it was clear that Jackson would most likely not become president of the United States. Although we have discovered no scientific data on this point from the "emergent" period, later studies suggest that adherence to this anti-Reagan strategic rationale as a basis for supporting a black candidacy, together with other references to improving of blacks' group image through having a black candidate run for president, strongly affected the black population.[60] In this sense the political system afforded blacks not only a specific instrumental opportunity for mobilization, it also characterized the continuing uniqueness of black politics, in that blacks apparently did not utilize the electoral system in precisely the same manner as the majority did, but for certain minority group, race-value ends. In the end, the existence of a strong group improvement rationale, which has always served as a sufficient motivating force for the initiation of black movements, is one of the soundest indications that the movement feature of the campaign had a potential for continuing far beyond the emergent period and becoming an important factor in the politics of the 1984 presidential campaign.

NOTES

1. Doug McAdam, *Political Process and the Development of Black Insurgency, 1930–1970* (University of Chicago Press, Chicago, 1982).

2. Richard Shingles, "Black Consciousness and Political Participation: The Missing Link," *American Political Science Review* 75, no. 1 (March 1981): 76–91.

3. McAdam, *Political Process*, p. 51.

4. Thomas Crawford and Murray Naditch, "Relative Deprivation, Powerlessness and Militancy: The Psychology of Social Protest," *Psychiatry* 33, no. 2 (May 1970): 208–33.

5. McAdam, *Political Process*, p. 41.

6. Ibid.

7. Sheila Rule, "Bush is Booed at N.A.A.C.P. Meeting," *New York Times*, July 16, 1983, I-7.

8. John Jacob, "Making 1985 a Better Year," *The Washington Afro-American*, January 5, 1985, p. 6.

9. McAdam, *Political Process*, p. 40.

10. *Blacks and the 1984 Democratic National Convention: A Guide, Election '84 Report #4* (Washington, D.C.: Joint Center for Political Studies, 1984). Includes data from the 1982 and 1984 Census Reports on elections.

11. M. Jean Terrell, *The Chicago Mayoral Election of 1983* (Chicago: Terrell, 1984).

12. James Compton, "Mobilizing the Black Vote in 1984," speech, August 1, 1983, New Orleans, La.

13. Abdul Alkalimat and Doug Gillis, "Black Power vs. Racism: Harold Washington Becomes Mayor," in *The New Black Vote: Politics and Power in Four American Cities*, ed. Rod Bush (San Francisco: Synthesis, 1984), pp. 78–79.

14. Ibid., p. 80.

15. Ibid.

16. Terrell, *The Chicago Mayoral Election of 1983*; *New York Times*, April 13, 1983, A-1.

17. Juan Andrade, Mid-West Voter Registration and Education Project, Speech, December 14, 1985, Chicago, Ill.

18. Nathaniel Sheppard, Jr., "Black-Oriented Radio, a Key in Chicago Election," *New York Times*, March 15, 1983, IV-24.

19. Alkalimat and Gillis, "Black Power vs. Racism," p. 85.

20. Nathaniel Sheppard, Jr., "Democrats Split on Support for Rep. Washington in Chicago," *New York Times*, March 14, 1983, I-11.

21. William Robbins, "Race Is a Muted Issue in Philadelphia," *New York Times*, April 12, 1983, I-16.

22. "A Philadelphia Story," *Newsweek*, April 11, 1983, p. 20.

23. Rod Bush, *The New Black Vote*, p. 37.

24. Manning Marable, *Black American Politics* (London: Verso Press, 1985), p. 274.

25. Bush, *The New Black Vote*; Marable, *Black American Politics*.

26. Kenneth Noble, "March in Capital Is Seen Spurring Vast Coalition," *New York Times*, August 29, 1983, I, A-12. See also Clarence Hunter, "Anti-Reagan Theme

Highlight of 1983 March on Washington," *Washington Afro-American,* August 30, 1983, p. 2.

27. Joint Center for Political Studies, "Largest Increase in BEOs Since 1976, *Focus* 12, no. 1 (January 1984): 8.

28. McAdam, *Political Process,* pp. 48–49.

29. Tom Madden, "Black Leaders Meet to Map Methods to Defeat Reagan," *Washington Afro-American,* March 15, 1983, p. 1.

30. Rev. Joseph Lowery *The Challenger* (Buffalo), March 16, 1983, p. 2.

31. Jacqueline Thomas, "Presidential Strategy Is Accelerated," *National Leader,* May 12, 1983, p. 1.

32. Christopher Edley, Jr., "Better No Black Candidate Than the Wrong One," *Washington Post,* April 29, 1983, A-29.

33. Thomas, "Presidential Strategy Is Accelerated."

34. The writer attended the meeting. See also "Seeking Votes and Clout," *Time,* August 1983, pp. 20–24, 26.

35. Milton Coleman, "Jackson Preaching Politics of Putting a Black Man in the White House," *Washington Post,* March 19, 1983, A-6.

36. Faye Joyce, "Jackson Moves Fast for One Who Hasn't Yet Decided to Run," *New York Times,* July 31, 1983, IV-4.

37. "Should a Black Run for President in 1984?" *Ebony,* October 9, 1983, p. 125.

38. Rob Gloster, "Jackson Leaves PUSH to Ponder Campaign," *National Leader,* October 6, 1983, p. 5.

39. Manning Marable, "Jesse Jackson for President?" *Washington Afro-American,* March 22, 1983; Ronald Walters, "Why Blacks Can't Wait," *Washington Post,* March 25, 1983; Edley, "Better No Black Candidate."

40. Milton Coleman, "Jackson Preaching Politics."

41. John Conyers, Jr., "Transforming Politics with a 'Coalition of the Rejected,' " *Washington Post,* July 21, 1983, A-23.

42. "A Black Candidate in 1984?" *Newsweek,* June 6, 1983, pp. 36–37.

43. Joyce, "Jackson Moves Fast."

44. "Should a Black Man Run for President in 1984?"

45. "Jesse Jackson Says He'll Decide by October," *National Leader,* September 22, 1983, p. 14.

46. *The Challenger,* September 7, 1983, p. 1.

47. "Seeking Votes and Clout," pp. 31–33.

48. "An Explosive Orator's Campaign Breeds Fusion and Fission for the Democratic Party," *People Weekly,* December 26, 1983–January 2, 1984, p. 30; "Is the U.S. Ready for a Black President?" *U.S. News and World Report,* July 25, 1983, pp. 21–22.

49. Michael Barone, "Running for President–or From Reality?" *Washington Post,* March 14, 1983, A-11.

50. Ibid.

51. M. Dowd, "Fresh Faces for an Old Struggle," *Time,* August 22, 1983, pp. 32–33; "Jesse Jumps In," *Newsweek,* November 14, 1983, p. 43; also Jean Thornton, "Jesse Jackson Shakes Up Race for the White House," *U.S. News and World Report,* December 19, 1983, pp. 35–37.

52. Adam Clymer, "Lessons for All Democrats," *New York Times,* February 24, 1983, II-11.

53. Thomas, "Presidential Strategy Is Accelerated," p. 3.

54. "Demo Leaders Tell Their Choices for '84," *U.S. News and World Report,* August 29, 1983, p. 21.

55. "Mondale and Jackson Camps Engage in Unusual Dialogue," *Washington Post,* July 23, 1983, A-4.

56. *CBS/New York Times Poll,* June 1983, CBS News, New York.

57. Hamilton Jordan, "Is Chicago Really So Important?" *Washington Post,* April 12, 1983, A-17. See also Tom Wicker, "Blacks and Chicago," *New York Times,* April 13, 1983, 31. His sentiment was that a black candidacy would result in a "considerable shake-up within the Democratic party," since whites constantly counsel blacks to "support the party," comforting themselves that blacks really have "no place to go."

58. McAdam, *Political Process,* p. 233.

59. "Jesse Jackson Wins Black Lawmaker's Backing," *Los Angeles Times,* September 30, 1983, I-18. Estimates from this meeting were that Jackson had the support of 11 to 13 members of the Caucus, who would support him as individuals, not as Caucus members. See also "Jesse Jackson Places Second in Straw Poll," *The Challenger,* December 14, 1983, p. 13. Article cites Jackson's close second place to Mondale in a poll of the New York State Public Employees Federation AFL-CIO, local 157.

60. Institute for Social Research, *National Black Election Study, Pre-election Survey* (Ann Arbor: University of Michigan, 1984).

PART II

The Constituents

Jesse Jackson's Campaign: Constituency Attitudes and Political Outcomes

3

William Crotty

E. E. Schattschneider defined democracy in *The Semi-Sovereign People* as "a competitive political system in which competing leaders and organizations define the alternatives of public policy in such a way that the public can participate in the decision-making process." The process is not neutral: some groups are represented, some are not; some have more weight in decisions and receive more of the rewards of the society than others. It is also not intrinsically representative or fair: each group fights for what it can get by backing leaders and policies that reflect its interests and then managing the scope of the conflict in such a manner as to maximize its chances of winning its objectives. "The development or expansion of conflict, the changing scope of the involvement and . . . the displacement of subordinate conflicts by dominant conflicts" are all important to the group and to the society for in "American politics . . . the scope of a conflict determines its outcome." "Every change in the scope of conflict has a bias: it is partisan in nature. That is, it must be assumed that every change in the number of participants is about something, that the newcomers have sympathies or antipathies that make it possible to involve them. By definition, the intervening bystanders are not neutral. Thus, in political conflict every change in scope changes the equation." [1]

Those in power—those with a comfortable control of decision-making—have much to lose through the "socialization" or "contagion," i.e., expansion, of conflict. The more people included in the process and the more organized demands put forward for consideration, the greater the challenge to those in charge of the management of the conflict. Organization through elections, on the other hand, is potentially the greatest single weapon available within the American political system for those on the fringes of political decision-making. It is their best opportunity to share power, to have their concerns addressed, and to win a proportionate distribution of the rewards the society has to bestow. Needless to say, any new mobilizations or efforts to expand the bounds of conflict will be resisted and resented by those dominant in the process.

Schattschneider's thesis has particular applicability to Jesse Jackson's campaign to win the Democratic party's presidential nomination in 1984. Jackson's constituency, as he represented it to the Democratic National Convention, was "the damned, disinherited, disrespected and the despised"; its purpose, to seek recognition: "They are restless and seek relief. . . . They have invested the faith, hope and trust that they have in us. . . . I pledge my best not to let them down." [2]

But such efforts are not easy. Any group attempting to mobilize political power and articulate its will has problems. According to Schattschneider, "The role of conflict in the political system depends . . . on the morale, self-confidence and security of the individuals and groups who must challenge the dominant groups in the community in order to raise an opposition." [3] Blacks, even more than most groups, face formidable difficulties. To address these problems and to place the Jackson campaign in an understandable perspective, this essay first looks at the context of American politics in which Jackson was to compete, with particular attention to (1) the attitudinal and societal barriers encountered by blacks that formed the environment in which the conflict was to take place and (2) the forces specific to the prenomination race of 1984 that established the immediate political climate in which Jackson was to contest. This discussion is followed by a review and analysis of the Jackson prenomination campaign bid.

The Context of the Jackson Presidential Race

The Candidate

Jesse Jackson's run for the Democratic party's presidential nomination is best seen in broad context. Jackson is not a politician nor is he an experienced national political figure. He was not a serious threat to other Democratic candidates for the nomination. In fact, within the contemporary political environment, a black's—any black's—chance of representing one of the major parties as its presidential nominee was, at best, infinitesimal. And Jesse Jackson was not just any black. He was a Protestant minister; a former follower of Martin Luther King, Jr., in the southern civil rights movement; the founder and head of Operation PUSH, an organization promoting black economic and educational advancement; and a highly visible spokesperson for the black community—particularly, as he saw it, an advocate for poor blacks. And he was controversial. The policy stands Jackson took; the confrontational manner in which he chose to dramatize them, using the media, and especially television, to personalize social problems many would have preferred to ignore; his seeming willingness to flaunt conventions, whether in meeting with Fidel

Castro in Cuba or the Sandinistas in Nicaragua or in flying to Syria to secure the release of an American prisoner, Navy Lt. Robert Goodman; his boldness in stepping forth, as he did in the presence of Ronald Reagan at the White House ceremony welcoming back Goodman, to state the need for leadership in the quest for peace; and, perhaps most of all, his forceful, even flamboyant, style in persistently voicing his views annoyed and even scared many. Whites, politicians of both parties, and even black leaders found much to criticize in Jackson's approach. He was not a conventional presidential candidate, and he did not run a traditional nomination campaign. His entry into the presidential race was not welcomed by the Democratic party nor by many black politicians who either had committed to a candidate or who felt he might prove an embarrassment to them and to the black community, strong enough to trigger a reaction that could hurt the concerns they all held in common.

Why then did Jackson run? The answer to this question and to questions concerning the type of campaign Jackson ran is best found in the web of American culture and its anomalous relationship to blacks.

The Long-Run Public Mood

In 1944 Gunnar Myrdal, a Swedish social economist, published a massive study, funded by the Carnegie Corporation, of "the Negro in America." The picture that emerged of the black's place in American society was not pleasant. By virtually any standards—economic, educational, social, legal, political— the black was at or near the bottom of the American social order, more a victim of the system than a partner in it. The findings in themselves were not surprising. What was new was the comprehensive documentation of the long-term severity of the problems encountered. Even more painful, for whites in particular, was the disparity between what Americans believed, what Myrdal called "the American Creed"—"American ideals and behavior"—and "American attitudes and actions with respect to the Negro." Myrdal's American Creed was familiar: those "ideals of the essential dignity of the individual human being, of the fundamental equality of all men, and of certain inalienable rights to freedom, justice, and a fair opportunity represent to the American people this essential meaning of the nation's early struggle for independence." [4] But the American Creed did not appear to apply to blacks. This disparity caused an enormous tension in the society and raised fundamental questions as to what the nation was all about in contrast to what Americans believed it represented. Hence Myrdal's title: *An American Dilemma*. Despite a world war and Vietnam, the civil rights acts of the late 1950s and 1960s and the Voting Rights acts, Franklin Roosevelt's New Deal and Lyndon Johnson's Great Society, despite Birmingham, Bull Connor, and Martin Luther King, Jr., despite the passage of four decades of virtually constant turmoil, the legacy of that "dilemma" remains.

There is no lack of studies to illustrate the problem and the continuing tension it produces. In 1942, about the time the Myrdal team was concluding their research, the National Opinion Research Center conducted a nationwide poll in which more than half of the respondents agreed that there should be separate sections for Negroes in street cars and buses (51 percent), Negro and white soldiers should not serve together in the Armed Forces (51 percent), there should be separate restaurants for Negroes and whites (69 percent), and there should be separate sections in cities and towns for Negroes and whites (84 percent).[5] Twenty-two years later (1964), Lloyd A. Free and Hadley Cantril in their study *The Political Beliefs of Americans* found that from 39 percent of the extreme liberals up to 71 percent of the extreme conservatives (the average for all of the groups in the population was 54 percent) believed that "most of the organizations pushing for civil rights have been infiltrated by the Communists and are now dominated by Communist trouble-makers."[6] The majority of respondents (56 percent) also felt that integration was going too fast (as against 18 percent who thought the pace "about right" and 20 percent who felt it was "not fast enough"). When the respondents were asked if blacks should have more influence in government and political matters than they did, 30 percent felt blacks should have more, 31 percent said "less," and 28 percent considered it was "about right." Since the authors believed "Negro influence was still minimal at the time of our survey in the fall of 1964," they saw the results as a confirmation of a country's racial bias.[7]

The 1980s are not the 1930s or even the 1960s. Attitudes can change. A series of studies published in the 1980s indicated a tolerance for civil rights for blacks, at least in the abstract.[8] Other attitudes resist change. When asked if more minority students should be admitted to college, over 80 percent of the respondents in both a mass and leadership sample said "only if normal standards of admission are met" and 83 percent of the mass sample and 50 percent of the elite sample opted for keeping children in their neighborhoods rather than busing them to achieve racial balance in schools (only 6 percent of the mass and 25 percent of the elite samples favored this option). When asked whether laws giving preferential treatment in hiring to minorities were "necessary to make up for a long history of discrimination" or were "unfair to qualified people who are not members of a minority," 76 and 62 percent of the mass and elite samples, respectively, believed them unfair and only 10 percent of the mass sample and 26 percent of the elite survey felt they were needed to overcome past discrimination. While just under 80 percent of the American public believed that minorities should not get special treatment in seeking jobs or getting into college, 60 percent felt the government should offer free special-education courses so minorities could do better in testing; slightly over 50 percent felt that if minorities did not receive equal treatment in jobs or housing, the government should intervene to see that they were treated the same as others; over 50 percent believed the government should support the right of blacks to patronize any hotel or restaurant they chose; and slightly under 50 percent took the "in between" option when asked if they were in favor of desegregation (35 percent said "yes"), segregation (14 percent said "yes") or "something in between." Things may have improved in some respects, but the intensity of support for black concerns is not great, and a sensitivity to the problems faced by blacks does not appear widespread (as the segregation-desegregation question suggests). Herbert McClosky and John Zaller conclude from their analysis that "contemporary Americans are far less prejudiced toward minorities . . . than they were forty or fifty years ago. Moreover, majorities now *favor* government action to combat many forms of discrimination once widely accepted as normal."[9] Still, an ambivalence remains—the continuation of the Myrdal dilemma in a different time frame but with basically the same issues at stake.

Further, blacks perceive themselves as a group, and are perceived by others, as being uninfluential, ranking close to the bottom (just above feminists) in a study of national leadership perceptions and views by Sidney Verba and Gary R. Orren. The authors write:

> When it comes to perceptions and values about influence, blacks . . . lose both ways. Their weakness is apparent both to themselves and to others. In addition, they must exercise more overt influence because their access to established channels is limited and they lack the special legitimacy of business. Just as established groups such as business get the double benefit of a reputation for considerable influence and the unobtrusive exercise of that influence, the challenging groups have the double disadvantage of a reputation for little influence and the need to be obtrusive in attempting to exercise what little influence they have.[10]

The Jackson campaign was to be obtrusive. It carried the accumulated weight of a historically ambivalent public and governmental attitude towards blacks. It was to be self-assertive in style and substance, not the tradition of black politicians within the parties; and it was to challenge the values, patience, and understanding of the more conventional political world into which it had intruded.

The immediate factors leading to Jackson's candidacy are well developed by Lucius Barker in the first essay in this book. They tie into and re-emphasize the anomalous position of blacks in American society. Ronald Reagan, the Republican incumbent seeking re-election, and his administration had given black concerns and programs relevant to black needs the lowest of priorities. If anything, these were the targets of his administration. The results of Reaganite policies were far-reaching, and blacks had little difficulty in affixing responsibility.[11]

The Democratic Party—ostensibly the party of black advancement and the advocate of the poor—did not welcome Jackson's candidacy. Many Democratic professionals hoped to settle early on front-runner Walter Mondale as their most formidable candidate. Mondale lay claim to the black vote and neither he nor many other Democrats welcomed another candidate into the race—especially one who threatened to reopen a dialogue over black interests and political allegiances (which Jackson did) and to make the road to the nomination that much harder and more contentious for the party's first choice.[12] All of this is, again, well captured in Lucius Barker's opening essay and needs no repeating here.

To further aggravate matters, there were other problems peculiar to the Jackson campaign. Late entry to the race; no organization; divided support from the established black leadership; no funding; no campaign master plan; policy appeals out-of-tune with the times; an often alienated and politically inactive core constituency; a flamboyant personal and oratorical style, unfamiliar and even threatening to whites; no major support from unions or PACs outside of the black community; and no previous track record in national politics—the Jackson campaign had little to recommend it.

Despite it all, Jackson entered the race. The Democrats were not pleased. A difficult campaign year had been made infinitely more trying.

Mondale won as expected, but not as comfortably or by the margin predicted. After ending the primary season within sight of the majority needed for the nomination, Mondale went on to receive 55 percent of the delegate votes cast at the national convention to Hart's 30 percent and Jackson's 11 percent. There were other setbacks for Jackson. The National Convention also rejected by decisive margins three of the four minority platform planks sponsored by the Jackson forces.

For Jackson, then, the campaign had to be the message.

The Prenomination Race

Jackson on the Attack

The Jackson approach was intense, emotional, galvanizing—in style and substance not the normal fare of presidential politics. With the fervor of the preacher, Jackson carried his appeals to the prenomination voters:

On domestic issues: concern and compassion

> Three million more on welfare. Four million more unemployed and more government-subsidized millionaires than ever before. In so many ways, a dark hour. Able, bright, brilliant young people turned away from colleges because they don't have scholarships. In so many ways a dark hour.
>
> We should not get trapped trying to color poverty. Poverty is not black, it's not brown, it's not white. Color poverty, pain, hurt, agony, ache, necessity, desperation, destitution.

If you're tired of hunger, vote about it. . . . If you want jobs, vote about it. If you want a better education, vote about it. If you want your children to go to school and not go to jail, vote about it. If you want peace and justice, vote about it.

They [steel companies] close a plant on workers without notice, that is violence. Ninety thousand corporations paid no taxes. That's wrong, that's violent, that's mean, that's cruel. That's irresponsible.

On foreign policy: tolerance, understanding, and leadership

Great moves in foreign policy are initiated by presidents and leaders.

Reagan is embracing a movement to overthrow a government in Nicaragua; a legitimate government in Nicaragua. . . . We need new leadership.

Stop killing in Central America. Stop killing in Grenada. Stop killing in Lebanon. Stop embracing South Africa. Let's go another way! Choose peace. Not war.

On Ronald Reagan: ridicule and rejection

The best way to keep Reagan from running is to announce he has to debate me. Let him come late, crippled or lame. David didn't back down, he faced Goliath. Goliath can't stand this power. Now our time has come.

We must be driven not by a negative—the fear of Reagan—but by the positive leadership and programs of the Democratic Party. It is not enough motivation just to vote against Reagan, we must inspire our constituency to vote for us. We must offer our people the vision of a just society and the dream of a peaceful world. We must inspire the American people with hope. We must put forth the vision of a government that cares for all of its people; the vision of a people at work rebuilding its nation.

On blacks, the Rainbow Coalition, and the future: hope

We can't ride to freedom on Pharaoh's chariot. It [freedom] means self-respect, self-government. It means an ideology in the human rights tradition. Black, yellow, red and white we are all precious in God's sight. It doesn't mean English or Spanish. A broken heart is the same language.

The fact is, I look at the missing windowpane, that's the slummy side. Train that youth to become a glazier and let him in the union, that's the sunny side. Whenever I see a missing brick, that's the slummy side. *Train* our youth to become brick masons and let them in the unions, that's the *sunny* side. When I see a missing door, that's the slummy side. Train our youth to become carpenters, that's the sunny side. All this writing on the walls! Let us become painters and artists and use our creativity. Just because it rains, you don't have to drown! [Italics in original]

Brown, black and white, we're all precious in God's sight. I AM SOME-BODY!

You are God's child. When I was in my mother's belly no father to give me a name . . . they called me bastard and rejected me. You are somebody . . . you are God's child.

What this campaign has shown above all else is that the key to our liberation is in our own hands, and in our dream and vision of a better world. It is the vision that allows us to reach out to each other and to redeem each other. It is the dream that sustains us through the dark times and the dark realities. It is our hope that gives us a "why" for living, when we do not see "how" to live.[13]

Such was the message of the Jackson campaign. The style was that of a Southern Baptist minister. The words could have come (as they often did) from the pulpit of a church. The message was repeated over and over throughout the prenomination campaign.

The Campaign Trail

Jackson announced his candidacy on November 3, 1983, a late entry into the race by recent standards. The first test of the 1984 presidential year came in the Iowa caucuses on February 20. Not expected to do well—his late start, his lack of organization in Iowa, and the absence of a natural constituency within the state all worked against him—Jackson received 1.5 percent of the vote. Mondale won decisively with 49 percent of the Democratic caucus vote, and Hart established himself as his principal contender with 17 percent of the caucus vote, a few thousand more than any of the other contenders.

The next test after Iowa was New Hampshire's first-in-the-nation primary eight days later (February 28). This primary firmly established Hart as a serious candidate. Gaining momentum in the last few days before the vote, Hart won 39 percent of the returns to Mondale's 29 percent. Jackson received a modest 5 percent (Table 1). After the New Hampshire results were in, Alan Cranston dropped out of the race, followed in early March by Ernest Hollings and Reubin Askew.

Hart did well in early March, winning the Wyoming caucuses and Vermont's nonbinding primary. Jackson showed little. On Super Tuesday I (March 13) primaries were held in five states (Alabama, Florida, Georgia, Massachusetts, and Rhode Island) and caucuses in four others (Hawaii, Nevada, Oklahoma, and Washington). Hart won again in New England, capturing the Massachusetts and Rhode Island primaries and winning an upset victory in Florida. He also won the West, taking the Nevada, Oklahoma, and Washington caucuses. Hart's showing on March 13 was to be the high-water mark of his campaign. Mondale won difficult primary fights in Alabama and Georgia and the Hawaii caucuses, enough to keep him firmly in the race. By mid-March Mondale was again in control and steadily, if unspectacularly, increased his delegate lead over Hart until the national convention. After Super Tuesday I, John Glenn and George McGovern also withdrew from the race, leaving the field to Mondale, Hart, and Jackson.

Super Tuesday I witnessed the first of the Jackson campaign's successes. Jackson finished third in Florida and Georgia and fourth in Alabama. Still, 45 percent of the eligible black population voted in Georgia (compared to 25 percent of the eligible white population) and Jackson received 21 percent of the vote in Georgia; 20 percent in Alabama, despite opposition from a number of black leaders who supported Mondale (including Mayor Richard Arrington of Birmingham); and 12 percent in Florida (see table 1). This was the Jackson campaign's first major breakthrough.

Jackson followed these successes by winning 70 percent of the black primary vote in his home state of Illinois on March 20. In a race won by Mondale with 41 percent of the primary vote, Jackson received an impressive 21 percent. In early April (April 3), Jackson took 26 percent of the New York primary vote (in a contest again won by Mondale with 45 percent of the vote) and 81 percent of the black vote—the Jackson campaign's most convincing win of the primary season. Jackson came back a week later (April 10) to win 72 percent of the black vote and 16 percent of the total vote in the Pennsylvania primary, a race again won by Mondale (with 45 percent of the vote).

On May 1, in the predominantly black District of Columbia, Jackson won 67 percent of the vote and his first primary victory, and he captured the Louisiana primary four days later with 43 percent of the vote in a race boycotted by significant numbers of whites. Jackson also captured 25 percent of the vote in Tennessee (May 1), and in the Super Tuesday II primaries on May 8 he received 14 percent of the vote in Indiana, 25 percent in North Carolina, 26 percent in Maryland, and 16 percent in Ohio. On the final primary day (June 5) he did well again, taking 20 percent of the California vote, 24 percent of New Jersey's, and 12 percent of New Mexico's.

All represented significant showings that served to re-emphasize the credibility of the Jackson effort and the strength of its appeal to blacks. However, as the campaign period entered its final stages, Mondale won consistently enough (Tennessee, Maryland, North Carolina, New Jersey, and West Virginia) to maintain a clear lead. Hart took enough contests (close races in Indiana, Ohio, California, and South Dakota and more decisive victories in Nevada, Oregon, Idaho, and New Mexico) to maintain the viability of his own effort and to deny Mondale an early nomination victory. Although Jackson did well as his campaign gained momentum in the later stages of the nominating season, most of the attention he received focused on the extent to which he would be a decisive factor at the national convention and the degree to which he might hurt the Mondale candidacy in the fall's general election. As it turned out, Jackson played a somewhat subdued role at the national convention, delivering a well-received speech, winning one of four platform fights, and sponsoring, along with the Hart delegates, a successful motion to establish a commission to reassess the nominating rules for 1988. In the fall election, Jackson supported Mondale and campaigned for the Democratic ticket.

Table 1. Primary Results, 1984 Democratic Prenomination Race

State	Estimated Turnout	% Hart	% Jackson	% Mondale	% Others	Uncommitted
New Hampshire (2/28)	101,131	37.3*	5.3	27.9	29.5	
Vermont (3/6)[a]	74,059	70.0*	7.8	20.0	2.2	
Alabama (3/13)	428,283	20.7	19.6	34.6*	24.1	1.0
Florida (3/13)	1,160,713	40.0*	12.4	32.1	15.5	
Georgia (3/13)	684,541	27.3	21.0	30.5*	20.8	0.4
Massachusetts (3/13)	630,962	39.0*	5.0	25.5	29.7	0.8
Rhode Island (3/13)	44,511	45.0*	8.7	34.4	10.9	1.0
Puerto Rico (3/18)	143,039	0.6		99.1*	0.3	
Illinois (3/20)	1,659,425	35.2	21.0	40.5*	3.3	
Connecticut (3/27)	220,842	52.6*	12.0	29.1	5.4	0.9
New York (4/3)	1,387,950	27.4	25.6	44.8*	2.2	
Wisconsin (4/3)[a]	635,768	44.4*	9.9	41.1	3.5	1.1
Pennsylvania (4/10)	1,656,294	33.3	16.0	45.1*	5.6	
District of Columbia (5/1)	102,731	7.1	67.3*	25.6		
Tennessee (5/1)	322,063	29.1	25.3	41.0*	2.5	2.1
Louisiana (5/5)	318,810	25.0	42.9*	22.3	3.7	6.1
Indiana (5/8)	716,955	41.8*	13.7	40.9	3.6	
Maryland (5/8)	506,886	24.3	25.5	42.5*	4.6	3.1
North Carolina (5/8)	960,857	30.2	25.4	35.6*	4.2	4.6
Ohio (5/8)	1,444,797	42.1*	16.4	40.3	1.2	
Nebraska (5/15)	148,855	58.2*	9.1	26.6	3.0	3.1
Oregon (5/15)	397,892	58.7*	9.3	27.7	4.3	
Idaho (5/22)[a]	54,722	58.0*	5.7	30.1	2.2	4.0
California (6/5)[b]	2,724,248	41.2*	19.6	37.4	1.8	
New Jersey (6/5)	676,561	29.7	23.6	45.2*	1.5	
New Mexico (6/5)	187,403	46.8*	11.8	36.1	4.5	0.8
South Dakota (6/5)	52,561	50.7*	5.2	39.0	2.6	2.5
West Virginia (6/5)	369,245	37.3	6.7	53.8*	2.2	
North Dakota (6/12)[a]	33,555	85.2*		2.8	12.0	
National Primary Total	17,845,659	36.2	18.3	38.6	6.2	0.7

Source: *Congressional Quarterly*

Note: Asterisk (*) indicates winner.

[a]Nonbinding primary, delegates selected by caucus process.

[b]No Democratic preference vote was held. The vote for each candidate's most popular delegate in each congressional district was aggregated to get a statewide total.

The Jackson Constituency

The major strengths and weaknesses of the Jackson candidacy can be seen in an analysis of the groups his campaign targeted. First, in the primaries Jackson's potential constituency, broadly defined as the disadvantaged for the moment, was limited (table 4). Jackson attempted to appeal to the young, the less educated, those least well-off economically, and liberals.[14] Judging from a look at the primary electorate (table 2), each of these groups makes up between 14 and 27 percent of those who participated, not in themselves encouraging numbers. Further, with the exception of liberals, each group is under-represented among primary voters compared to their proportionate strength among Democrats as a whole. This is not surprising: these groups (possibly excepting liberals) would be expected to participate less than others in primary or general elections. It is a difficult, even unpromising, base on which to build a presidential campaign.

Blacks and Whites: Two Different Political Worlds

The black constituency, which formed the base of Jackson's support, differed significantly on issues and in priorities from the white electorate. Yet to piece together a true Rainbow Coalition Jackson was going to have to appeal to both whites and blacks. The effort to unite the disadvantaged of the two races introduced a tension into the campaign that was never adequately resolved. Questions for the future may center on whether the differences can be bridged. Is another Jackson-style effort feasible?

The problems are fundamental.[15] The races agree on little. A poll on black/white differences commissioned by the Joint Center for Political Studies during the 1984 election and carried out by the Gallup organization, sheds some light on fundamental differences (see table 3).

Socio-Economic Profile. Demographically, fewer blacks than whites have jobs (almost one-half of the blacks surveyed are unemployed) and, when working, are less likely to be employed full-time. Significantly fewer blacks than whites are married, but blacks are more likely to have children living in the household and more of them. Considerably more whites than blacks own, rather than rent, their homes. Blacks are less well educated; most have attended high school, but only one in four (as against 44 percent of the whites interviewed) entered either college or a post-secondary trade school. Blacks earn significantly less than whites, the modal category being incomes below $10,000, while most whites earn $20,000 or more. Not surprisingly, given all of this, the modal category of blacks believe themselves economically worse off than four years ago while the modal category of whites see themselves as in improved financial conditions.

Table 2. Demographic groups' proportionate share of 1984 Democratic party's primary electorate, Democratic party's membership and U.S. population

		Primary voters		Group as percent of all Democrats	Group as percent of total population
		In millions	In percent		
Sex	Men	7.85	46	46	48
	Women	9.09	54	54	52
Race	White	13.14	78	75	84
	Black	3.05	18	22	12
	White men	6.21	37	35	40
	White women	6.92	41	40	44
	Black men	1.31	8	10	5
	Black women	1.83	11	12	6
Age	18–29	2.89	17	25	30
	30–44	5.20	31	26	28
	45–59	4.02	24	24	21
	60 and older	4.82	28	25	21
	Men under 45	3.63	21	24	28
	Men 45 and older	4.17	25	22	20
	Women under 45	4.46	26	27	30
	Women 45 and older	4.68	28	26	22
Family Income	Under $25,000	9.18	54	61	55
	$25,000 and over	7.78	46	39	45
	Men under $25,000	3.99	24	27	26
	Men $25,000 and over	3.90	23	20	23
	Women under $25,000	5.13	30	33	28
	Women $25,000 and over	3.91	23	19	22
Education	Less than high school	2.41	14	32	27
	High school graduate	5.54	33	41	40
	Some college	4.51	27	16	17
	College graduate	4.48	26	11	16
Ideology	Liberal	4.49	27	21	16
	Moderate	7.97	47	47	44
	Conservative	3.54	21	25	31
Union household		5.57	33	30	25

Source: *New York Times*, June 17, 1984, p. 4E. The data reported are from a variety of sources including network and newspaper exit polls, secretaries of state, and *Congressional Quarterly*.

Political attitudes. The attitudes toward government of both blacks and whites should not inspire confidence. For both groups, they are negative, although substantially more negative for the black population. More than seven out of ten black respondents are dissatisfied with the way things are going in the country (as against 43 percent of the whites), believed public officials do not care what people think (as against 52 percent of the whites), feel that those elected to Congress lose touch with their constituents (as against 64 percent of the whites), and agree that political parties are only interested in a person's vote (as against 53 percent of the whites). Two out of three of both races believed government is too complicated to understand and slightly more than one-half of the blacks feel they do not have a say in government while roughly the same proportion of whites believe they do. Both groups may be right. Blacks certainly exhibit little confidence in political processes. Government, they feel, is not concerned with their problems. White respondents are not necessarily enthusiastic about government in general but they clearly feel they have a stronger voice in political decision-making.

Issue positions. The issue positions of blacks and whites again differ markedly. Pronouncedly more blacks than whites disapprove of the Reagan administration's handling of the economy (85 percent to 38 percent), the budget deficit (77 percent to 59 percent), the employment problem (89 percent to 40 percent), foreign policy (67 percent to 40 percent), relations with the Soviet Union (63 percent to 37 percent) and the crisis in Central America (66 percent to 43 percent). Even more polarized are the racial divisions as to the Reagan administration's handling of civil rights (82 percent of the blacks disapprove to 29 percent of the whites) and its approach to poor people (94 percent of the blacks disapprove to 56 percent of the whites).

Far and away the most important problem facing the nation for blacks is unemployment. One-half as many white respondents as black rank this number one along with the budget deficit. Other differences are noticeable in the priorities attached to civil rights, inflation, government programs for the poor, and nuclear policy. When asked to rank themselves on a seven-point scale relating to government spending for defense, better than one-half of the blacks cluster toward the less spending alternatives while 60 percent of the whites position themselves in the middle of the scale, apparently believing the current levels of investment in defense are about right. Using the same type of scale, on social programs the majority of white respondents cluster in the middle, again appearing to support administration policies of bare-bones social outlays as they did the recent heavy emphasis on military expenditures. Three out of four blacks take the most extreme scale positions in favor of a heavily increased emphasis on social programs.

To review such statistics, one has to remind oneself that both groups are operating in the same political environment at the same point in time. The responses on policy and the emphasis given and support for administration actions present a mirror image for each of the racial groups. Blacks and whites appear to inhabit two different economic and issue worlds.

Political patterns. Politically, both groups have about the same interest in politics and concern over the election outcome. Although blacks turn out with somewhat less frequency than whites, better than eight in ten of both races intended to vote in the 1984 election. Most whites interviewed see themselves as politically moderate to slightly conservative (62 percent) while most blacks interviewed see themselves as moderate to very liberal (73 percent). Blacks affiliate overwhelmingly with the Democratic party while whites divide themselves roughly evenly among Independents, Democrats, and Republicans. In data not reported in the table, two out of three blacks said they believed Reagan did not care about blacks and that another Republican administration would be much the same. Seventy percent said they could expect more help from a Democratic administration, evidence of the extremely close ties of blacks to one party—a relationship that may hurt their bargaining position within a two-party competitive situation and one that may also keep them from forming an independent political group or third party.[16] Given the forgoing, and not unexpectedly, blacks overwhelmingly disapproved of Reagan's conduct of the presidency, while the majority of whites approved (57 percent). Most blacks supported Jesse Jackson in the Democratic race. Four percent of the white respondents did.

In relation to the perception of and qualities associated with Reagan, Mondale, and Jackson, again the racial differences are major. Black respondents believed Reagan racially prejudiced, unfair, insensitive to their problems, lacking in compassion, ineffective (from their vantage point), quick to rely on military force, and indebted to a number of political groups. Clearly, blacks do not like Ronald Reagan. The picture is almost universally negative. The best black respondents could say was that about one-half thought the president was knowledgeable.

Whites, on the other hand, like Reagan. They see him as informed, hardworking, a strong leader able to get things done, fair and unprejudiced, and, although less intensely, compassionate, clear on his positions, and sensitive to the concerns of people like themselves.

The polar extreme of such views can be found in the perceptions of Jesse Jackson. Blacks like him, see him as representing their interests, and assess him in the most positive of terms. On the average, nine out of ten black respondents feel he is a strong leader, fair, unprejudiced, caring, compassionate, knowledgeable, hard-working, and so on. Although white respondents also believe Jackson to be hard-working, they see little else to admire. Most ap-

pear willing to concede that he represents a new way of thinking and that he
may be knowledgeable and compassionate, but beyond this they are decidedly
lukewarm to negative in their perceptions (over one-half, for example, state
they felt he was prejudiced, unresponsive to their interests, and owed a lot of
favors).

Voters' perceptions of Walter Mondale fall somewhere in between. Black
and white respondents are comparatively close in their assessments of Mondale, although blacks are considerably more favorable in their views than
whites. White respondents liked Ronald Reagan. For them, Mondale was a
poor second. Blacks were extremely positive in their evaluations of Jesse
Jackson and far stronger in their support of the Democratic nominee, Walter
Mondale. In terms of the candidates and qualities associated with them, the
two races polarized: it is difficult to conceive of them being much further apart
in their perceptions.

Finally, blacks and whites see racial issues in quite different perspectives.
As vivid a demonstration of this as any is the question whether the situation
of blacks has improved in the last five years. Sixty-eight percent of the white
population thought it had gotten better, and, all told, 90 percent thought it
either better or the same. If there is no problem, then there is no reason for
complaint or for special concern. Whites appear to see no problem. They also
do not see themselves as racist; 43 percent believe most white people would
like to see blacks receive a better break, and another 30 percent believe most
whites did not care one way or the other whether blacks improved their lot or
were kept down. Blacks do not see matters in the same light. Roughly one-half
of the blacks tend to favor job preferences for minorities; three out of four
whites tend to oppose these.

Three out of four whites would vote for a "qualified" black candidate for
president. Ninety percent of the blacks would. Interestingly, 18 percent of the
white population said they would not vote for a black. The figure is probably
much higher, but at a minimum one out of five whites would refuse to support
a black candidacy under any conditions. This could well be an indication of the
hardcore racist sympathies. The problem, of course, is broader. Most whites
do not believe themselves anti-black yet at the same time see no black problem
and support policies and an administration that blacks reject emphatically. Such
perceptions reveal fundamental differences in policy concerns and political
positions that offer no obvious common grounds.

The different emphases carry over to perceptions of the Jackson campaign.
Two out of three blacks said that Jesse Jackson's campaign had made them
more likely to vote in November; the same proportion of whites said it had
no effect on their intentions. Better than one-half of the black respondents
felt that Jackson's endorsement of the Democratic ticket helped solidify their
support for it; most whites reported that the endorsement had no effect on

Table 3. Political views of blacks and whites, 1984

Social Profile	% Blacks	% Whites
Employment status		
Employed full-time	40	47
Employed part-time	10	12
Not employed	48	38
Own or rent home		
Own	46	71
Rent	49	24
Other arrangement	4	4
Formal education (highest level completed)		
Grade 0–4	4	1
5–7	7	3
8	5	7
9–11	23	10
12	25	36

Social Profile	% Blacks	% Whites
Technical, trade, business school	4	7
Some college	15	17
College graduate	8	20
Family income		
Less than $10,000	43	18
$10,000 – $20,000	30	29
Over $20,000	24	53
Marital status		
Married	45	68
Single	31	16
Divorced	10	6
Separated	5	6
Widowed	9	8

Social Profile	% Blacks	% Whites
Children living in household		
None	41	55
1	18	18
2	18	15
3	13	6
4	5	2
5 or more	3	0
Financially better off than a year ago		
Better off	30	46
Worse off	43	25
About the same	24	27
Don't know	2	2

Attitudes toward the political system	% Blacks	% Whites
Generally satisfied with the way things are going in the United States		
Satisfied	14	48
Dissatisfied	79	43
No opinion	7	9
Voting is the only way people like me have a say in the government		
Agree	75	60
Disagree	20	30
Don't know	5	3

Attitudes toward the political system	% Blacks	% Whites
Politics and government too complicated to understand		
Agree	67	67
Disagree	29	31
Don't know	4	2
Public officials don't care what people think		
Agree	72	52
Disagree	23	42
Don't know	5	6
People like me don't have a say in what government does		
Agree	53	38

Attitudes toward the political system	% Blacks	% Whites
Disagree	43	58
Don't know	4	4
Those elected to Congress lose touch with people		
Agree	78	64
Disagree	14	30
Don't know	8	6
Parties are only interested in people's vote		
Agree	74	53
Disagree	20	40
Don't know	6	7

Issue Positions	% Blacks	% Whites
Approve or disapprove of Reagan handling:		
Economic Conditions		
Approve	10	54
Disapprove	85	38
No opinion	5	8
Budget Deficit		
Approve	8	24
Disapprove	77	59
No opinion	15	17
Unemployment		
Approve	7	52
Disapprove	89	40
No opinion	5	8
Foreign policy		
Approve	11	41
Disapprove	67	40
No opinion	22	19
Relations with Soviet Union		
Approve	13	47
Disapprove	63	37
No opinion	24	16
Situation in Central America		
Approve	7	29
Disapprove	66	43
No opinion	27	28
Situation of poor people in United States		
Approve	3	31
Disapprove	94	56
No opinion	3	14
Civil rights of minority groups		
Approve	10	48
Disapprove	82	29
No opinion	8	23
Most important problem facing nation		
Unemployment	40	20
Budget deficit	5	20
Civil rights of minorities	10	1
Inflation	7	14
Protecting American jobs	6	9
U.S. role in Central America	1	1
Relations with Soviet Union	2	7
Defense spending	2	5
Government programs to help poor	14	6
Quality of public education	2	2
U.S. nuclear weapons policy	4	11
U.S. relations with Soviet Union	0	0
Government spending on defense		
Spend much less 1	27	11
2	11	10
3	17	16
4	18	29
5	11	16
6	6	7
Spend much more 7	7	9
Don't know	4	3
Government spending on social programs		
Cut back 1	3	9
2	1	10
3	2	15
4	6	21
5	12	19
6	17	10
Spend more 7	57	15
Don't know	1	2

Table 3. (*Continued*)

Political Characteristics	% Blacks	% Whites
Interest in politics		
Great deal	29	23
Fair amount	41	49
Little	22	24
None	8	4
How often vote		
Always	35	38
Part of the time	22	30
Seldom	13	11
Other	1	1
Never	16	10
Plan to vote in November election		
Yes	85	86
No	9	9
Don't know	6	5
Approval of Reagan as president		
Approve	8	57
Disapprove	82	32
No opinion	11	11
Party affiliation		
Republican	3	30
Democrat	76	32
Independent	19	36
Other party	1	1
Degree of concern with outcome of election		
A great deal	56	51
Some	26	33
A little	11	10
Not at all	6	5
Don't know	1	1
Choice for Democratic Party's presidential nominee		
Gary Hart	4	40
Walter Mondale	30	36
Jesse Jackson	58	4
Don't know	7	20
Placement on liberal-conservative scale		
Very conservative 1	9	8
2	1	3
3	5	8
4	3	7
5	17	30
6	14	12
7	12	11
8	11	9
9	6	2
Very liberal 10	13	4
Don't know	8	5

Racial Perceptions	% Blacks	% Whites
Vote for qualified black for president		
Yes	91	74
No	5	18
Don't know	3	8
Support for job preference for blacks		
Strongly support 1	30	27
2	8	2
3	17	5
4	21	14
5	10	9
6	6	15
Strongly oppose 7	11	50
Don't know	3	3
Jackson impact on policies of Democratic party		
A great deal	67	22

Racial Perceptions	% Blacks	% Whites
Some	20	45
Little	6	20
Almost none	3	8
Don't know	4	5
Did Jackson campaign make you more likely to vote in November?		
More likely	65	20
Less likely	3	7
No effect	30	69
Don't know	2	4
Jackson endorsement of Mondale-Ferraro ticket make you more likely to vote Democratic in November?		
More likely	56	10
Less likely	4	17
No effect	37	68

Racial Perceptions	% Blacks	% Whites
Don't know	3	5
Press coverage of Jackson fair?		
Yes	50	79
No	41	9
Don't know	10	12
Situation of blacks improved over last five years?		
Better	37	68
Worse	30	4
Same	31	23
Don't know	2	5
Do white people want to see blacks		
Get better break	23	43
Keep down	40	18
Don't care	29	30
Don't know	8	9

Source: Joint Center for Political Studies, 1984 survey of black and white political attitudes conducted by the Gallup Poll.

their decision. Two out of three blacks believed the Jackson campaign had a significant influence on the Democratic party's policies. White respondents, while conceding some impact, were less sure of the extent of the campaign's influence. Eight out of ten white respondents felt the media had given the Jackson campaign fair coverage; a significant portion of the black population (41 percent) disagreed.

Overall, whites are relatively satisfied with the Reagan administration, its policies, and their own situations. Blacks most emphatically are not. There are two political worlds evident here that had consequences for the 1984 election. Jackson spoke to a disaffected minority that needed an advocate. He spoke both to them and for them. His chance for fashioning a broader coalition including any significant number of white voters was foredoomed. Walter Mondale, on the other hand, needed to placate the black constituency—a difficult thing to do given their alienation—and also to appeal to enough white voters, supportive of the Reagan policies, to put together an electoral majority. Obviously, he failed. It is worth speculating whether any candidate could have successfully bridged the polarization in perception of the two races. In 1984 it was unlikely. For Jackson, this meant that, at most, he could expect to speak for, and appeal to, blacks. This is basically what happened. A look at the poll results from selected primaries illustrates the point.

The Jackson Appeal in Selected Primaries

I have selected four primaries for an examination of the manner in which Jackson voters, and those supporting the other two remaining Democratic candidates, perceived their choices. The CBS poll results indicate the qualities associated with the candidates and the factors that held their coalitions together. Two of the primaries are in southern states, the Alabama and Georgia primaries held on Super Tuesday I (March 13), and two are in northern states, Illinois on March 20 and New York on April 3. In all, Jackson did well. He took 19.6 percent and 21 percent respectively in the Alabama and Georgia primaries, 21 percent in Illinois, and 25.6 percent in New York, his most dramatic showing.

The pattern of Jackson support is similar in each of the primaries (Tables 4,5,6). Jackson did best, first and foremost, among blacks (an average of 83 percent in the two northern states; in the South, he shared a portion of the black vote with Mondale). He held no appeal for white voters (for reasons that should be clear from the foregoing discussion, an average of only 3 percent of the whites voted for him in the four states).

The racial division of the vote is the key to the Jackson candidacy and its appeal, an indicator of its strength and its limitations. His was a constituency of disadvantaged blacks, liberals, the poor, and the less educated. Jackson voters saw themselves as worse off than they were a year ago, were strongly anti-Reagan, and were most likely to vote for the Democratic nominee (Mondale or Hart) regardless of who won the nomination.

Table 4. Profile of the candidates

	Reagan		Mondale		Jackson	
Percent describing the candidate as	Black	White	Black	White	Black	White
Knowledgeable	51	75	79	74	89	58
Prejudiced	72	31	13	17	15	56
Hard-working	33	72	77	77	93	78
Exciting	15	34	38	16	88	53
Can get things done	35	71	58	37	87	49
Compassionate	14	54	66	58	89	57
Owes a lot of political favors	65	40	38	49	23	34
Cares about people like me	8	49	63	49	94	37
Clear on issues	23	51	66	41	84	33
Too quick to use military force	72	39	11	10	10	15
Represents new ways of thinking	20	31	57	30	89	62
Fair	16	64	78	66	92	46
A strong leader	29	69	62	32	89	45

Jackson voters were also the most intensely committed. For example, they were considerably more likely to indicate they knew all along their choice for the nomination. They were also substantially more likely to isolate attention on their primary issue concerns—programs for the poor and unemployment —indicating relatively little support for other issue areas (outside of nuclear weapons). The Mondale and Hart voters had a wider spread of policy concerns they associated with their candidates and a lesser intensity and clarity of focus. Jackson reached his constituency on the issues of importance to him and them. Data bearing this out appear in the qualities supporters associated with their candidates. Jackson was perceived as a strong leader who cared about people and had something new and interesting to say. Those voting for Hart liked his "new ideas," a theme of his campaign, and, more so than with the other contenders, felt he could beat Ronald Reagan in the general election. Mondale supporters associated a broad range of qualities and issue positions with their candidate, possibly an indication of his inability to emotionally excite voters and the relative blandness that goes with running a front-runner campaign. Jackson took clear advantage of the issue configurations in the black community and, based on these poll results, was seen as a clear and forceful spokesman for their perspective.

Winning—Sort Of: The Jackson Campaign and the Nominating Rules

Even when Jackson won, he did not win all that he could have, due to an imbalance between votes won in a state and the proportion of national convention delegates awarded candidates. Jackson was not the only loser; all candidates other than the front-runner were disadvantaged through such rules as winner-

Table 5. Candidate support patterns in Alabama and Georgia Democratic primaries, 1984

	Total	% Glenn	% Hart	% Jackson	% Mondale
Race					
Alabama					
White	56	32	37	1	29
Black	40	1	1	50	47
Georgia					
White	69	25	38	1	32
Black	28	1	5	61	30
Sex					
Alabama					
Men	45	22	22	20	35
Women	53	16	23	23	37
Georgia					
Men	45	22	30	15	28
Women	54	14	27	22	34
Age					
Alabama					
18–29	17	16	18	35	28
30–44	25	22	25	28	23
45–59	23	16	26	18	40
60 or over	32	20	20	11	48
Georgia					
18–29	14	12	30	27	26
30–44	30	18	34	21	22
45–59	23	21	25	17	35
60 or over	29	18	25	14	40
Education					
Alabama					
Less High School	21	13	17	21	48
High School Grad	34	17	24	20	39
Some College	22	24	24	22	28
College Grad & more	19	23	23	26	27
Georgia					
Less High School	17	7	21	26	44
High School Grad	33	12	31	21	33
Some College	22	21	33	14	27
College Grad & more	24	31	29	14	24
1983 family income (in thousands of dollars)					
Alabama					
Under 12.5	33	7	18	30	44
12.5–24.9	24	19	19	17	43
25–34.9	18	29	23	21	26

Table 5. (*Continued*)

Total	% Glenn	% Hart		% Jackson	% Mondale
35–50	10	30	36	16	18
Over 50	5	39	27	10	24
Georgia					
Under 12.5	24	7	18	30	41
12.5–24.9	26	15	33	22	28
25–34.9	19	20	35	13	29
35–50	15	28	33	9	25
Over 50	8	39	27	7	24
Family financial situation					
Alabama					
Better	23	33	29	19	19
Worse	30	8	15	35	42
Same	45	19	23	14	42
Georgia					
Better	26	26	33	11	24
Worse	23	9	25	25	37
Same	48	17	29	19	33
Party ID					
Alabama					
Democrat	72	12	18	26	44
Independent	19	40	29	13	16
Republican	6	32	50	4	11
Georgia					
Democrat	67	11	27	23	38
Independent	24	31	35	9	19
Republican	7	41	29	7	15
Political philosophy					
Alabama					
Liberal	18	4	22	32	42
Moderate	42	16	21	21	42
Conservative	31	33	24	16	26
Georgia					
Liberal	21	4	31	33	30
Moderate	43	16	30	16	35
Conservative	30	32	27	12	24
When vote was decided					
Alabama					
Last 3 days	25	33	37	19	18
After New Hampshire	6	5	17	4	2
Earlier this year	24	23	30	20	23
Knew all along	39	35	11	52	51

Table 5. (*Continued*)

Total	% Glenn	% Hart	% Jackson	% Mondale
Georgia				
Last 3 days	32	49	40	16	26
After New Hampshire	11	3	28	4	5
Earlier this year	25	26	21	35	22
Knew all along	27	18	8	40	41
Are you any of the following:				
Alabama				
Catholic	6	15	35	22	27
Female working				
outside home	14	14	26	24	34
Member of a union				
household	28	13	15	23	48
Military veteran	16	21	23	17	37
Born-again Christian	44	21	24	17	37
Teacher	8	14	21	17	46
Born in Alabama	67	18	20	24	37
Georgia				
Catholic	7	23	26	7	40
Female working				
outside home	20	20	30	22	28
Member of a union				
household	16	13	24	23	36
Military veteran	18	23	29	11	33
Born-again Christian	41	19	28	17	32
Teacher	9	22	32	16	29
Born in Georgia	60	15	27	22	34

Source: CBS News

take-all district or primary rules, bonus votes, at-large appointment of ex officio delegates, nonelected positions reserved for "superdelegates," and an increased emphasis on caucus nominating systems (as against primaries), more sensitive to direction from party professionals and less likely to attract many participants. The rules were not intended to be antiblack or racist. They were designed to be pro-front-runner, to produce a consensus behind a centrist-moderate that would provide a mobilization point for the Democratic party's coalition. All helped the 1984 front-runner, Walter Mondale.

The problem was evident in the first of the contests, Iowa, which illustrated Jackson's weakness in caucus nominating states. A heavy emphasis was placed on caucus states in 1984 (Table 7). Twenty-seven states and five other electoral jurisdictions that chose delegates to the national convention (Democrats

Table 6. Candidate support patterns in Illinois Democratic primary, 1984

	Total	% Hart	% Jackson	% Mondale
Sex				
Men	48	33	24	40
Women	51	34	23	39
Age				
18–29 years	20	35	29	32
30–44 years	30	34	26	36
45–59 years	23	37	23	37
60 or over	27	31	16	51
Are you any of these:				
Catholic	41	38	8	52
College Grad	21	43	19	33
Female working outside the home	17	38	24	35
Member of union household	37	32	18	46
Blue collar worker	13	32	26	39
Race				
White	69	45	4	47
Black	25	4	79	17
Party ID				
Democrat	68	32	26	40
Independent	26	43	17	36
Political philosophy				
Liberal	24	37	29	31
Moderate	48	35	19	43
Conservative	22	29	25	43
Family financial situation				
Better today	16	47	12	39
Worse today	34	28	31	38
Same as one year ago	47	35	20	41
1983 family income (in thousands of dollars)				
Under 25.5	27	24	36	37
12.5 to 24.9	26	36	22	40
25 to 34.9	20	42	14	41
35 to 50	12	43	14	38
Over 50	5	35	10	51
1980 presidential vote				
Carter	53	28	28	42
Reagan	27	43	7	47

Table 6. (*Continued*)

Total	% Hart	% Jackson	% Mondale
Anderson	8	60	11	21
Didn't vote	8	33	43	21
Qualities describe choice				
Can beat Reagan	24	31	16	25
Has new ideas	22	42	18	6
Experience	21	3	5	45
Strong leader	20	12	33	19
A very smart man	10	8	15	7
Cares about people	24	14	36	25
To try something new	12	21	11	6
Not tied to special interests	7	13	3	4
No opinion	9	8	10	10
Issues mattered in voting				
Helping poor people	43	29	70	40
Nuclear weapons	24	30	19	23
Central America	4	7	2	3
National defense	13	17	2	15
Dealing with Russia	6	7	2	7
Federal deficit	21	29	9	20
Unemployment	44	41	47	44
No opinion	9	9	7	9
When vote decided				
After Tues. primaries	19	23	14	18
After NH primary	11	25	3	6
Earlier this year	29	29	28	28
Knew all along	36	17	48	45
No opinion	5	6	7	4
Reagan handling job				
Approve	25	31	5	30
Disapprove	71	65	89	67
No opinion	4	4	6	3
1984 election choices				
Reagan	23	19	6	36
Hart	67	78	79	52
No opinion	10	3	16	12
1984 election choices				
Reagan	22	38	5	18
Mondale	68	49	81	78
No opinion	9	12	14	4

Table 6. (*Continued*)

	Total	% Hart	% Jackson	% Mondale
Unions too much power in politics				
Yes	49	59	40	46
No	45	37	52	49
No opinion	5	4	8	5

Source: CBS News

Abroad; Latin American Democrats) used caucuses predominantly, and 37 percent of the total number of national convention delegates at stake were decided through caucuses; both figures are the highest in over a decade (up from 24 percent in 1976 and 29 percent in 1980). Jackson did poorly in the caucus states and was especially weak outside of the South (see table 9). Overall, he won only two. One-third of his total national convention delegates came from caucus states. He won only 9 percent of the caucus delegates at stake in these contests (compared, for example, to Mondale's 41 percent). Caucus selection systems respond to political organization—over 70 percent of Mondale's supporters in Iowa had been personally contacted by the Mondale campaign [17]— and are more responsive to direct influence from party professionals. Both factors worked against the Jackson campaign. Jackson's political organization was weak throughout the campaign year, and he was not the favorite of the party establishment.

The problem with the ratio of popular votes to the proportion of delegate seats won was evident in the primaries also (table 9). The impact of the rules —i.e., the extent to which they distorted the popular vote—varied by state (table 9). In New Hampshire Hart received 37 percent of the primary vote, and Mondale 28 percent. Each received an equal division of New Hampshire's national convention delegation. In the Maryland, Illinois, Florida, Alabama, North Carolina, and Pennsylvania primaries, Mondale received an average of 39 percent of the popular vote but 58 percent of the national convention delegate seats. In Maryland and Pennsylvania Hart received 25 and 35 percent of the vote, respectively, but only 5 and 9 percent of the national convention delegates. Jackson took 21 percent of the vote in Illinois and 12 percent in Florida but received no national convention delegates in either state. In the six primary states identified, Hart captured 31 percent of the popular vote and 20 percent of the national convention delegates. Jackson took 37 percent of the popular vote and 10 percent of the delegates. Results like these brought many to question the implicit biases built into the nominating rules and the Democratic party's wisdom in adopting them. The disparity between popular

Table 7. Candidate support patterns in New York Democratic Primary, 1984

	NEW YORK				WHITE VOTERS		
	% Total	% Hart	% Jackson	% Mondale	% Hart	% Jackson	% Mondale
Sex							
Men	42	28	24	48	35	6	58
Women	58	27	29	43	37	6	56
Age							
18–29 years	16	29	42	27	47	8	42
30–44 years	32	29	34	37	43	6	51
45–59 years	23	27	26	46	36	7	57
60 or over	28	25	11	64	27	4	68
Race							
White	70	36	6	57	—	—	—
Black	23	3	87	10	—	—	—
Party ID							
Democrat	81	26	26	47	36	4	60
Independent	16	32	29	36	40	14	43
Political philosophy							
Liberal	35	28	31	40	38	8	53
Moderate	45	28	21	51	35	4	60
Conservative	14	25	30	43	35	5	58
Family financial situation							
Better today	22	36	17	45	44	4	52
Worse today	26	19	41	38	31	6	61
Same today	51	28	23	49	35	7	58
1983 family income (in thousands of dollars)							
Under 12.5	18	20	36	44	31	5	64
12.5 to 24.9	28	24	34	41	36	7	56
25 to 34.9	19	31	24	44	39	8	54
35 to 50	16	34	19	46	41	5	54
Over 50	12	32	10	57	35	4	62
1980 presidential vote							
Carter	61	23	29	48	33	4	62
Reagan	21	34	10	53	38	5	57
Anderson	6	56	15	29	57	11	32
When vote decided							
Last three days	18	20	15	18	21	33	19
Last two weeks	20	25	14	20	26	27	19

Table 7. (*Continued*)

	NEW YORK				WHITE VOTERS		
	% Total	% Hart	% Jackson	% Mondale	% Hart	% Jackson	% Mondale
After New Hamp.	8	19	4	4	19	6	4
Earlier in year	23	22	25	24	22	17	24
Knew all along	29	11	39	32	10	12	32
Are you any of the following							
Catholic	39	34	14	51	39	5	56
Jewish	24	27	5	68	27	5	68
College grad	36	33	19	46	39	9	51
Women work outside home	21	31	36	33	46	9	45
Irish	10	48	3	48	49	4	47
Italian	7	34	8	56	36	6	56
Attend religious serv. last month	31	26	30	43	36	6	57
Are you or anyone else in your household a member of a labor union							
Yes	41	22	30	48	30	7	63
No	56	31	24	44	40	6	54
Koch's job approval							
Approve	58	64	32	71	65	42	73
Disapprove	33	25	62	20	23	47	18
Education							
Not HS grad	10	23	27	50	33	1	66
HS grad	26	24	26	49	32	4	64
Not coll grad	25	25	37	37	38	5	57
Coll grad	36	33	19	46	39	9	51
Cuomo job approval							
Approve	74	71	66	81	71	78	81
Disapprove	19	22	23	14	22	6	14
Qualities describe choice							
Can beat Reagan	25	38	9	28	—	—	—
Has new ideas	23	46	27	7	—	—	—
Experience	28	3	3	59	—	—	—
Keep US strong	10	6	11	11	—	—	—
Endorsements	7	4	5	11	—	—	—

Table 7. (*Continued*)

| | NEW YORK | | | | WHITE VOTERS | | |
	% Total	% Hart	% Jackson	% Mondale	% Hart	% Jackson	% Mondale
Cares/people	25	11	46	20	—	—	—
Something new	9	18	9	2	—	—	—
Not tied to							
Spec interests	6	14	7	1	—	—	—
Well in debates	8	5	16	5	—	—	—
No Opinion	13	11	15	13	—	—	—
Issues mattered in voting							
Helping poor	38	24	65	31	—	—	—
Nuclear weapons	32	43	22	32	—	—	—
National defense	12	16	4	14	—	—	—
Dealing w/Russia	6	7	3	7	—	—	—
Federal deficit	13	18	2	16	—	—	—
Unemployment	30	23	42	27	—	—	—
Support Israel	9	7	1	15	—	—	—
Treat women fair	7	6	7	8	—	—	—
No opinion	16	15	16	17	—	—	—
Who was your second choice							
Hart	30	—	25	51	—	—	—
Jackson	9	16	—	11	—	—	—
Mondale	24	50	38	—	—	—	—
No 2nd choice	30	30	30	31	—	—	—
No answer	7	5	7	7	—	—	—
1984 election choices							
Reagan	14	8	8	21	—	—	—
Hart	73	89	72	64	—	—	—
No opinion	13	3	21	15	—	—	—
1984 election choices							
Reagan	13	26	8	6	—	—	—
Mondale	79	64	75	90	—	—	—
No opinion	9	10	17	3	—	—	—
Hart's new ideas mean he has							
Specific ideas	7	10	5	7	—	—	—
Diff. approach	28	45	22	21	—	—	—
Both	14	29	12	6	—	—	—
Neither	42	10	50	57	—	—	—

Table 7. (*Continued*)

| | NEW YORK | | | | WHITE VOTERS | | |
	% Total	% Hart	% Jackson	% Mondale	% Hart	% Jackson	% Mondale
Should your candidate pick a woman vice president							
Yes	15	12	21	13	—	—	—
Depends	66	71	64	65	—	—	—
No	17	16	11	21	—	—	—

Source: CBS News

vote and delegate vote led Jackson and, more indirectly, Hart to fight against the rules up through the national convention.

Overall, Jackson received 19 percent of the primary vote and 10 percent of the delegates selected through primaries. He received an estimated 12 percent of the caucus vote and 11 percent of the delegates selected through caucus systems. Mondale received 39 percent of the primary vote and 49 percent of the primary delegates selected and 43 percent of the caucus votes and 52 percent of the delegates selected through caucuses.[18] Mondale also received approximately 85 percent of the nonelected "superdelegates" (about 500 of 568) appointed by party committees or specially designated bodies (mayors' and governors' associations, the congressional Democrats).

The nominating rules used in 1984 were influential: they did have an impact on the outcome of the race, and they did favor Walter Mondale's candidacy. They decreased Jackson's representation at the national convention, and they weakened his bargaining position in relation to the platform and the Democratic party's policy commitments.

Jackson entered the campaign late, with no organization of consequence early in the race and no campaign experience at the national level. And yet, despite nominating rules that worked against him and a targeted constituency that may be the most difficult to mobilize in politics, Jackson did surprisingly well. His showings in Georgia, Alabama, Illinois, New York, the District of Columbia, Tennessee, Louisiana, Maryland, North Carolina, California, and New Jersey, in particular, established his credibility in the campaign and the validity of his claim to speak for blacks. The Jackson campaign themes were particularly suited to the needs and views of the black population. However, given the gulf between blacks and whites on policy questions, perceptions of

Table 8. Official Democratic Caucus Results, 1984

	Mondale	Hart	Jackson	Uncommitted	Others
Total delegates won	1648	1162	350	682	91
Percent won	41.9	29.5	8.9	17.3	2.3
Caucus delegates won	597	393	131	343	1
Percent won	40.8	26.8	8.9	23.4	0.1
Percent caucus delegates won versus total delegates won	36.2	33.8	37.4	50.3	1.1
Number of caucuses won	13	13	2	4	0
Percent Won	40.6	40.6	6.3	12.5	0.0

Source: ABC News

Notes: The total required for nomination was 1,967 votes. The ABC Estimated Count was as follows:

Mondale	Hart	Jackson	Uncommitted	Others
2048	1237	378	210	60
52.1	31.5	9.6	5.3	1.5

the problems facing the nation, and the adequacy of the Reagan administration's approach, Jackson had little attraction for whites, winning a negligible proportion of their vote and destroying any possibility of a viable "Rainbow Coalition." Overall, Jackson, running an unorthodox campaign, did mobilize his constituency (poor blacks) and proved himself to be an able campaigner with fine political instincts. For many, the most interesting and unusual aspect of the 1984 election year was the Jackson candidacy.

Did the Jackson Campaign Make a Difference?

The Jackson effort had its ups—the primary successes in northern states like New York and the South and the proportion of the black vote won—and its downs—the "Hymie"/"Hymietown" remarks and the controversy over Jackson's relationship with Louis Farrakhan, leader of the Black Muslims. Still, in trying to place the campaign in perspective, E. E. Schattschneider's words are appropriate. Democracy is a competitive struggle for attention and for a fair share of what the nation has to offer. Leaders and organizations, through electoral campaigns and other forms of expression, define the priorities and target the potential solutions. To have a voice, a group must be organized, assertive, and ably led. The Jackson campaign expanded the bounds of political discourse and the substance of the political conflict. It provided an outlet for minority concerns, and it forced a media and a dominant white population

Table 9. Democratic caucus results by region, 1984

East	Total	Mondale	Hart	Jackson	Uncommitted	Others
New England						
Maine	27	10	12	0	5	0
Vermont	17	4	6	3	4	0
Total	44	14	18	3	9	0
% Total Dels		31.8	40.9	6.8	20.5	0
Mid-Atlantic						
Delaware	18	10	4	0	4	0
Democrats						
Abroad	5	0	0	0	5	0
Total	23	10	4	0	9	0
% Total Dels		43.5	17.4	0	39.1	0
Regional	67	24	22	3	18	0
%Total Dels	1.7	35.8	32.8	4.5	26.9	0
% of all 3,933						
delegates					1.7	
% of all 1,465						
caucus delegates					4.6	

Midwest	Total	Mondale	Hart	Jackson	Uncommitted	Others
West Central						
Iowa	58	29	20	0	8	1
Kansas	44	20	16	0	8	0
Minnesota	86	50	0	0	36	0
Missouri	86	46	9	13	18	0
North Dakota	18	6	3	0	9	0
Total	292	151	48	13	79	1
% Total Dels		51.7	16.4	4.5	27.1	0
East Central						
Michigan	155	78	49	9	19	0
Wisconsin	89	48	25	5	11	0
Total	244	126	74	14	30	0
% Total Dels		51.6	30.3	5.7	12.3	0
Regional	536	277	122	27	109	1
% Total Dels		51.7	22.8	5.0	20.2	0.2
% of all 3,933						
delegates					13.6	
% of all 1,465						
caucus delegates					36.6	

Table 9. (*Continued*)

South	Total	Mondale	Hart	Jackson	Uncommitted	Other
Border South						
Arkansas	42	19	9	7	7	0
Kentucky	63	19	3	6	35	0
Oklahoma	53	19	24	0	10	0
Virginia	78	21	14	22	21	0
Total	236	78	50	35	73	0
% Total Dels		33.1	21.2	14.8	30.9	0
Deep South						
Mississippi	43	14	0	10	19	0
South Carolina	48	6	6	17	19	0
Texas	200	94	40	35	31	0
Latin America	5	0	0	0	5	0
Virgin Islands	6	2	0	1	3	0
Total	302	116	46	63	77	0
% Total Dels		38.4	15.2	20.9	25.5	0
Regional	538	194	96	98	150	0
% Total Dels		36.1	17.8	18.2	27.9	0
% of all 3,933 delegates					13.7	
% of all 1,465 caucus delegates					36.7	

West	Total	Mondale	Hart	Jackson	Uncommitted	Others
Mountain West						
Arizona	40	15	17	1	7	0
Colorado	51	0	43	0	8	0
Idaho	22	7	11	0	4	0
Montana	25	7	12	0	6	0
Utah	27	2	14	0	11	0
Wyoming	15	4	8	0	3	0
Total	180	35	105	1	39	0
% Total Dels		19.4	58.3	0.6	21.7	0
Pacific West						
Alaska	14	6	4	1	3	0
Hawaii	27	19	0	0	8	0
Nevada	20	6	9	0	5	0
Washington	70	26	34	1	9	0
American Samoa	6	3	0	0	3	0
Guam	7	2	1	0	4	0
Total	144	62	48	2	32	0
% Total Dels		43.1	33.3	1.4	22.2	0

Table 9. (*Continued*)

West	Total	Mondale	Hart	Jackson	Uncommitted	Others
Regional	324	97	153	3	71	0
% Total Dels		29.9	47.2	0.9	21.9	0
% of all 3,933 delegates					8.2	
% of all 1,465 caucus delegates					22.1	

Source: ABC News

to take notice, however reluctantly, of issues not currently popular and of a serious black candidacy for the presidency, however novel and unfamiliar. It brought more blacks to the polls; it may have served to give them more of a stake in the system; and it could provide the base for future black candidacies and political movements of consequence.[19]

In *An American Dilemma* Gunnar Myrdal wrote: "Man is a free agent, and there are no inevitabilities. All will depend upon the thinking done and the action taken. . . . History can be made. It is not necessary to receive it as mere destiny." [20] These thoughts were put down over forty years ago, and they were meant to refer to the political reactions of southerners to blacks. They could also apply to the future role of blacks in national politics.

Throughout the campaign Jackson was followed by allegations that he could not win. Why then run? Jackson's answer:

Winning is new people running.
Winning is also new voters.
Winning is more young voters.
Winning is providing hope.
Winning is winning Congressional districts across this country that progressives have never won, which gives us the ability to change the face of Congress.
Winning is expanding participation.
Winning is knowing that I have the ability to compete at this level. I have done more with fewer resources than my opponents have.
We're not just running for an office.
We're running for freedom.[21]

Jesse Jackson's 1984 campaign made a start toward this type of winning.

Table 10. Imbalance between popular vote and proportion of national convention seats received, selected Democratic primaries, 1984

	Total vote	% of vote	Delegates	% of delegates
Alabama	419,455		52	
Mondale	144,129	34	26	50
Hart	88,005	21	12	23
Jackson	81,218	19	9	17
Other, uncomm.	106,103	25	5	10
Connecticut	220,300		52	
Mondale	64,136	29	18	35
Hart	116,076	53	33	64
Jackson	26,044	12	1	2
Other, uncomm.	14,044	6	0	0
Washington, D.C.	99,489		15	
Mondale	25,345	25	4	27
Hart	7,053	7	0	0
Jackson	67,091	67	11	73
Florida	1,117,602		123	
Mondale	338,216	32	61	50
Hart	458,523	39	35	28
Jackson	142,520	12	1	—
Other, uncomm.	178,343	15	26	21
Georgia	684,167		70	
Mondale	208,191	30	24	34
Hart	188,825	27	28	40
Jackson	143,622	21	17	24
Other, uncomm.	145,529	21	1	—
Massachusetts	621,746		100	
Mondale	160,101	26	35	35
Hart	243,227	39	52	52
Jackson	31,452	5	0	0
Other, uncomm.	186,966	30	13	13
New Hampshire	101,129		18	
Mondale	28,173	28	9	50
Hart	37,702	37	9	50
Jackson	5,311	5	0	0
Other, uncomm.	29,943	30	0	0
New York	1,350,247		252	
Mondale	604,993	45	132	52
Hart	369,118	27	73	29
Jackson	343,529	26	47	19
Other	32,607	2	0	0
North Carolina	960,691		75	
Mondale	341,366	35	43	57
Hart	289,276	30	19	25
Jackson	243,717	25	13	17
Other, uncomm.	86,332	9	0	0
Ohio	1,448,845		154	
Mondale	583,876	40	67	44
Hart	608,505	42	79	51
Jackson	237,166	16	8	5
Other	19,298	1	0	0

Table 10. (*Continued*)

	Total vote	% of vote	Delegates	% of delegates		Total vote	% of vote	Delegates	% of delegates
Illinois	1,659,425		171		Pennsylvania	1,516,883		172	
Mondale	670,951	41	95	55	Mondale	711,830	47	117	68
Hart	584,579	35	41	23	Hart	529,198	35	16	9
Jackson	348,843	21	0	0	Jackson	251,332	17	15	9
Other, uncomm.	55,052	3	35	20	Other, uncomm.	24,523	2	24	14
Indiana	693,950		77		Rhode Island	45,135		22	
Mondale	283,832	41	36	46	Mondale	15,871	35	10	45
Hart	291,711	42	38	50	Hart	20,419	45	12	55
Jackson	92,464	13	3	4	Jackson	3,550	8	0	0
Others	25,943	4	0	0	Other, uncomm.	5,295	12	0	0
Louisiana	318,810		57		Tennessee	320,627		65	
Mondale	71,162	22	14	25	Mondale	131,836	41	29	45
Hart	79,593	25	19	33	Hart	93,092	29	20	31
Jackson	136,707	43	24	42	Jackson	80,847	25	16	25
Other, uncomm.	31,348	10	0	0	Other, uncomm.	14,852	5	0	0
Maryland	480,799		62						
Mondale	209,330	44	42	68					
Hart	119,861	25	3	5					
Jackson	127,659	27	17	27					
Other, uncomm.	23,949	5	0	0					

Source: *New York Times*, May 20, 1984, 19.

NOTES

I wish to thank Thomas E. Cavanagh, Milton Morris, the Joint Center for Political Studies, and the editors of this volume for varying forms of assistance in the development of this chapter.

1. E. E. Schattschneider, *The Semi-Sovereign People* (New York: Holt, Reinhart & Winston, 1960), pp. 141, 114, 7, 4–5.

2. Jesse Jackson, speech to the 1984 Democratic National Convention, printed in the *Congressional Quarterly Weekly Report,* July 21, 1984, p. 1785.

3. Schattschneider, *The Semi-Sovereign People,* p. 8.

4. Gunnar Myrdal, *An American Dilemma* (New York: Harper & Row, 1944), pp. LXXXII, 4.

5. These results are reported in Lloyd A. Free and Hadley Cantril, *The Political Beliefs of Americans* (New Brunswick, N.J.: Rutgers University Press, 1967), pp. 120–21. See also Samuel A. Stouffer, *Communism, Conformity, and Civil Liberties* (New York: Doubleday, 1955); and more recently: John L. Sullivan, James Pierson, and George E. Marcus, *Political Tolerance and American Democracy* (Chicago: University of Chicago Press, 1982).

6. Free and Cantril, *The Political Beliefs of Americans,* p. 122. See also Albert H. Cantril and Charles W. Roll, Jr., *Hopes and Fears of the American People* (New York: Universe Books, 1971); Donald R. Matthews and James W. Prothro, *Negroes and the New Southern Politics* (New York: Harcourt, Brace & World, 1966); V. O. Key, Jr., *Public Opinion and American Democracy* (New York: Alfred A. Knopf, 1961); and Wilson Carey McWilliams, *The Idea of Fraternity in America* (Berkeley: University of California Press, 1973).

7. Free and Cantril, *The Political Beliefs of Americans,* pp. 123–24.

8. Herbert McClosky and Alida Brill, *Dimensions of Tolerance* (New York: Russell Sage Foundation, 1983), pp. 286–87.

9. Herbert McClosky and John Zaller, *The American Ethos* (Cambridge, Mass.: Harvard University Press, 1984), pp. 93, 95.

10. Sidney Verba and Gary R. Orren, *Equality in America* (Cambridge, Mass.: Harvard University Press, 1985), pp. 216–17.

11. For discussions of the Reagan administration's orientation and impact and how it related to blacks, see Gerald M. Pomper, ed., *The Election of 1984* (Chatham, N.J.: Chatham House, 1985); Michael Nelson, ed., *The Elections of 1984* (Washington, D.C.: CQ Press, 1985); and Salim Muwakkil, "Civil Rights Leaders Shift Course Inwards," *In These Times,* August 7–20, p. 5.

12. See William Crotty, "The Presidential Nomination Process and Minority Candidates: The Lessons of the Jackson Campaign" (Washington, D.C.: The Joint Center for Political Science, April 30, 1985) and on the Democratic Party's nominating rules Crotty, *Party Reform* (New York: Longman, 1983).

13. These quotations are taken from various speeches given during the campaign by Jesse Jackson and reported in: Jon Margolis and George E. Curry, "The Paradox of Jesse Jackson," Chicago *Tribune,* July 15, 1984, Section 5, pp. 1, 4; Myra MacPherson, "Pain and Passion: The Mystique of Jesse Jackson," Washington *Post,* May 21, 1984, pp. D1, D8; Tatiana Goodman, "Jackson's Oratory: Visions of Apocalypse,"

Congressional Quarterly Weekly Report, January 7, 1984, p. 10; Timothy B. Clark, "Jackson's Message," *National Journal,* March 24, 1984, p. 575; Myra McPherson, "Jesse Jackson: The Fire and the Faith," Washington *Post,* May 22, 1984, pp. E1, E4; and "For the Record," *National Journal Convention Special,* July 21, 1984, p. 25.

14. The proportion of the primary electorate least well-off economically cannot be determined from the data in Table 4. The dichotomy is established at over and under $25,000. This is a higher income than most blacks and most Jackson supporters would earn (see Table 3). For a clearer indication of the candidate support patterns based on income and the low income primary voters support for Jackson, see the CBS exit polls (tables 4, 5, 6).

15. See also the poll results in "How Blacks and Whites Differ on Election Issues," *New York Times,* July 10, 1984, p. 10; William Schneider, "The Dividing Line Between Delegates Is Age," *National Journal Convention Special,* July 21, 1984, p. 12; and Thomas E. Cavanagh, *The Reagan Referendum: The Black Vote in the 1982 Elections* (Washington, D.C.: Joint Center for Political Studies, April, 1983).

16. See the discussions in Hanes Walton, Jr., *Invisible Politics* (Albany: State University of New York Press, 1985), pp. 131–66; and Walton, *The Negro in Third Party Politics* (Bryn Mawr, Pa.: Dorrance, 1969).

17. CBS News, "Iowa Caucus Poll, February 20, 1984" (New York: Mimeo, 1984).

18. Gary Hart's totals were in line with his grassroots party support. He received 36 percent of the primary vote and 36 percent of the national convention delegates selected through the primaries and 31 percent of the caucus vote and 33 percent of the delegates selected through caucuses.

19. For various statements and data supporting these views, see Barry Commoner, "Jackson's Historic Campaign" *New York Times,* July 10, 1984, 27; Robert A. Jordan, "Jackson Gave Them New Hope, Blacks Assert," *Boston Globe,* July 20, 1984, 7; Juan Williams, "Dejected Jackson Contemplates Turning PUSH to Politics," *Washington Post,* July 22, 1984, A-10; Dom Bonafede, "Though He Can't Win the Nomination, Jackson Will Leave His Political Mark," *National Journal,* March 24, 1984, 562–65; Ronald Smothers, "Jackson's One Sure Legacy Is New Voters," *New York Times,* October 21, 1985, E-3; Salim Muwakkil, "Rainbow Coalition Seeking Ways to Carry on the Fight," *In These Times,* May 8–14, 1985, p. 3; Smothers, "Jackson Backers Map Future Efforts," *New York Times,* July 21, 1985, 15; Gary R. Orren, "The Nomination Process: The Vicissitudes of Candidate Selection," in Nelson, ed., *The Elections of 1984,* pp. 59–60; Rod Bushrod, ed., *The New Black Vote* (San Francisco: Synthesis Publications, 1985); and Thomas E. Cavanagh, "Black Mobilization and Partisanship" (Washington, D.C.: Joint Center for Political Studies, April 30, 1984).

20. Myrdal, *American Dilemma,* p. 520

21. "On the Road: Jesse Jackson on Winning," *New York Times,* May 5, 1984, 8.

Through the Prism of Afro-American Culture: An Interpretation of the Jackson Campaign Style

4

Joseph P. McCormick II
and Robert C. Smith

As the essays in this volume indicate, Jesse Jackson's campaign for president in 1984 may be analyzed from a variety of philosophical, theoretical, methodological, and substantive foci. In this essay we examine the Jackson campaign style. Through a focus on style we interpret the Jackson campaign as emblematic of certain features of Afro-American culture. In an attempt to illustrate how selected features of Afro-American culture shaped Jackson's campaign style, which in turn influenced the decision-making process of his campaign, we also discuss Jackson's decision to go to Syria to seek the release of Navy Lt. Robert Goodman.

Afro-American Culture and Its Political Significance

In *The Politics of the Black "Nation,"* Matthew Holden addresses a number of factors that shape and condition the internal politics of the Afro-American community. Among these factors are what he calls certain "partially distinctive attributes" of Afro-American culture.[1] Holden argues that what black political leaders do and how they do it is significantly influenced by Afro-American culture and he identifies five politically significant attributes of Afro-American culture.[2]

The hope for deliverance, Holden's first attribute, is perhaps the single most common theme in all Afro-American culture.[3] The faith that "God will deliver us," that the "Lord will make a way" or that "We Shall Overcome" is rooted in the black church and its spirit of evangelical Protestantism. The rhetoric of black leaders as seemingly diverse as Frederick Douglass, Nat Turner, Martin Luther King, Jr., Malcolm X, Louis Farrakhan, and Jesse Jackson all suggest that, doctrinal content apart, blacks would overcome their oppression, whatever the obstacles, through the intervention of divine providence.

The second theme of Afro-American culture identified by Holden is *the wish for defiance*—the belief that within blacks there is the capacity to go against the odds, to take risks, and to endure in order to overcome their oppression.[4] This spirit of "defiant heroism," or risk-taking, predisposes some black leaders to take actions that a more cautious examination of alternatives would perhaps foreclose.

Dionysian individualism—a passion to maintain one's honor or pride in the face of attack—is the third theme of Afro-American culture posited by Holden. This theme involves three elements: *self-expressive assertion, authoritarian leadership,* and *segmentation* and *secession.* The first element, self-expressive assertion, relates to the fact that "black culture is a culture in which, relatively speaking, oratorical debating competence is more praiseworthy than technical bureaucratic skill or the investment of one-self in the tedium or organizational detail."[5] Authoritarian leadership, the second element, deals with the "tendency—found in all sorts of organizations, black and white in any case—for leaders to run their organizations with a minimal sense of due process and maximal sense that their followers ought to do as they are told."[6] The third element, segmentation and secession, is a mode of behavior derived primarily from the black church. Many blacks have learned their organizational behavior in the Baptist church, where there is a strong tendency toward de facto autocracy. Holden writes that "the defense against autocracy—legitimated by the doctrines of the church—is withdrawal to form a new and purer unit."[7]

Moralism, Holden's fourth theme, also derives from the Protestant religious tradition. This theme expresses the notion that black people seem to possess, in contrast to whites, a greater "sensitivity," a greater "humanness" or (in one version) "more soul."[8] Moralism demands of black leaders that they "do right" and be seen as doing right by those they would claim to lead. Moral authority, like oratorical skill, thus becomes an important ingredient in Afro-American leadership.

The final theme of Afro-American culture identified by Holden as having some political significance is *cynicism-and-fear:* "The same experience that teaches people to wish for defiance and hope for deliverance also teaches them to be cynical about the prospects and fearful of trying. . . . One may admire other people's defiance and yet recognize the likelihood that such defiance will be destructive to oneself."[9] As a result, Holden maintains, there is a relatively low level of mass trust in the leadership and an ever present fear of a sell-out.

The Protestant religious tradition runs as an undercurrent through Holden's five cultural attributes. Central to this cultural analysis of Afro-American politics are the roles played by the black church and the black preacher.[10]

The Church and the Clergy in Afro-American Politics

Three aspects or dimensions of the black preacher's role in the politics of black America are relevant to this inquiry: (1) the *moral authority* commanded by the black preacher; (2) the tendency for the leadership style of the black preacher to be authoritarian, and (3) the centrality of the preacher's oratorical skills.

In *The Negro's Church,* Mays and Nicholson argue that the clergy has had a distinct advantage over other professions that would aspire to positions of leadership among black people: "Not only did it have historical precedence and hold a unique place because of prominence and disinterested service, but it also had a 'divine sanction' from the very beginning. This combination of forces made the Negro minister supreme among leaders. . . . [T]he Negro minister did not have to achieve acceptance by the group, for he was accepted and in full authority from the start." [11]

The second dimension of the black preachers' role is their tendency to be authoritarian in their leadership style. Holden writes: "The clerical dictatorship in an ordinary Baptist church (not to mention the National Baptist Convention) could teach lessons to many a ward boss. . . . In the Baptist experience—where ever so many blacks have learned their organizational behavior—there is a strong tendency toward de facto autocracy, even though the Baptist polity emphasizes the equality of conscience of each man." [12]

The third dimension of the black preacher's role is the centrality of the preacher's oratorical skills, the ability to be a "good talker"—"to speak the word." As Hortense Spiller, writing on the tradition of black preaching, puts it: "The minister weaves analogy and allegory into the sermon, comparing and juxtaposing contemporary problems in morality with and alongside ancient problems in morality. These build toward an emotional pitch and climax that are made possible by the minister's sense of timing and dynamics." [13]

These three dimensions of the political behavior of the black clergy further clarify the religious motif which runs through the five cultural attributes advanced by Holden. We now turn to an application of these attributes to an interpretation of the style of the Jackson campaign. [14]

The Style of the Jackson Campaign

The Hope for Deliverance and the Wish for Defiance

Rev. Jackson traces the origins of his 1984 quest for the Democratic presidential nomination to the 1983 Chicago mayoral election. When Senator Edward Kennedy supported Richard M. Daley and former Vice President Mondale supported then mayor Jane Byrne, rather than a black candidate, former congressman Harold Washington, Jackson told *Playboy* magazine, "I couldn't believe it. How can progressive Democrats make a commitment to Chicago—which is 40 percent black and 15 percent Hispanic and only three percent Irish—and choose two Irish candidates over the black candidate?" In other words, in Jackson's view, "the progressive wing of the Democratic Party was moving to the right. . . . So what could you do? You can't go Republican; that's too devastatingly right wing. Can't stay with the Democrats as they are, right? So . . . take them on in the primaries! Aha! The best of both worlds. You can act, challenge the Democrats in their own primaries, challenge the Republicans in the general election, do all of it." [15]

Jackson's decision to seek the nomination involved defiance not only of the Democratic party but of important elements of the black leadership establishment in the United States as well. As the idea of a black running for president began to circulate in black leadership circles, substantial opposition emerged in the press and among Democratic party officialdom, supporters of former Vice President Mondale, the leaders of national civil rights organizations, and some black mayors and members of Congress. Opposition from these quarters involved objection to both the idea in principle of a black running for president and the Jackson candidacy specifically. Thus, in order to act Jackson had to defy black and white power brokers in the Democratic party.

Given this range of opposition, Jackson embarked upon a year-long campaign to build grassroots enthusiasm and leadership support for his candidacy. Central to Jackson's explanation of his candidacy was the necessity to alter the "captive" status of the black vote in the American two-party system. Writing in *The Washington Post* in early 1983, Jackson noted: "The fundamental relationship between blacks and the Democratic party must be renegotiated. No longer can blacks allow Democrats to take them and their votes for granted." [16] Implicit in this statement was the possibility of an independent, or third-party, challenge in the event that the outcome of the negotiations with the Democratic party were not successful. Although Jackson was under enormous pressure from the outset to rule out an independent challenge, he generally refrained from explicitly doing so until the end of the Democratic convention. In its origin and purpose, therefore, the Jackson campaign represented a *defiance* of establishment political leadership and opinion.

This theme of defiance was ever present in Jackson's campaign. From the beginning Jackson characterized his candidacy as more a "crusade" than a campaign. When Mondale strategists outlined for Jackson the difficulties of organization, fund raising, the party's threshold provision—which required a candidate to win 20 percent of the primary or caucus vote in order to win any delegates—Jackson would often respond by invoking the organizational strength of the black church, the enthusiasm of the masses, and his faith in God.

Dionysian Individualism

A passion for honor or respect was also a thread running throughout the Jackson campaign. In an April 1983 *Washington Post* article, Jackson made the point that in spite of the fact that black voters had supported Democratic candidates for public office throughout the country white Democratic leaders and voters had not reciprocated. In this regard, Jackson observed: "In the last year black Democrats have won primaries in South Carolina, North Carolina, Mississippi, California, and Chicago, yet significant numbers of white Democratic leaders and voters have chosen to support white Republicans over those black Democrats. If black people and their leaders support Democrats without regard to race but others cannot reciprocate, then the character and viability of the party must be called into question." Jackson went on to say that when "black leaders have attempted to remedy these problems through the Democratic party . . . too often they have been ignored or treated with disrespect." [17]

Jackson's oratorical skill caused the most frequent comment in the press regarding his campaign style. His campaign stump speeches, like those of his mentor, Martin Luther King, Jr., were really sermons, involving a weaving of poetry, scripture, and political analysis in the tradition of old-time black preaching. Traditional preaching should be heard rather than read because its ultimate effectiveness is in the preacher's sense of timing. However, the following excerpts from a Jackson "stump" sermon in Baltimore in May 1984 provide some insight:

> Yesterday was a day of mixed emotions for me. Jesus was crucified on Friday, resurrected on Sunday. That's great joy because the stone was rolled away. But for the poor of Baltimore, for the malnourished of our nation, for the poor mothers who cannot get a breakfast program or lunch programs, for the youth who can't get a skill, they were crucified on Sunday, crucified on Monday. The hands are still bleeding, the thorns are still in their heads. I say it's time for the poor to realize resurrection, to stop the hammers, stop the nails, wheel away the stone.[18]

Jackson's leadership style in decision-making has been described by one of his biographers as "authoritarian." [19] According to Barbara Reynolds, as head of Operation Breadbasket and Operation PUSH Jackson reserved all decisions to himself and was reluctant to delegate any real authority. The Jackson campaign organization was unconventional and very diverse, including a range of individuals representing the major ethnic elements of Jackson's Rainbow Coalition as well as the various ideological tendencies within the black "nation." The staff decision-making process on major controversies encountered during the campaign—the Syrian mission, the second primary, Jackson's response to the "Hymietown" incident, and the Farrakhan controversies—solicited a range of opinions and advice *prior* to decisions being made. Nevertheless, Jackson was indisputably the head of the entire operation. Jackson appeared willing on more than one occasion to make decisions against the advice of many of his staff and personal advisors. Our discussion below on the Syrian mission sheds some light on this point.

Moralism

During the course of the campaign Jackson displayed a dramatically different worldview from that of his fellow candidates for the presidency. Jackson argued that his view of the nature, causes, and solutions to the major politically relevant conflicts of the time derived from the unique history and circumstances of Afro-Americans. For example, in announcing his candidacy on the television broadcast "60 Minutes," Jackson said that his was "a national campaign growing out of the black experience and seen through the eyes of a black perspective—which is the experience and the perspective of the rejected." During the campaign Jackson frequently told the press that he was "born in occupied territory" and that in South Carolina he spent his growing years "under apartheid." As a result, he argued, he had a special empathy and identification with the poor and oppressed at home and abroad. Jackson argued that blacks in America had a unique *moral responsibility* to "save the human race." This sense of moralism requires black leadership, especially its clergy, to be "apocalyptic advocates of the poor" and to "preach the gospel to defend the poor"—"a Canaan bound gospel that shakes the foundations upon which our slave masters stand." [20] A frequent refrain in the campaign was Jackson's capacity to "test the moral character of the nation" or to "shake the moral foundations of the nation."

Jackson's controversial relationship with Nation of Islam leader Louis Farrakhan may also be interpreted within the thematic context of moralism. Following the reporting of Jackson's "Hymietown" remarks in the *Washington Post,* Minister Farrakhan in a weekly radio broadcast vowed to "make an example" of Milton Coleman, a black reporter who had initially reported the remarks to a *Washington Post* colleague. However, when asked, on "Meet the Press" on April 8, 1984, whether he would repudiate Farrakhan because of those remarks, Jackson couched his response in a moral context: "I'm not going to do that. I don't think that its fair for you to attempt to make me do that. . . . All of us who live in the public domain do make errors. . . . My approach is to separate the sinner from the sin." Subsequent remarks by Minister Farrakhan on Israel, supporters of Israel, and Judaism, made during another radio broadcast, did eventually lead Jackson to publicly denounce him.[21]

It is our view, however, that Jackson's sense of his moral authority among the Afro-American masses resulted in his ambivalence in dealing with Minister Farrakhan. This points to the dual pressures that the campaign confronted: the *external* pressure of the broader white political establishment, which was hostile to Jackson's candidacy at the outset and even more so following his "Hymietown" comments, and the *internal* pressure of the national black community, which invariably demands that its would-be leaders be strong and resist capitulation in the face of external attack and criticism. The nature of this internal pressure is more clearly illustrated in our discussion of Holden's final theme, cynicism-and-fear.

Cynicism-and-Fear

Jackson's initial unwillingness to repudiate Minister Farrakhan can also be interpreted in the context of the theme of cynicism-and-fear. There is among the masses of Afro-Americans, Holden argues, a lack of trust of black leadership —a fear of what is ritualistically called a "sell-out," a fear that black leaders will in the course of their interaction and cooperation with the structure of white power betray the interests of the race. Thus Jackson was concerned that if he was seen through the media as having denounced Farrakhan as a result of pressure from the white establishment not only would he lose support among an important segment of the national black community, but such an act would also contribute to cynicism about the moral authority and integrity of black leadership in general and Jackson in particular.

Jackson also had to contend, throughout the campaign, with the fear that his campaign would end in failure. Operationally, this meant that Jackson's effort would be seen as leading to the nomination of a more conservative Democrat or the re-election of the incumbent Republican president. There was also the fear that Jackson himself might not have been up to the intellectual and emotional challenges that accompanied the first credible campaign for the presidency by a black person. These kinds of fears may have had some impact on Jackson in his early debate performance and his repeated talk of being treated with respect and as an equal to his seven counterparts in the Democratic nomination process.

As the booing of Atlanta mayor Andrew Young at the San Francisco convention vividly demonstrated, many blacks harbored a sense that Jackson (and thus the 85 percent of the black electorate that supported him) had been betrayed by black leadership. Indeed on the convention floor, when Mayor Young spoke against the Jackson minority plank on the second primary, many black delegates shouted "traitor" and "sell out." Many of the black Jackson delegates left the convention feeling that Jackson (and therefore blacks generally) had not been treated with respect by the leadership of the Democratic party or by its nominee, Walter Mondale. This sense of rejection among Jackson delegates probably was also reflected at the mass level and may have contributed to the lower-than-expected turnout in the general election, especially among Jackson's more enthusiastic supporters.[22]

Jackson's Syria Mission: An Act of Faith

Perhaps more than any other decision of major significance made by Jackson during the course of the campaign, the decision to go to Syria unambiguously carried his stylistic imprint. Three of Holden's cultural themes are particularly relevant to an interpretation of this decision.

Holden's first attribute of Afro-American culture—the hope for deliverance —carries with it the notion that *faith in God* is an essential ingredient in overcoming all obstacles. As we have previously indicated, this theme of religious optimism is rooted in the black church and its spirit of evangelical Protestantism. Consider, for example, the language of faith and moralism Jackson chose to use prior to his departure for Syria: "We do not have a signed contract [guaranteeing meetings with Asaad and Goodman]. . . *we must go on faith.* I certainly hope to bring Lt. Goodman back, . . . We're doing the right thing. Citizens have the right to do something or do nothing. We chose to do something." [emphasis added].[23]

Further evidence of this moral theme may be seen in a statement released by Rev. Jackson shortly before his departure:

I have met with President Asaad . . . on a previous occasion. I have known religious leaders there and I have visited Syria. Our moral appeal for the release of Lt. Goodman has meaning, therefore, for both Americans and Syrians. We appeal to President Asaad to release Lt. Goodman as a gesture of good faith, as a way of relieving some of the special tensions and to enhance the focus of the peace negotiations and de-emphasize the use of military solutions. . . . Our *collective wisdom* must get us to the negotiating table and away from the combat zone, toward peace for all in that region of the world [emphasis original].[24]

This statement reflects the moral tone that Jackson attempted to display throughout the course of the campaign, particularly in matters of U.S. foreign policy. Given the close association of this cultural theme of moralism with the black Christian experience, it is doubtful that such explicit evidence of this theme would have been seen in Jackson's oratory had he not been a minister.

Under a third theme, Dionysian individualism, Holden discusses three separate elements. One of these elements, authoritarian leadership, has some relevance to what we know about the process by which the decision to go to Syria was made.[25]

Jackson was in Memphis, Tennessee, in late December 1983 for a one-day summit conference of black religious leaders to enlist their support in his presidential bid. In what appears to have been an impromptu meeting held with a group of activist black clergy who had come to Memphis for this summit conference, Jackson told his audience: "I don't know whether you know it or not, but there's a black Navy flier who's a prisoner of war in Syria and the United States has forgotten about him. . . . I took it upon myself to send a cable to Asaad asking for Goodman's release on humanitarian grounds. . . . I do think that if a delegation of high profile religious leaders would go to Syria, we may be able to get them to turn him loose." [26] All available evidence indicates that the decision to go to Syria was a unilateral one, made by Jackson against the advice of his staff and in the face of overwhelming opposition from the establishment press and from the foreign policy elite within the United States. Thus this case illustrates the influence in the campaign of cultural attributes of authoritarian leadership, religious faith, optimism, and moralism.

In a summary discussion of the cultural themes that we have utilized in this interpretation, Holden writes, "The hope for deliverance, the wish for defiance, and moralism jointly produce a disposition to treat the problem of racial liberation as a morality play rather than as a pragmatic problem in political tactics." Holden goes on to say:

> At the same time, Dionysian Individualism and cynicism-and-fear undermine the capacity of individuals to participate on a large scale and responsibly. The passion for honor diminishes the willingness of leaders to extend due process to followers. . . . The political morality play is also a form of collective psychiatry, which makes the participants feel better about themselves in a hostile world. It encourages members of the group to believe that all failures are a function of "bad" leaders or malevolent adversaries. The net effect is to diminish the capacity to make prudent use of those limited resources which are available in a hostile world, for that task is very difficult to carry out under a combination of very high demands and very low support.[27]

Through an examination of Jackson's rhetoric and behavior, we have uncovered evidence that the five cultural themes advanced by Holden have some interpretive value. We observed that the theme of religiously grounded optimism and faith was frequently tapped to both inspire and mobilize support. Jackson also brought to the campaign a defiant attitude toward the Democratic party, its leadership, and the status quo rule structure. Organizationally, he approached the presidential campaign as an exercise in mass mobilization in which he relied on both religious and secular sociopolitical networks within black America in order to challenge elements of both the black and white political establishments.

Much of Jackson's rhetoric during the campaign was clearly expressed in a style that reflected Holden's theme of *moralism*. In Jackson we saw a black preacher-politician who approached a presidential campaign as an exercise in "doing right." As we pointed out above, Jackson's rationale for the Syrian mission clearly reflected this theme. These three themes—moralism, the wish for defiance, and the hope for deliverance—can all be seen in Jackson's oratorical style—familiar to many Afro-Americans—which served as an effective tool in mobilizing black voters and stimulating black interest in his candidacy. This style had been heard in the oratory of Jackson's mentor, Martin Luther King, Jr., and it is ever-present in the sermons of the black Baptist church. In terms of *self-expressive assertion* Jackson proved to be the master orator throughout the campaign.

Even in the face of reservations expressed by doubting staff members, Jackson typically took the initiative in making many of the key decisions which confronted the campaign. Such a decision-making style can be characterized as *authoritarian*. It is also apparent that Jackson was prepared to take risks that a more conventionally-oriented politician would in all likelihood have ruled out.

Throughout the campaign, Jackson's rhetoric reflected a preoccupation with personal and collective self-respect for blacks from whites who commanded and controlled the Democratic party. This preoccupation with self-respect and recognition parallels what Holden sees as the essence of Dionysian individualism, a concern with *honor* or *the maintenance of pride*. In those instances where honor could not be reconciled within the context of a given organizational structure, Holden reminds us, segmentation and secession might be pursued. Toward the final weeks of his campaign, when it became obvious that the Democratic party's leadership and its eventual nominee would make no concessions on his challenges concerning the delegate selection and second primary issues, Jackson began to reiterate the need for "self-respect" from the party as an essential condition for a pledge of support for the party's nominee. While Jackson never spoke of a walkout from the Democratic convention—an act that could have been seen as tantamount to secession—he nonetheless spoke after the convention of not actively campaigning for the Mondale-Ferrarro ticket until they, in Jackson's words, sent a "message to the masses." Such a message never emerged, and while Jackson endorsed the Democratic ticket, he did not actively campaign on the nominees' behalf. We suspect that in his support of the party's nominees and in his unwillingness to withdraw from the convention, Jackson did not wish to be characterized as a spoiler and thus be blamed for aiding the Republican incumbent in the general election. We also suspect that Jackson wished to preserve any options for future efforts in influencing the nomination of the Democratic party's presidential candidate. Outright secession and/or confrontation with the party's leadership might have foreclosed such options.

Our interpretation of the Jackson campaign in terms of Holden's cultural themes leads us to conclude that there is some validity to his hypothesis that various aspects of Afro-American culture—many historically rooted in the black church—lead black leaders to treat the problem of racial liberation in America as a morality play rather than a pragmatic problem in political tactics.

The major concerns of the Jackson campaign were to add issues of importance to black Americans to the Democratic party's issue-agenda, to gain greater party support for black Democratic candidates at the state and local levels, and to expand the base of black political power within the party. These issues were frequently expressed by Jackson in a rhetorical style that reflected the particular cultural themes of the hope for deliverance, the wish for defiance, and moralism. This confluence of themes tended to portray Jackson's efforts to treat the multifaceted problem of racial liberation as though it were a morality play—i.e., an exercise in "doing right" and getting one's adversaries to "do right" rather than as problems in pragmatic politics.

There can be little doubt that the 1984 presidential candidacy of Jesse Jackson will leave its mark on the pages of the history of Afro-American politics. The Jackson campaign has provided students of black politics with some valuable insights on the possibilities and limits of Afro-American culture as a base for influencing the presidential nomination process and expanding the base of black political power within the larger polity.

NOTES

1. Matthew Holden, Jr., *The Politics of the Black "Nation,"* (New York: Chandler, 1973), p. 16.

2. Holden writes, "Since culture is behavior learned in cohorts, it follows that when two groups are separated by legal or behavioral frontiers over any significant time, some tendency toward cultural difference must develop." Ibid., p. 17. There is, however, considerable dispute among specialists on the status of Afro-American culture in the United States. For a review of the controversy see Nathan Huggins, "Afro-American History: Myths, Heroes and Reality," in *Key Issues in the Afro-American Experience,* ed. Martin Kilson, Daniel Fox, and Nathan Huggins (New York: Harcourt Brace and Jovanovich, 1971), pp. 5–19.

3. Holden, *The Politics of the Black 'Nation,"* p. 17.

4. Ibid., pp. 18–20.

5. Ibid., p. 21.

6. Ibid., p. 22.

7. Ibid., p. 23. Jackson's departure from the Southern Christian Leadership Conference (SCLC) and subsequent formation of Operation PUSH is an example of this pattern of segmentation and secession in black organizational life. See Barbara Reynolds, *Jesse Jackson: The Man, The Movement and the Myth* (Chicago: Nelson Hall, 1975), pp. 312–16 for a discussion of the SCLC-Jackson segmentation and the subsequent formation of Operation PUSH.

8. Holden, *The Politics of the Black "Nation,"* pp. 23–24.

9. Ibid., pg. 24.

10. There is a substantial literature on the role of religion and the clergy in black

politics. See for example Gary Marx, "Religion: Opiate or Inspiration of Civil Rights Militancy among Negroes," *American Sociological Review* 32 (February 1967): 64–72, and Larry Hunt and Janet Hunt, "Black Religion as Both Opiate and Inspiration: Putting Marx's Data to the Test," *Social Forces* 55 (1977): 1–14. See also W. Berenson, K. Elifson, and T. Tollerson, "Preachers in Politics: A Study of Political Activism among the Black Ministry," *Journal of Black Studies* 6 (March 1976): 379–92, and Arnold Vedlitz, J. Alston, and C. Pinkele, "Politics and the Black Church in a Southern Community," *Journal of Black Studies* 10 (March 1980): 367–75.

11. Benjamin Mays and Joseph Nicholson, *The Negro's Church* (New York: Institute of Social and Religious Research, 1933), p. 38.

12. Holden, *The Politics of the Black "Nation,"* p. 22.

13. Hortense Spiller, "Martin Luther King and the Style of the Black Sermon," *Black Scholar* 3 (1971): 14.

14. For another, more critical view of the role of religion and the church in black politics in general and the Jackson campaign in particular, see: Adolph Reed, Jr., *The Jesse Jackson Phenomenon* (New Haven: Yale University Press, 1986): 41–60.

15. *Playboy Magazine*, "Interview with Jesse Jackson," (July, 1984): 66.

16. Jesse Jackson, "Hey You Democrats: We'll All Benefit If a Black Runs for President," *The Washington Post,* April 10, 1983, C-1.

17. Ibid.

18. John E. Yang, "Campaigning in Free Verse," *Time Magazine,* May 7, 1984, p. 41.

19. See Barbara Reynolds, *Jesse Jackson: The Man, The Movement and the Myth* (Chicago: Nelson Hall, 1975).

20. Jesse Jackson, "Ministers as Apocalyptic Advocates of the Poor," *Journal of Religious Thought* 40 (Spring 1983): 23–24.

21. See Fay S. Joyce, "Jackson Criticizes Remarks Made by Farrakhan as 'Reprehensible,' " *New York Times,* June 29, 1984, A-1.

22. See Robert C. Smith and Joseph P. McCormick II "The Challenge of a Black Presidential Candidacy: An Assessment," *New Directions* 12 (April 1985): 25–26.

23. See Rick Atkinson, "Jackson Begins 'Pilgrimage' to Syria," *Washington Post,* December 30, 1983, A-1.

24. Quoted in Wyatt T. Walker, *The Road to Damascus: A Journey of Faith* (New York: Martin Luther King Fellows Press, 1985), p. 139.

25. Our understanding of the Syria mission is drawn from Wyatt Walker's account (see note 24) and interviews with Jackson campaign staff.

26. Walker, *The Road to Damascus,* p. 25.

27. Holden, *The Politics of the Black "Nation,"* p. 26.

28. Ibid.

The Jackson Campaign in the Hispanic Community: Problems and Prospects for a Black-Brown Coalition

5

Armando Gutierrez

For some time now black and Hispanic leaders have spoken of the need to build a coalition between the nation's two largest minority groups. Both groups have been victimized by racism, classism, and economic policies that seldom take the needs of the poor into account. Additionally, both have been strong supporters of the Democratic party, often constituting the margin of victory in local, state, and national races. Yet the Democratic party has paid only perfunctory attention to the needs of these two groups. Indeed, the status of blacks and Hispanics in the party has usually been that of clients to white patrons. To be sure, in the last decade or two the two groups have increased their number of elected and appointed officials, both in government generally and in the Democratic party specifically. Yet even with such gains both groups are far from achieving parity.

Past attempts at coalition building have been largely ad hoc, haphazard, and ineffective. Within local, state, and national policy-making bodies cooperation between the two groups has been the rule. Black elected officials have generally been allies in legislative struggles launched by Hispanics and vice versa. In the economic sphere the covenant signed with the Southland Corporation by Operation PUSH and the League of United Latin American Citizens (LULAC) in 1981 represented a major breakthrough in business cooperation between blacks and Hispanics. But little has been done since to expand the relationship.

The Jesse Jackson presidential campaign offered a unique opportunity for effective coalition building. Although his experience with Hispanics was limited, Rev. Jackson's history of involvement and knowledge of key leaders and issues was far greater than that of most black leaders. Moreover, his campaign spoke most directly to the issues that struck at the heart of the Hispanic community.

Due to both internal and external factors, the Jackson campaign met with limited success in attracting Hispanic voters. Nevertheless, the campaign could predicate the future of minority politics in the United States.

In this essay I will explore these topics in terms of perspectives and experience I gained as a staff member with the Jackson campaign organization.[1] The essay begins with a demographic profile of the nation's 20 million Hispanics, a profile that emphasizes the diversity of the group. Next it looks at the Jackson campaign strategy as regards its appeal to Hispanics. The essay then looks in more detail at the case of Rev. Jackson's trip to Central America in the summer of 1984, the rationale behind the trip, and its political impact. Finally, it analyzes the successes and failures of Rev. Jackson's Hispanic strategy and the implications for the future of coalition building between blacks and Hispanics.

Hispanics: A Demographic Profile

Particularly for political purposes, it is critical to break down the composition of the United States' Hispanic population. According to the 1980 census, the breakdown is as follows: Mexican Americans, 59.8 percent; Puerto Ricans, 13.8 percent; Cuban Americans, 5.5 percent; and other Hispanics, 20.9 percent. All but one of these composition groups, Cuban Americans, have historically voted overwhelmingly Democratic. For example, the *Chicago Tribune* estimated that some 90 percent of Hispanics in Dade County (Miami), Florida voted for Ronald Reagan in 1984.[2]

In a more general sense, perhaps the most salient characteristic of Hispanics is their growth rate. The 1980 census reported a total Hispanic population of some 14,608,673. This number represents a 61 percent increase over the 1970 count of 9,073,237. By comparison, the growth rate for whites during this period was 6 percent; for blacks, 18 percent. If this growth rate (a combination of immigration and an inordinately high fertility rate) continues into 1990, Hispanics will number 24,503,690. In fact, by the end of the century Hispanics would become the nation's largest minority population (see table 1).[3]

Another characteristic of Hispanics is their heavy population concentration. Two of every three Hispanics reside in just four states: California has 31.1 percent; Texas has 20.4 percent; New York has 11.4 percent; and Florida has 5.9 percent of the total. The first two of these states alone have over half of the nation's Hispanics.

Additionally, Hispanics are a largely urban population. In 1980, 62 percent of all Hispanics lived in ten markets. Overall, some eight of every ten Hispanics resided in just twenty markets (see table 2).

The 1980 census estimated the median family income for Hispanics at $14,711. Nearly 24 percent of all Hispanics lived below the poverty level,

Table 1. Population growth trends, 1970–1980–1990

	1970	1980	1990
Whites	178,119,221	189,079,281	200,713,737
Blacks	22,539,362	26,504,985	31,168,327
Hispanics	9,073,237	14,608,673	24,503,690

Source: Hispanic Policy Development Project, *The Hispanic Almanac* (NY: 1984)

Table 2. Twenty largest U.S. Hispanic markets, 1985

City	Rank	Hispanic Population
Los Angeles	1	4,459,499
New York	2	2,400,053
Chicago	3	962,196
Houston	4	892,299
San Francisco	5	823,261
Miami	6	821,412
San Antonio	7	818,892
McAllen	8	624,171
Albuquerque	9	509,854
El Paso	10	499,499
San Diego	11	474,174
Fresno	12	393,026
Phoenix	13	385,783
Sacramento	14	367,573
Dallas–Fort Worth	15	361,982
Denver	16	328,507
Corpus Christi	17	289,972
Philadelphia	18	230,894
Tucson	19	210,894
Austin	20	206,668

Source: Hispanic Policy Development Project, *The Hispanic Almanac* (NY: 1984)

compared with 30.2 percent of blacks and 9.4 percent of whites. The white median family income was $20,840 in 1980, while for blacks it was $12,618 (see tables 3 and 4).

In educational attainment, Hispanics lag behind both whites and blacks. For example, looking at the portions of all three groups that have only an elementary school education, we find that only 16.6 percent of whites and 27.7 percent of blacks fall into this category. Yet 40.9 percent of Hispanics have completed only elementary school.[4]

Table 3. Comparative incomes, 1979

Group	Median family income	% below proverty level
Whites	$20,840	9.4
Blacks	12,618	30.2
Hispanics	14,711	23.8

Source: Hispanic Policy Development Project, *The Hispanic Almanac* (NY: 1984)

Table 4. Comparative median family income of Hispanic subgroups, 1979

Subgroup	% of total	Median family income
Mexican American	59.8	$15,200
Puerto Ricans	13.8	9,900
Cuban Americans	5.5	17,500
Other Hispanics	20.9	15,500
All Hispanics	100.0	14,711

Source: Hispanic Policy Development Project, *The Hispanic Almanac* (NY: 1984)

The Hispanic Electorate

A corollary of the population concentration of hispanics is the fact that some 85 percent of all voting-age Hispanics reside in just nine states. What's more, these states comprise a total of 193 electoral votes, nearly three-fourths of the votes needed to win the presidency.

The composition of the hispanic population also correlates with a regional division. Mexican Americans are located largely in the Southwest, with nearly three of four in just Texas and California. Puerto Ricans are concentrated in the Northeast; half of all Puerto Rican Americans reside in New York alone. Cuban Americans are heavily concentrated in Florida, where six of every ten can be found.

As mentioned earlier, during the decade of 1970 to 1980, hispanics increased by 61 percent. Large as this figure is, the number of voting age Hispanics grew by an even greater margin of 77 percent (see table 5). Approximately 9 million Hispanics were voting age in 1980. Hispanics are a very young population— the median age in 1980 was 22.1 years, compared to 31 among non-Hispanics. This means, of course, that in the near future a disproportionate number of Hispanics will be entering the voting age population. Hence, Hispanic voting proportions will increase significantly relative to other population subgroups. However, registration for Hispanics is less than for both whites and blacks. Some 50 percent of eligible Hispanics were on the registration rolls in 1980. Of these, 60 percent actually voted.

Table 5. Growth of Hispanic voting age population: 1970–80

State	Number of Hispanics (1980)	% Growth
Arizona	256,688	+ 88
California	2,775,170	+ 11
Colorado	204,301	+ 70
Florida	629,292	+ 130
Illinois	379,208	+ 73
New Jersey	307,321	+ 85
New Mexico	292,714	+ 82
New York	1,061,852	+ 35
Texas	1,756,971	+ 82

Source: Hispanic Policy Development Project, *The Hispanic Almanac* (NY: 1984)

Table 6. Percent of eligible registered voters by group: 1972–82

Group	1972	1974	1976	1978	1980	1982
White	76	66	71	66	71	68
Black	67	56	60	59	62	61
Hispanic	66	51	56	49	54	52

Source: Hispanic Policy Development Project, *The Hispanic Almanac* (NY: 1984)

Table 7. Percent of eligible voters participating by group, 1972–82

Group	1972	1974	1976	1978	1980	1982
White	67	50	63	49	63	52
Black	54	35	50	38	52	44
Hispanic	55	34	47	35	44	37

Source: Hispanic Policy Development Project, *The Hispanic Almanac* (NY: 1984)

While the rate of Hispanic support for the Democratic party is not as high as that of blacks, it is nevertheless disproportionately high. In 1980 nearly 25 percent of all Hispanics voted for Ronald Reagan. In 1984 the figure increased to 33 percent. If we factor out the Cuban American voter, however, the rate of Hispanic support for the Democratic party presidential candidate remains at about 75 percent. In fact, in the 1982 congressional elections, eight of every ten Hispanic voters supported Democrats.[5]

The Jackson Campaign and Hispanics

Early in the campaign a "Hispanic desk" was set up in the national office. This desk sought to pinpoint issues, organizations, and actors in the Hispanic community. Initially concentrating on Puerto Rican issues for the New York primary, the desk later expanded to focus on Mexican Americans and on issues related to South and Central America and the Caribbean.

Probably the most important endorsements of Rev. Jackson by Hispanics came from former and then current LULAC presidents, Tony Bonilla and Mario Obledo respectively. Several Hispanic local and state elected officials from throughout the country also endorsed the campaign.

It is curious, given the generally progressive politics of most Hispanic congresspeople, that none endorsed Rev. Jackson. This was due to several factors. First, virtually all of the Hispanic congresspeople are heavily tied into the Democratic party establishment. Since the hierarchy had almost unanimously endorsed the Mondale candidacy, no Hispanic was willing to buck the party's wishes. Second, Jackson entered the race relatively late. By the time Hispanics were approached, most had committed to particular candidates. Third, the initial Jackson campaign hierarchy was devoid of Hispanics. Hence there was little appreciation or knowledge of how best to seek out such endorsements. By the time this problem was resolved, endorsements had already been made.

Table 8. Hispanic legislators by state, 1983

State	% Hispanic Population	% Hispanic Legislators
Arizona	16	13
California	19	6
Colorado	12	7
Florida	9	9
Illinois	6	1
New Jersey	6	1
New Mexico	37	29
New York	10	3
Texas	21	14

Source: Hispanic Policy Development Project, *The Hispanic Almanac* (NY: 1984)

"Latinos for Jackson" chapters sprang up throughout the country, but particularly in New York, New Jersey, and Pennsylvania among the heavily Puerto Rican populations and in Texas, California, Arizona, Colorado, and New Mexico among the heavily Mexican American population. These chapters were organized largely by the most progressive elements within the Hispanic community—those segments concerned with both domestic and foreign policy questions.

Several issues were key to Hispanics during the campaign. No candidate addressed these issues in as direct and forthright a manner as Rev. Jackson.

Reagan cutbacks. Like other minority and poor communities, Hispanics were heavily impacted by the Reagan administration cutbacks in school lunch programs, federal subsidies for the poor, health, housing, food stamps, etc. While other Democratic party candidates addressed these issues, none focused on them as clearly and relentlessly as Rev. Jackson. His call for a 20 percent reduction in defense spending, with the resultant savings to be targeted for social service, job training and development, and education, offered the only realistic plan for remedying this problem area.

Unemployment. Hispanic unemployment has consistently been some 50 to 100 percent higher than for whites. The Reagan administration policy of "solving" the country's recession by increasing unemployment hit hardest in the black and Hispanic communities. Even eventual Democratic nominee Walter Mondale had no job creation program as part of his national campaign strategy. Again, only Jackson developed such a plan.

Education. Hispanics, of course, are impacted like other poor groups by cutbacks in education. Of particular note, cutbacks in Pell Grants for minority college aspirants, school lunch programs, and other educational programs were key issues in the campaign. For Hispanics, however, bilingual education has become the litmus test for candidates. Of late, bilingual education has become a favorite whipping boy for those who perceive a "depurification" of American society away from the white, Anglo-Saxon, Protestant tradition. By contrast, liberals have found it easy to make perfunctory declarations of support for bilingual education as a transitional mechanism to monolinguality—that is, the prevailing liberal view is that Spanish is to be used as a mechanism to facilitate the learning of English so that the child will eventually become monolingual in English. This view does not regard Spanish language retention or Mexican and Puerto Rican culture as assets but rather as liabilities. The only difference between this view and that of conservatives is that the latter take the "sink or swim" attitude while the former acknowledge the need to be more sensitive to the realities of learning for non-English speakers.

Only Rev. Jackson went beyond the liberal view and specifically called for the *promotion* of bilingualism and biculturalism as official government policy. He also analyzed opposition to such programs both as part of the xenophobia of the past and as a key link in foreign policy analysis. This view, he argued, was symptomatic of the United States' unilateral and insensitive dealings with the third world.

Immigration. During the presidential campaign the issue of immigration to the United States was heavily debated. The Congress was debating the Simpson-Mazzoli bill which, among other things, would have created legal sanctions against employers who hire the undocumented. This provision of the bill was particularly onerous to Hispanics as it would have led to blatant discrimination against anyone "Hispanic looking."

Rev. Jackson not only took the most progressive position in opposition to Simpson-Mazzoli but also went further in analyzing immigration from an econopolitical context and calling for a comprehensive and humanistic approach to its resolution. His analysis thus included a consideration of the United States' defense spending, the international debt and the policies of the International Monetary Fund (IMF), and the hypocrisy and racism of an immigration policy that set one standard for European-looking people and another for blacks and Hispanics and that used arbitrary classifications for political and economic refugees.

In fact, Democratic nominee Mondale refused to condemn the Simpson-Mazzoli bill until the final hour of the Democratic convention, when his Hispanic delegates threatened a massive boycott of the first ballot—a move that would have cost him the nomination.[6] Even the exhortations of such Hispanic "heavyweights" as Henry Cisneros and Polly Baca could not stem the tide of resentment toward Mondale's refusal to publicly condemn Simpson-Mazzoli.

Central America. Perhaps no issue better illustrated the distinction between Rev. Jackson and his opponents than Central America. Rather than condemning the liberation movements in the region, Rev. Jackson effectively argued that such movements were the inevitable result of oppression and exploitation and that the United States had historically far too often consciously supported its perpetrators. He unhesitatingly condemned as illegal and immoral the mining of Nicaraguan harbors.

Jackson became the favored candidate of the peace movement and of Hispanics who recognized that war would put United States Hispanics on the front lines of battle against cultural, linguistic, and historical brothers and sisters. Indeed, there were some who felt that Jackson alone stood against a possible United States invasion of Nicaragua.

The Latin America Trip: A Case Study

To say the least, Rev. Jesse Jackson's candidacy for the Democratic party presidential nomination was anything but orthodox and conventional. Not only was it the first serious run for the presidency by a black American, but also his sharp delineation of issues ran against the conventional campaign wisdom that moderate and innocuous stances on issues is the formula for success. By contrast, strong stances on controversial issues is generally seen as sure doom for candidates. Given the unconventional nature of the campaign, then, it should not have surprised many—but it did—that he would embark on a trip to

Central America at a time when the other candidates were busy solidifying their hold on delegates and raiding the delegates of others. Two major imperatives compelled such a trip for Rev. Jackson. One of these forces was domestic, the other Latin American.

As the campaign for the presidential nomination moved in the latter months into states with large Hispanic populations, the need to address issues of relevance to that community became crucial. In particular, the Simpson-Mazzoli bill loomed as the single most important issue to Hispanics. While the general hysteria surrounding the immigration question had generated a sense of urgency about "controlling our borders"—a hysteria that was fueled by thinly veiled racism—it was Rev. Jackson's position that the cure in this case was worse than the illness. A bill that would sanction blatant discrimination against latinos and other "foreign-looking" people, that would usher in an era of passbooks akin to South Africa, was anathema not only to its most immediate victims, the 20 million Hispanics in the United States, but also to any civil libertarian.

In addition, the immigration issue clearly had to be considered within the context of Latin America's grave economic crisis. The $350-billion debt of the Latin American countries has compelled the chief lending institutions— the International Monetary Fund and the World Bank—to demand austerity programs in the debtor nations. The situation has grown to the point of absurdity. Nations are having to borrow money to pay the interest on loans, thus furthering their indebtedness. For most of these nations, more than half of all export earnings go to pay their debt, thus precluding important development projects and social programs aimed at alleviating the daily food, health, and housing needs of a large portion of their populations. This social and economic stagnation in its turn compels both rebellion and immigration.

In Jackson's analysis of the situation, to close the borders without addressing the internal economic problems of the sending countries was to invite political instability. Hence the rebellion question. Although it has been for some time the position of the United States generally, and of the Reagan administration specifically, that the cause of unrest in Central America is Soviet and Cuban subversion, it was important for Rev. Jackson to go to the sources and sites of the unrest and find out from them their views of regional instability. What's more, a good many Hispanic groups were also quite concerned about the possibilities of war in the Central American region. They recognized that Hispanics in the United States share a great deal in common with their Latin American brothers and sisters—language, history, culture, and blood. Hence, for Hispanics to be sent to Central America to fight a war, particularly when the issues were obscure and highly debatable, was to invite serious self-doubt for many. It also meant, of course, that Hispanics would probably be called to fight in record numbers, since they would enjoy a linguistic advantage over their anglo and black counterparts.

Concern for the possibility of regional war was also a primary preoccupation with some of the principal supporters of Rev. Jackson's candidacy—peace activists. Early in the campaign this group had expressed their belief that the Reagan administration was gearing up for a major armed confrontation in Central America. Troop buildups, military maneuvers, the evolution of Honduras into a virtual United States' military encampment, the expansion of the war to even normally neutral Costa Rica, the mining of Nicaraguan harbors, murder manuals, and the escalated war rhetoric of the president all portended a grim summer and fall. The peace movement was convinced that Reagan's war moves along Nicaragua's borders were intended to provoke that country into retaliatory action that could be interpreted as an excuse for armed intervention with United States' troops. In particular, they saw the fall of 1984 as a vital period. Not only would the rainy season be over in the region, but also it would be just before election time, and on the strength of American public reaction to the Grenada invasion and Reagan's cold war view that the public would rally around a president "forced" to take action against an aggressor, Reagan would see his re-election chances as virtually assured with such an invasion. Moreover, Congress would not be in session in October, hence the one source of a counter view on such an action would be effectively muted.

Rev. Jackson was less concerned with what this scenario might mean for the re-election chances of Ronald Reagan than with what it meant in possible American and Central American casualties because, unlike Grenada, there was little doubt that the Nicaraguan people would defend their revolution to the death. There was every reason to believe, then, that armed intervention in Nicaragua would lead to an outbreak of violence unlike any we had seen since the darkest days of Vietnam. And while some would label this scenario as overly alarmist, at this point Rev. Jackson's position was that in such instances it was better to err on the side of caution than to wait until it was too late, as we had in Vietnam.

But beyond the domestic pressures for Rev. Jackson to undertake a trip to Central America there existed an intense sense of urgency among Latin American forces. Although there had been contact between Rev. Jackson and the Nicaraguan government (Mrs. Jackson had already visited the country) and the FMLN/FDR from El Salvador had written letters requesting his intervention, the first real thrust toward a trip to the region came on May 14 when he briefly crossed into Mexico in Tijuana, Baja California. The reaction of the Mexican people and press gave a clear indication that people south of the border had been following Rev. Jackson's campaign with intense interest. No other candidate would have generated the same kind of excitement.

On the heels of this brief foray a larger and more intense trip to Mexico City was planned. This trip at the end of May allowed Jackson to meet with extremely high level Mexican officials, including Mexico's most influential senators, Foreign Minister Bernardo Sepulveda, and various leading Latin American intellectuals. It also afforded the opportunity to gauge Mexican press reaction to Rev. Jackson.

What emerged from that trip, in spite of predictably negative United States press reaction, was a realization that many in Latin America, including moderate forces such as Mexico and other Contadora nations, saw Reagan administration policy in Central America as ill conceived at best and agonizingly dangerous at worse. Moreover, significant elements in the region clearly perceived Rev. Jackson as the *only* force on the United States' political scene with the political clout and will to curb Reagan administration policy before it was too late. Without exception, all of the Mexican officials with whom he spoke—from the right, the left, and the center of the ideological spectrum—agreed that the causes of revolt in Central America had nothing to do with Soviet or Cuban subversion. Instead the overwhelming view was that the outrageous policies of the IMF with the complicity of the United States, and the devastating effects that such policies had in limiting development and social service programs in the Latin American countries, combined with years of oppression, exploitation, repression, hunger, and disease, had much more to do with unrest than any other forces. The Mexicans also were convinced that the United States had seriously undercut the Contadora process by granting the Duarte government in El Salvador an additional $61 million in military aid. They argued that such aid would not help the army win the war but would only prolong the killing before both sides realized that only a negotiated settlement could resolve the conflict. They also argued that such actions were typical of Reagan administration policies—that is, policies that were publicly supportive of the Contadora process but that were privately committed to its failure.

With the termination of the Mexico trip, then, forces within the campaign began to realize the way in which Rev. Jackson was seen outside of the United States. In particular, the belief crystallized among a diverse set of actors, both of the center and of the left, that Rev. Jackson was the only hope of averting outright regional warfare in Central America. The pressures to undertake a larger trip to the region began to intensify.

By this time, of course, it had become evident that Walter Mondale had all but sewed up the Democratic party nomination. While within the Jackson camp voices called for a stepped-up campaign to solidify his hold on delegates and to press his claims for internal party justice by going to as many state party conventions as possible, the need for an extended trip to Central America lingered. Rev. Jackson concluded that an effort to avoid war in Central America far outweighed a handful of delegates for his candidacy. The decision was made to go to Central America during the latter half of June.

The timing of the trip was crucial. To go before the Democratic convention in July was to seriously cut into time that might have been used to fortify Rev. Jackson's internal party position. On the other hand, to wait until after the convention was to risk a dissolution of Rev. Jackson's command of the press and of public attention. In terms of the goals of the trip, public exposure was an absolute necessity. While he was quite aware that some would label such a trip as opportunistic, his belief was that such a trip at this time was in fact opportune. In such efforts, he knew that timing was critical because if the Mexican perception that Reagan was looking to a fall offensive in the region was accurate to wait any longer was not only to assure additional deaths but also to risk having to try to end the conflict *after,* rather than before, it had intensified. Hence, events and circumstances dictated that the trip be undertaken before the Democratic convention.

I initiated the idea of each Latin American trip. Although I had to wage a continual battle with higher campaign officials, in the end I was able to convince Rev. Jackson of the urgency and necessity of each trip. These other advisors focused on the costs of such excursions, both financial and political. Although none of the trips was paid for with campaign monies, since this was prohibited by federal election laws, the time spent in raising the money from private sources was seen as much too valuable to spend on such a tenuous proposition. Additionally, some felt Rev. Jackson's time would better be spent campaigning in the United States. They also believed the press would not treat such a trip positively, focusing instead on the issue of "theatrics" and "sensationalism." These arguments, to be sure, were not without merit.

My position, however, was that the potential benefits of such trips, particularly as regards attracting Hispanic voters, were worth the risks. Jackson had to put distance between himself and the other candidates. He had to force their hand on Hispanic and Central American questions. He had to demonstrate a boldness in confronting such difficult issues. Finally, he had to put his words into action—talking and negotiating were better than shouting and fighting. After lengthy debate and struggle, the latter view prevailed.

Once Rev. Jackson had decided that the trip would indeed be made before the convention, the next consideration was which countries to visit. First, we wanted a broad cross section of countries—that is, we did not want to visit only countries identified as leftist. In order to receive a representative sample of views on the conflict in the region as well as an honest appraisal of United States' policy, countries identified as friendly to the United States as well as those not so friendly would have to be included on the trip. Additionally, because Jackson had already visited one Contadora country, Mexico, we felt it necessary to meet with another in hopes of convening all of the foreign ministers of the Contadora nations. His first choice was Colombia, but simple geography said that Panama made more sense. Not only was Panama in Central America, but also it was a country friendly to the United States and also a country generally identified as conservative. Indeed, when we did in fact go to Panama, we were criticized by leftist forces in the United States for having selected a country with such a strong military influence. Later Jackson learned that Panama had undertaken ongoing, if semisecret, talks with all of the forces in the Central American region, including the FMLN/FDR, Salvodoran President Duarte, and the Honduran and Costa Rican and Nicaraguan governments to try to bring all of the relevant forces to the bargaining table. In short, Panama turned out to be an inspired choice.

The decision to go to El Salvador was perhaps the most difficult of all. Rev. Jackson was determined to meet with President Duarte in spite of his outspoken criticism of United States' military aid to the government. In the first place, Salvadoran labor leader Hector Bernabe Recinos had been imprisoned without any formal charges for some four years. During campaign stops in California, Rev. Jackson had been introduced to Recinos's three sons and had invited them on a march against the Simpson-Mazzoli bill in Los Angeles. He was thus committed to making every effort to win the release of Recinos. Secondly, in spite of his criticism of United States' military aid to the Salvadoran government and his belief that such aid only served to prolong the war, Rev. Jackson made it clear that he had no reason to question the personal integrity of President Duarte. Hence, to meet face to face with him and receive his personal assessment of the conflict was an absolute necessity. Thirdly, El Salvador was at the center of the conflict in Central America—the scene of the most intense fighting—and thus its internal political, military, and economic situation was vital to the resolution of conflict in the region. Finally the FMLN/FDR had been in continuing contact with Rev. Jackson and had sent several letters requesting a meeting. Moreover, they expressed their willingness to make new proposals for the resolution of the conflict, using Jackson as the conduit for such proposals. The possibility for such a break in the hostilities was too vital to avoid. In spite of grave apprehensions regarding Rev. Jackson's safety from the Salvadoran right wing, El Salvador had to be a stop in Central America.

Jacqueline Jackson had already visited Nicaragua. This country was clearly key to the entire Central America conflict. Indeed, if there was one country where the United States was most likely to intervene with troops, it was Nicaragua. It existed in many ways as a nation under siege. Jackson had already been informed by his other Central American sources, including Mexico, that United States' maneuvers on its borders and support for the Contra forces made up largely of the old Somoza national guard troops were intense attempts to provoke a war. He also saw Nicaragua as a nation at a critical crossroad in its development. It had yet to fully consolidate its revolution. Many elements in the country still were not fully convinced that the Sandinistas were truly committed to building a more egalitarian society. Some in the Church had continued to criticize the government, and the Sandinista reaction to the Pope's visit had done little to endear the government to a significant element of its population. Additionally, the United States had made the case that the Sandinistas were at the center of arms shipments to the Salvadoran guerrillas, in spite of the fact that no such shipments had been interdicted by United States and Salvadoran forces for over three years. The Nicaraguan government was thus most vulnerable to destabilization and intervention. It seemed the most likely place where an outright confrontation with the United States would occur. And since even the CIA agreed that most Nicaraguans would defend their country, it was likely that a large-scale bloodbath might be in the offing. For if the Nicaraguan people were as yet unsure of their total commitment to the Sandinistas, they were of like mind that the ouster of military strongman Anastacio Somoza, who had remained in power for so long because of United States support, was the best thing that had ever happened to the country. The prospect of the United States reinstating a similar kind of government was enough to make even lukewarm supporters of the Sandinistas take up arms.

Finally, Rev. Jackson was committed to the idea of including Cuba as one of the stops on his trip. There is no other country in the hemisphere, no other leader, about which United States perceptions are so influenced by myth, stereotype, and unabashed propaganda as Cuba and Fidel Castro. We know ludicrously little about this island, its people, and President Castro. Moreover, what is known is usually colored by such an obvious disdain that it becomes useless for any kind of objective assessment. Yet every source of information that Jackson had made contact with, from the Mexicans to the FMLN/FDR to the United States' state department, agreed that Cuba was key to any settlement of regional conflict. It was a central element of Rev. Jackson's approach to foreign policy that dialogue between conflicting elements is key to any rational resolution. Yet for twenty-seven years the United States has failed to recognize Cuba diplomatically. This policy has insured that the two sides talk at and about each other. It has also meant that mutual perceptions are based on the crassest of propaganda. Rev. Jackson was convinced that propaganda is not the kind of element upon which foreign policy should be based. Besides, if the United States had reached a stage where it could talk and trade with the Chinese, the largest Communist country in the world and a country about which we once held many of the same misconceptions regarding life style and foreign policy intentions, why could we not do the same with a tiny island ninety miles away? Surely logic and common sense should be made to prevail in this instance.

After he announced that Cuba would be one of the stops on his trip, another factor came into the picture—prisoners. Almost immediately we began to receive numerous phone calls from family members who had relatives in Cuban prisons. Most of the calls were from Americans, but some also came from Cuban Americans wishing to secure the release of Cubans who were political prisoners. For the rest of his life Rev. Jackson may well be a victim of the "Goodman Syndrome"—wherever he goes there will be desires and expectations that prisoners will be released as a consequence.

So as the decision of when and where to go on his Central American trip was made, there was a mood of caution and optimism. That there would be criticism from some quarters was to be expected.

Rev. Jackson made a decision early on that the state department would be kept apprised of his plans both before he left as well as during the trip. Nothing was kept from Undersecretary Michael Armacost during his meeting of June 12, 1984. While Armacost and his Central American experts were cordial and informative, they offered little hope that significant movement could be made in the general atmosphere and events in the Central American region.

We were, of course, intensely aware that the timing of the trip was opportune for Rev. Jackson to make a difference. Certainly he could not be ignored. We anticipated no fewer than seventy-five members of the press to accompany us on the trip. In this instance, truly the world would be with him. The Reagan administration would be unable to ignore his peace efforts, and the Democratic Party would be compelled to take a strong and progressive stance on the Central American question in its platform. Elements within the party were calling for the presidential nominee to out-Reagan Reagan on the issue of Central America. Rev. Jackson believed that such a course was a formula for failure. He hoped that his trip to the region would help solidify a clearly progressive policy stance on this vital issue. We also believed that to move *now* was crucial in averting disaster in the fall. If either the United States or the FMLN/FDR was prepared to launch a military offensive after the rainy season, the prospects for an ugly and bloody military confrontation were grim.

The trip was watched closely by the United States' hispanic community. Leaders from throughout the country privately praised the peace efforts. To be sure, the Cuban American community, maintaining its hard-line anti-Castro stance, predictably chastised Rev. Jackson's trip to Cuba as a propaganda ploy for President Castro and charged that Jackson had been "used" by the Cuban leader. Most Cuban Americans trace their migration to the United States directly to the triumph of the Cuban Revolution in 1959. As the revolutionary government of Fidel Castro expropriated private holdings and instituted a socialist government, the Cuban bourgeoisie migrated en masse to southern Florida. For example, over half of the island's medical doctors migrated shortly after the revolution. This group and their descendants continue to harbor rabid anti-Castro views. This also explains their 9 to 1 voter turnout for the

Republican party, which has historically taken a much more bellicose position vis-à-vis Cuba.

Upon Jackson's return the reaction of the Hispanic community, again with the exception of Cuban Americans, was uniformly enthusiastic. Jackson was praised for his boldness of vision and his sensitivity to Hispanic concerns. In particular, his willingness to meet with Latin American leaders on their own terms struck a resonant chord. Hispanics in the United States, like their Latin American counterparts, are all too familiar with the historical tendency for United States politicians, liberal and conservative alike, to treat them with disrespect and heavy-handedness, imposing a point of view, an ideology, and a demand to meet on United States turf and terms. Jackson was a deep breath of fresh air.

While reliable data is impossible to obtain, sociologist Tatcho Mindiola, Jr., of the Mexican American Studies Program at the University of Houston, estimates that Rev. Jackson averaged some 30 percent of the Hispanic vote, excluding the Cuban American community.[7] At first glance and given the foregoing analysis, this support appears most disappointing. However, the political primary process is heavily stacked in favor of party regulars—those citizens who regularly participate in the electoral process. In particular, in states such as Texas, where the caucus system is in use, it is exceedingly difficult to attract to the polls the disillusioned and disaffected—the very people to whom Rev. Jackson appealed. In the black community a greater enthusiasm for a fellow black and the support of the black church helped to overcome these barriers. No such factors were at play in the Hispanic community.

One cannot assume that Hispanics, any more than their black counterparts, will automatically give their enthusiastic support to a candidate of color who is not specifically from their own racial/ethnic group. In the Black community Rev. Jackson had a track record that was over two decades old. Key black leaders, political, religious, and social, were intimately familiar with the man and his accomplishments. Such was not the case in the Hispanic community. It was to be expected that his candidacy would be greeted with some degree of skepticism by Hispanics. Overcoming this skepticism would have taken a monumental and time-consuming effort. That some progress was made within the terribly confining limits of a presidential campaign is rather remarkable.

This overview should prove that much can be done to unite the black and brown communities. The fact that over 80 percent of all Hispanics are concentrated in the twenty largest hispanic markets has several critical implications for coalition-building attempts. First, this is a very manageable number of areas; it is quite feasible to visit each of these market areas and build a strong local Hispanic support system. Second, this concentration allows a representative of the individual or organization seeking to build the coalition to be in each of these communities on a relatively regular basis as part of an overall plan to build black-Hispanic unity. Third, anyone able to build a strong progressive organization at a time when most Democrats are moving to the right is likely to be the only figure on the national scene speaking directly and forcefully to the issues that hit closest to the Hispanic community.

A potential candidate could easily visit each of the twenty cities (see table 2) more than a half dozen times before the next elections, building the base and the network among key community activists—not necessarily the establishment Hispanic politicians—who could mobilize Hispanics even in the face of party rules designed to discourage mass participation. In this sense the Hispanic community is no different from the black. It surprised no one, except black establishment politicians and the whites who have historically sponsored them, when the black community en masse defied black endorsements for Mondale and voted for Jackson anyway. Hispanics have the potential for reacting similarly, as shown at the Democratic convention when Mayor Cisneros and Senator Baca proved ineffective at persuading the Hispanic delegates to support Mondale in spite of his refusal to condemn Simpson-Mazzoli. But in order for this to occur, much grass roots work must be undertaken to build an effective support system.

Never in the history of this country have the forces critical to the building of a strong black-Hispanic coalition been as operative as they are today. The social, economic, educational, and political conditions of both groups bring them together naturally. If these natural allies can be forged into a voting and acting bloc, the politics of this country can be forever changed. Up to now, however, no leader capable of forging this alliance into a reality has emerged.

Eighty-five percent of all voting age Hispanics can be found in nine states. These nine states control a total of 193 electoral votes—71 percent of the 270 votes needed to win the presidency. By the turn of the century, in New York, Texas, California, and Illinois blacks and Hispanics will form in combination a majority of the voting age population. These four states alone control 136 electoral votes. In these and other key states coalition politics is the key to increasing the number of blacks and Hispanics in local, state, and national offices.

What is clear is that sooner rather than later Hispanics and blacks will begin to be elected in increasing numbers. Already Democrats and Republicans are beginning to *select* their own blacks and Hispanics to elect and appoint. We stand on the threshold of one of the most historic periods of America's political life. Blacks and Hispanics will either see their collective futures controlled and dictated by white-selected functionaries, or they will select their own leaders and course. Rev. Jackson currently stands as the most likely leader and beneficiary of black-Hispanic coalition building. But this could change as new efforts are undertaken to harness the substantial strength of these two natural allies.

NOTES

1. I served the Jackson presidential campaign in various capacities—initially as a consultant on Hispanic affairs, then as the deputy press secretary, and finally as a principal speech writer and advisor on Hispanic and Latin American affairs. I conceived of, organized, and participated in Rev. Jackson's trips to Mexico and Latin America.

2. As reported in *Hispanic Monitor* 1 (November 1984).

3. Bureau of the Census, *Persons of Spanish Origin by State: 1980* (August, 1982).

4. Ibid.

5. Hispanic Policy Development Project, *The Hispanic Alamanac* (New York: 1984).

6. This period was perhaps the most frustrating for me. Up to this point I had virtually total access to Rev. Jackson at will. At the convention, however, I had to fight to be housed in the same hotel with him. Even then I was on a different floor from him, without the security key needed to get on his floor. By this time all of the key campaign "heavyweights" (Marion Barry, Richard Hatcher, Walter Fauntroy, Maxine Waters, and others) had sequested Rev. Jackson and controlled access to him. After attending two latino caucus meetings, I realized that Mondale's refusal to publicly condemn Simpson-Mazzoli could, if played correctly, cost him enough Hispanic delegates to deny him the nomination on the first ballot, which would have effectively denied him the nomination. The nearly 300 Hispanic delegates pledged to Mondale were ready to bolt but needed to be approached individually or in small groups by Rev. Jackson and persuaded of the utility of boycotting the first ballot. I was able to get a list of all the latino delegates and the hotels in which they were housed. However, two full days of relentless efforts to get to Rev. Jackson proved fruitless and on Thursday, July 19, Mondale finally had no choice but to take a public stance condemning the Simpson-Mazzoli bill, thus averting a Hispanic boycott of the first ballot. It is obvious that Rev. Jackson's bargaining position, with 465 delegates, would have been substantial had Mondale not won the nomination on the first ballot.

7. More reliable data is not yet available. However, Dr. Mindiola's figures do match with estimates given to the author by Jackson campaign staff.

PART III

The Voters

The 1984 Presidential Primary Campaign: Who Voted for Jesse Jackson and Why?

6

Michael B. Preston

Black voters, once known for their political quiescence, are now becoming politically active. The same voters who were expected to stay at home on election day because of their low socioeconomic status and their lack of attachment to and understanding of the linkages between the political process and policy outcomes are today providing the fuel for a new era of political activity.

The Voting Rights Act of 1965 provided the catalyst for an increase in black voter registration and turnout. This was especially true in the South. In 1980 a Republican presidential candidate hostile to black interests pushed that participation even higher. The momentum continued in 1982 and accelerated in 1983, when Harold Washington was elected mayor in Chicago and Wilson Goode became mayor of Philadelphia. Jesse Jackson's candidacy for president further intensified the momentum. The tremendous outpouring of blacks for black candidates has brought criticism from some. Yet why shouldn't blacks take pride in voting for their own? Other ethnic groups and regional groups have done this for years. The Irish and Catholics poured out for Kennedy. Southerners voted heavily for Lyndon Johnson and Jimmy Carter. The symbolic value of a minority person running for the highest executive position elicits pride for the group and in the individuals that make up that group. This point cannot be overstated, because it also helps explain why low-income groups who traditionally have voted less are suddenly voting more.

This essay will describe and analyze the black vote for Jesse Jackson in the 1984 presidential primary campaign. To do this, we shall first develop a framework that puts the Jackson campaign in a broader perspective. In general, we are suggesting that black voter turnout in the Jackson campaign was built on the momentum that developed after the inception of the Voting Rights Act of 1965. More specifically, we are suggesting that the Jackson campaign was fueled by the "new black voter" of the 1980s. Second, we shall analyze who voted for Jesse Jackson and why. We shall also investigate whether there was a "black establishment vote" for Mondale that suppressed Jackson's support among certain segments of the black population.[1]

The New Black Voter: Background and Characteristics

The steady increase in black voter registration and turnout after 1965 led to a renewed emphasis on electoral politics in 1982. Voter registration campaigns took on a new urgency and slogans abounded—from Lu Palmer's "We Shall See in '83" to the NAACP's "3 million more by '84." The momentum gained during this period has not abated. In 1984 it helped cause the near defeat of one of the country's most popular Republican governors, Jim Thompson of Illinois.

The most remarkable testimony to the resurgence of black voters took place in Chicago during the 1983 primary and general elections. The new black voter can take major credit for the election of Chicago's first black mayor. This was followed by the election in Philadelphia of that city's first black mayor as well as the election of several other black mayors in smaller cities. The new black voter has also provided the fuel for the campaign of the first serious black candidate for president of the United States. Indeed, one might well argue that the new black voter has shifted the emphasis from the civil rights revolution to the electoral revolution.[2]

The new black voter may be categorized into two groups: (1) previously registered voters who have developed a stronger sense of political efficacy and group consciousness and (2) newly registered voters who now see some linkages between political process and product. Charles Hamilton has called this the *P* paradigm—i.e., when *process* (political activity, however defined) leads to a *product* (more jobs, better schools, ethnic pride, or, conversely, negative outcomes), then *participation* is likely to increase.[3] The newly registered black voters are significant because they represent the groups that in previous times were the least likely to register and vote: the young, the poor, women, and the elderly. Today they are beginning to believe, like many of their middle-class brethren, that they can make a difference. This is especially true when the choices presented seem to attack their ethnic pride or group identity or when opposing forces are seen as hostile to black interests.

The important point here is that this is not an episodic or isolated response by black voters; it is patterned and is likely to be sustained for some time to come. The serious possibility of a black running for president (or governor, or some other high office) every four years should have a profound influence on future elections. And in the short run it may lead to new party alignments. In any case, the poor, the powerless, and the dispossessed have found their "voice" and will probably never return to the quiescent state in which they existed in the past.

The demographics of the black electorate provide further evidence of their potential influence. According to the 1980 census blacks represent 10.8 percent of the total voting age population. This percentage translates into 17 million blacks of voting age in the United States, many of whom are concentrated in industrial areas of the northern states.[4]

The Resurgence of Black Voters: 1982–84

Figures from the 1982 election indicate another important political development: black turnout actually exceeded white turnout in eight states—California, Illinois, Indiana, Kentucky, Louisiana, Missouri, South Carolina, and Tennessee. In several other states—Michigan, Mississippi, Ohio, Oklahoma, Pennsylvania, Texas, and Virginia—black and white turnout was about equal. Nationwide, the gap in turnout between the races was the lowest it has been in twenty years (6.9 percent).[5]

What accounts for this resurgence? According to Eddie Williams, president of the Joint Center for Political Studies, three factors explain the increase in black voting: (1) registration and get-out-the-vote drives targeted at blacks, (2) more black major candidates in significant races, and (3) black opposition to President Reagan and his policies.[6] The intensity of black opposition to Reagan and his supporters was perhaps most evident in the 1982 Chicago registration and voting drive which contributed to a 64 percent black turnout statewide, as opposed to 54.2 percent among whites.[7] However, while the explanation provided by the Joint Center makes a good deal of sense, it is limited. Moreover, the phenomenon of the resurgence needs to be put in a broader theoretical framework.

A good argument can be made that the new emphasis on electoral politics is an extension of the civil rights movement. One reason for its intensity at this time is the hostile political environment that existed for so long. Because black interests have not been reflected in the political system at the local, state, or national levels, and given the fact that the old civil rights movement has largely disappeared, blacks are now transferring their fervor to the electoral arena.

One of the more interesting aspects of the increase in black voting is that it is not fully accounted for by the SES model used so prominently by political scientists. For example, Verba and Nie, Erickson, and others argue that people of higher socioeconomic status and education vote more than those of lower education and status.[8] That model does not really account for the increase in voting by low-income and younger black voters. However, the work of Verba and Nie on group and/or racial consciousness does shed more light on race and class as determinants of mobilization and participation in electoral success. They suggest that socioeconomic status is closely related to race. It is interesting to note that Verba and Nie's data indicate that consciousness of race (either as a problem or as the basis for conflict) appears to bring blacks *up to a level of participation equivalent to that of whites*. For example, in their measurement of group consciousness, 64 percent of their black respondents mentioned race spontaneously in response to a question about group consciousness and political participation, and 24 percent mentioned race more than once. In comparing the rates of participation of blacks at varying levels of group consciousness with the average participation of whites, the key variable in the group consciousness model tended to be group consciousness itself.[9] This awareness on the part of blacks tends to *overcome the socioeconomic disadvantages* of blacks and makes them as active as whites.

The importance of "group consciousness" is particularly evident in Nie's recent empirical analysis of the correlation between wealth and voter turnout in elections from 1922 to 1966.[10] In contravention to what the SES model would predict, turnout among low-wealth voters was as high as and often higher than turnout among high-wealth voters from 1922 to 1950; only between 1956 and 1966 is there a strong positive relationship between wealth and voter turnout. The authors explain this result by stressing the importance of political machines as an organizational force in the early years covered by the study (1922 to 1934); they also stress the importance of the New Deal in drawing voters together. Some of these same factors, especially the emphasis on issues and ethnicity, are contributing to the emergence of the new black voter.

It seems clear then that the standard SES models, as useful as they are, cannot be used as a basis for explaining increases in black voter turnout. A better explanation is found in an increase in group consciousness. It becomes especially apparent when a serious black candidate runs for a high political office and when the election is highly competitive. According to Verba and Nie: "If blacks participate more than one would expect of a group with a similar socioeconomic status (SES), the explanation may lie in the fact that they have, over time, developed an awareness of their own status as a deprived group, and this self-consciousness has led them to be more political than members of the society who have similar socioeconomic levels but do not share the group identity." [11]

While group consciousness is an important determinant of increased black participation, other factors are needed to help specify under what conditions group consciousness is likely to lead to higher participation. One such factor is the incentives that spur people to action. These incentives include pertinent issues, symbols of ethnic identification, and the competitiveness of the election. These incentives provide a more concrete basis for analyzing and interpreting Harold Washington's and Wilson Goode's elections and the high turnout for Jesse Jackson. Ronald Terchek argues that the presence of an incentive structure increases a group's participation:

1. With the introduction of more *pertinent issues* into (local, state and national) campaigns, the incentive to participate should increase and result in a higher turnout.
2. The *symbolic* dimension of elections and candidates also provides an important incentive for participation. Ethnic affinity has long been an important symbolic component of American politics, and ethnic identification has often provided an incentive for otherwise inactive voters to vote for a representative of their ethnic community. The presence of a minority member on the ballot might be expected to increase minority group participation, particularly when the candidate is running for an office that is considered important (such as *mayor* rather than clerk of courts), when the office has not been traditionally filled by members of the minority, and where the ethnicity of a candidate becomes an issue.
3. Relevant issues, ethnic identification, and the *competitiveness* of the election define the incentive structure for voting and should be coupled with Charles Hamilton's organization structure for minority group participation. Incentives and organization structures are not independent of one another. The very factors that make a candidate appealing to previously inactive voters also tend to generate other expressions of support, such as volunteer activity, money, and endorsements that serve to build an organization.[12]

Congruent with Terchek's discussion, Nie, Erbring, and Hamburg find that more than one of these incentives must be present: "Organization must become the vehicle of a salient dimension of political conflict, with clear-cut partisan alternatives, if it is to mobilize voters. Yet a clear issue separation between parties alone appears to be equally insufficient to engage individual electoral participation, at least among lower-status voters, in the absence of organizational support." [13] Therefore, Jesse Jackson's success can be explained by heightened group consciousness and incentives to participate. For example: (1) some of the *pertinent issues* included the plight of the poor in America, South Africa, unemployment, and Reagan's record on civil rights; (2) the *symbolic* importance of a black running for president was not lost on most black voters; and (3) the *competitiveness* of the primaries meant that blacks would have to vote if Jackson was to be competitive with other candidates.

According to Cavanagh,

The biennial Census Bureau surveys have recorded a large increase in black registration and turnout during the four years of Reagan's presidency. Reported black registration surged from 9.8 million to 12.2 million during this period, driving the black registration rate (as a percentage of voting age population) from 60.0 to 66.3 percent, a gain of 6.3 percentage points. During the same four-year period, white registration increased only marginally, from 68.4 to 69.6 percent (or 1.2 percentage points). Thus, descriptive data alone strongly suggest a race-specific effect; as Verba and Nie would predict, a period of heightened black awareness of racial differences in policy outputs is marked by black participation rates much more closely approaching those of whites. Looked at another way, the gap between black and white registration rates has shrunk from 8.4 percentage points in 1980 to only 3.3 percentage points in 1984, the lowest such gap ever recorded in a national election.[14]

Who Voted for Jesse Jackson and Why

If Harold Washington helped prove the thesis about the new black voter, Jesse Jackson's candidacy added strong reinforcement. For even though Jackson, like Washington, did not have the support of some black politicians, he did receive the support of these new voters, and while he received votes from all segments of the black community, his support among younger voters was especially strong (see table 1).[15]

Jackson's percentage of votes in the primaries climbed steadily: he moved from a mere 0.4 percent of the primary vote in Maine to 3 percent in Iowa, 5 percent in Massachusetts, 8 percent in Vermont, 8.9 percent in Rhode Island, 12 percent in Florida, 20 percent in Alabama, 21 percent in Georgia, 25 percent in South Carolina, and 34 percent in Arkansas. His support among black voters was particularly evident in Illinois, where he won 79 percent of the black vote. In one of his most spectacular victories Jackson won 87 percent of the black vote in New York; he followed this up by winning 77 percent in Pennsylvania. In New York he captured 34 percent of the New York City vote and 26 percent statewide.[16] In Georgia he won 61 percent and in Alabama 50 percent. It is significant that in the last two he was opposed by two very popular black mayors.[17]

By April 1984 Jesse Jackson had received 1.4 million votes in the Democratic primaries, or 17 percent of all votes cast. Another measure of his success may be seen in the survey results released on April 17 by the NBC News exit poll (see table 2).

The NBC poll data provide a brief overview, but the National Black Election Study (NBES) data allow us to take a more detailed look at who voted for Jackson by age, sex, education, income, party, and region. Before turning to our specific findings, a brief explanation of that study is in order.[18]

The NBES

The 1984 National Black Election Study was the first in-depth investigation of the attitudes, perceptions, and electoral behavior of a large, representative, national sample of blacks. It included interviews with a voting age member of each of 1,155 cooperating black households. Pre-election telephone interviews were conducted between July and October 1984, and post-election interviews started on November 7, the day after the presidential election. The 1984 NBES will be of special interest to students of American politics as it replicates many

Table 1. Votes among "young" and "old" black voters

	% under 50 years old	% over 50 years old
Alabama		
Mondale	26	51
Hart	4	3
Jackson	67	45
Florida		
Mondale	26	43
Hart	7	7
Jackson	67	51
Georgia		
Mondale	21	26
Hart	4	5
Jackson	74	68
Illinois		
Mondale	15	16
Hart	9	7
Jackson	74	76
Connecticut		
Mondale	12	37
Hart	8	17
Jackson	80	42
New York		
Mondale	5	17
Hart	2	2
Jackson	93	81
Pennsylvania		
Mondale	16	23
Hart	7	12
Jackson	77	65

Source: NBC News Poll, April 17, 1984.

of the questions used in the National Election Studies conducted by the Center for Political Studies at the University of Michigan.

NBES interviewers asked respondents which candidate they voted for in the 1984 presidential primaries and, if they did not vote, which candidate they would have supported had they gone to the polls. We focus on those respondents who voted for Jesse Jackson or Walter Mondale, as 91.6 percent of the respondents in the 1984 NBES voted for one of these candidates. Respondents who would have supported Jackson or Mondale are also included. Thus the dependent variable measures both voting and nonvoting support for

Table 2. Percent of Jesse Jackson's vote in the Democratic primaries

	Mondale	Hart	Jackson	% blacks in Democratic primary electorate
Black voters				
New Hampshire	—	—	—	—
Alabama	34	4	60	30
Florida	32	5	62	13
Georgia	24	5	70	24
Maine	15	18	57	3
Rhode Island	10	22	66	5
Illinois	16	8	74	28
Connecticut	19	11	69	9
New York	9	2	89	20
Wisconsin	22	8	70	5
Pennsylvania	17	8	75	13
White voters				
New Hampshire	28	41	5	
Alabama	31	34	1	
Florida	33	49	3	
Georgia	32	37	2	
Maine	26	37	2	
Rhode Island	34	49	4	
Illinois	44	47	4	
Connecticut	31	63	7	
New York	57	36	7	
Wisconsin	43	48	7	
Pennsylvania	53	43	4	

Source: NBC Poll, April 17, 1984.

these two candidates. We turn now to the demographic breakdown of the primary results.

Age

NBES respondents were placed in four age cohorts: 18 to 26 years of age, 27 to 44 years, 45 to 64 years old, and those respondents 65 years of age and older. Table 3 displays the percentage of votes cast during the primaries for Jackson and Mondale by each cohort, along with the percentages of those who did not vote but would have if they had gone to the polls.

Several important findings can be drawn from this table. First, Jackson outpolled Mondale in each of the four age cohorts. The ratio of Jackson votes to

Table 3. Vote cast or candidate preference by age group, 1984 Democratic primaries

	18–26	27–44	45–64	65+
Voted for Jackson	26.5%	51.0%	46.9%	38.6%
Would have voted for Jackson	34.5	25.9	11.7	11.4
Voted for Mondale	13.3	16.2	33.6	31.8
Would have voted for Mondale	25.7	6.9	7.8	18.2
	100.0%*	100.0%	100.0%	100.0%
N = 545				

Source: NBES, 1984

*Columns may not add exactly to 100% due to rounding.

Mondale votes is highest among those voters 27–44 years of age; in this group Jackson outpolled Mondale by more than three to one. Voters 18-26 years old favored Jackson two-to-one over Mondale. Second, it is clear that despite the tendency of younger cohorts to support Jackson strongly, large numbers of respondents in these age categories never made it to the polls. More than half of the 18–26 group and roughly one-third of those in the 27–44 category would have voted either for Jackson or Mondale. The large vote margins for Jackson among younger voters is therefore tempered by the fact that support for Jackson was not efficiently converted into votes. This is especially true of the youngest group. Only 40 percent of this group actually voted for *either* candidate and more than one-third would have voted for Jackson. This is the highest figure for any of the four age groups.

The tendency of older voters actually to vote is readily apparent in table 3. Eighty percent of respondents 45–64 years of age voted for either Jackson or Mondale in the 1984 primaries along with 70 percent of those sixty-five years or older. Jackson outpolled Mondale in both of these cohorts but not by the margins he received from the younger cohorts. This is attributable to the substantially stronger support that Walter Mondale received from older voters. Mondale received roughly one-third of the votes cast by each of the two senior cohorts.

Collapsing the four age cohorts into two (18–44 and 45+) makes these tendencies clearer (see table 4). The percentage of votes cast for Jackson in the two age categories is nearly identical. Voting support for Mondale is much stronger among older than among younger respondents. The crucial point in both tables is that the younger cohorts gave Jackson impressive vote margins. At the same time respondents in the younger cohorts were those most likely to say that they "would have voted for Jackson" but failed actually to vote.

Table 4. Vote cast or candidate preference by age group, 1984 Democratic primaries

	18–44	45–91
Voted for Jackson	43.3%	44.8%
Would have voted for Jackson	28.6	11.6
Voted for Mondale	15.3	33.1
Would have voted for Mondale	12.8	10.5
	100.0%	100.0%

Source: NBES, 1984

Table 5. Vote cast or candidate preference by education level, 1984 Democratic primaries

	No high school	Some high school	Some college
Voted for Jackson	25.6%	47.0%	48.0%
Would have voted for Jackson	19.8	23.8	23.5
Voted for Mondale	30.2	13.2	20.9
Would have voted for Mondale	24.4	15.9	7.5
	100.0%	100.0%	100.0%
N = 539			

Source: NBES, 1984

In other words, the young blacks who voted in the 1984 primaries voted for Jackson.

Education

Education level is also helpful in explaining the support Jesse Jackson received from blacks in the 1984 primaries. We distinguished respondents who never attended high school from those who received some high school education and those who attended or graduated from college, respectively (see table 5). Jackson's support in both the high school and college groups is nearly twice that of those who did not attend high school. Mondale actually outpolled Jackson among the least-educated respondents. Voting support for Mondale was weakest among high-school educated respondents. Only 13 percent of this group voted for Mondale compared to 20.9 percent of those with some college education.

Investigating the relationship between voting behavior and education is enhanced by "controlling" for the age groups introduced previously. Tables A,

Table 6. Vote cast or candidate preference by region, 1984 Democratic primaries

	South	Non-South
Voted for Jackson	40.2%	49.2%
Would have voted for Jackson	23.7	20.5
Voted for Mondale	24.1	16.9
Would have voted for Mondale	12.0	13.3
	100.0%	100.0%
N = 539		

Source: NBES, 1984

B, C, D in the appendix show these relationships. The youngest respondents (18–26, table A) are characterized by their failure to vote for either candidate. It is somewhat surprising to find Mondale staying relatively close to Jackson among college-educated voters in this youngest age cohort. Nonvoting respondents who would have voted for Jackson slightly outnumber nonvoting Mondale supporters in the 18–26 age group.

Jackson votes are most pronounced among the high school and college groups in the 27–44 and 45–64 age groups (see tables B and C). Note especially the large Jackson-to-Mondale vote ratios in both the high school and college groups among those 27 to 44 years of age. These groups also show substantial numbers of nonvoting respondents who "would have voted for Jackson," thereby making even clearer the intensity and breadth of support for the Jackson candidacy among those 27 to 44 years of age. Mondale voters, in contrast, tended to be 45 to 64 years of age at each of the three education levels (see table C).

Region

That voting and nonvoting support for the Jackson candidacy was strong in the major demographic categories of age and education is not surprising given Jackson's overwhelming appeal in the entire black community. Another perspective on conception of black voting behavior in the 1984 primaries can be gleaned from the anomalous case of the black Mondale supporter. An examination of Jackson support in the southern and nonsouthern regions of the country shows that Jackson led Mondale in both votes cast and nonvoting support (see table 6). While nonvoting support is nearly identical between the two regions, Jackson voters were noticeably more common in the non-South, but Mondale voters, while still only one-fourth of all respondents, were largely located in the South. Two reasons might be offered to explain this. First, Mondale may have benefited from his identification with Jimmy Carter, who remains especially popular with southern blacks. More probable is the possi-

Table 7. Vote cast or candidate preference by sex, 1984 Democratic primaries

	Male	Female
Voted for Jackson	48.5%	40.3%
Would have voted for Jackson	24.7	22.0
Voted for Mondale	13.9	25.6
Would have voted for Mondale	13.0	12.1
	100.0%	100.0%
N = 544		

Source: NBES, 1984

bility that Mondale benefited in the South to some degree from his association with such elected leaders as Atlanta mayor Andrew Young; Birmingham, Alabama, mayor Richard Arrington; and the active support of Coretta Scott King. Jackson, conversely, may have also benefited from the support he received from Chicago mayor Harold Washington,[19] Gary mayor Richard Hatcher, and the endorsement of the Congressional Black Caucus, whose members for the most part represent "nonsouthern" congressional districts.

Gender

Another intriguing difference in votes cast for Jackson and Mondale emerges in considering voter sex. Among male respondents, 48.5 percent voted for Jackson compared to only 14 percent who voted for Mondale (see table 7). Jackson's support among women voters fell to 40 percent, and Mondale support jumped to 25.6 percent. Since nonvoting support is nearly identical, the differences in voting support between men and women become clear. Mondale's voting support among women becomes more significant when the higher turnout rates of black women compared to black men are taken into account.

Mondale's relatively better showing among women is attributable to his receiving unusually strong support from women 45 years of age and older (see table 8). Men and women under the age of 45 voted for Jackson at a two-to-one rate, as did men over 45. Women over 45 favored Mondale by a 40.4 percent to 34.3 percent margin. Women in the 45–64 group favored Mondale 42.7 percent to 37.3 percent (data not shown). Jackson's support was unusually strong among men 27–44, who voted for Jackson over Mondale at a 6-to-1 ratio (53.5 percent to 8.8 percent data not shown).

The "Establishment"

Given the breadth and depth of Jackson's support among blacks, it is not surprising to note that Jackson received 46.3 percent of the "strong Democrat" vote, while Mondale received only 27.3 percent. But controlling for age once

Table 8. Vote cast or candidate preference by sex (respondents 18–45 years of age), 1984 Democratic primaries

	Male	Female
Voted for Jackson	44.9%	42.2%
Would have voted for Jackson	32.1	26.0
Voted for Mondale	9.6	19.6
Would have voted for Mondale	13.5	12.3
	100.0%	100.0%
N = 360		

Source: NBES, 1984

Table 9. Vote cast or candidate preference by sex (respondents 45–91 years of age), 1984 Democratic primaries

	Male	Female
Voted for Jackson	58.3%	34.3%
Would have voted for Jackson	8.3	14.1
Voted for Mondale	23.6	40.4
Would have voted for Mondale	9.7	11.1
	100.0%	100.0%
N = 171		

Source: NBES, 1984

again produces some very interesting results. Mondale voters increase from 14.0 percent of strong Democrats in the 18–26 age group to 22.4 percent of the 27–44 group, to 42.1 percent of the 45–64 age group. In the 45–64 age group Mondale actually outpolled Jackson, albeit by a margin within polling error. Along with the support Mondale received from older black women, this is the only "major" condition under which Mondale "caught" Jesse Jackson among black voters.

Collapsing the four age categories into two makes these findings clear. Among strong Democrats 18–44 years of age, Mondale received 19.9 percent of the vote. Mondale also received 39.5 percent of the vote of strong Democrats 45 years of age and older. Jackson outpolled Mondale 49.2 percent to 19.9 percent in the 18–44 age group. In the senior group (45–91) Jackson and Mondale finished within polling error: Jackson's 40.3 percent to Mondale's 39.5 percent (see tables A, B, C, D, and E).

While definitive conclusions about the relative importance of variables such as education, party ID, and age in the Jackson/Mondale vote choice cannot be drawn from this presentation, it certainly does appear that Mondale tended to

Table A. Vote cast or candidate preference by education level (respondents 18–26 years of age), 1984 Democratic primaries

	No high school	Some high school	Some college
Voted for Jackson	25.0%	22.2%	28.9%
Would have voted for Jackson	62.5	37.0	28.9
Voted for Mondale	0.0	3.7	18.4
Would have voted for Mondale	12.5	37.0	23.7
	100.0%	100.0%	100.0%

Source: National Black Election Study (NBES). ISR. Ann Arbor: University of Michigan, 1984. Less than high school N = 8, High school N = 27, College N = . . . , N = 111

Table B. Vote cast or candidate preference by education level (respondents 27–44 years of age), 1984 Democratic primaries

	No high school	Some high school	Some college
Voted for Jackson	15.8%	51.4%	54.8%
Would have voted for Jackson	15.8	30.0	25.5
Voted for Mondale	21.1	10.0	18.5
Would have voted for Mondale	47.4	8.6	1.3
	100.0%	100.0%	100.0%

Source: NBES, 1984
Less than high school N = 19, High school N = 70, College N = 157, N = 246

draw his support from older, better educated, and more strongly partisan black voters. Given these considerations and given Mondale's personal identification with the civil rights tradition and its leaders, such as Coretta Scott King and Andrew Young among others, we might conclude that Mondale benefited from a "black establishment" type vote.

If it is granted that Jesse Jackson was never in a position to win the Democratic nomination for president, then we might see that the support given to Mondale by this "black establishment" as strategic votes meant to help Mondale (the "traditional" Democrat) beat Gary Hart (a relatively unknown quantity). Black establishment support for Mondale need not be interpreted as a turning of the back on the Jackson candidacy. It does suggest that another Jackson candidacy or an attempt to form a black political party might meet strong resistance in a segment of the black community that is in the best position to help either cause in its organizational and/or administrative stages.

These findings also demonstrate that the appeal of the Jackson candidacy

Table C. Vote cast or candidate preference by education level (respondents 45–64 years of age), 1984 Democratic primaries

	No high school	Some high school	Some college
Voted for Jackson	22.2%	56.4%	58.8%
Would have voted for Jackson	19.4	10.3	7.8
Voted for Mondale	44.4	25.6	29.4
Would have voted for Mondale	13.9	7.7	3.9
	100.0%	100.0%	100.0%

Source: NBES, 1984
Less than high school N = 36, High school N = 39, College N = 51, N = 126

Table D. Vote cast or candidate preference by education level (respondents 65–91 years of age), 1984 Democratic primaries

	No high school	Some high school	Some college
Voted for Jackson	40.9%	54.4%	20.0%
Would have voted for Jackson	4.5	9.1	30.0
Voted for Mondale	27.3	18.2	50.0
Would have voted for Mondale	27.3	18.2	0.0
	100.0%	100.0%	100.0%

Source: NBES, 1984
Less than high school N = 22, High school N = 11, College N = 10, N = 43

Table E. Vote cast by or candidate preference of all strong Democrats, strong Democrats 18–45 years of age, and strong Democrats 46–91 years of age, 1984 Democratic primaries

	All strong Democrats	Age: 18–45 strong Democrats	Age: 46–91 strong Democrats
Voted for Jackson	46.3%	49.2%	40.3%
Would have voted for Jackson	16.3	21.5	9.3
Voted for Mondale	27.3	19.9	39.5
Would have voted for Mondale	10.1	9.4	10.8
	100.0%	100.0%	100.0%
	N = 239	N = 156	N = 77

Source: NBES, 1984

was strongest among voters below the age of 45. The appeal of the Jackson candidacy among younger respondents overrode even the strongest partisan identification. This cannot be said of those over 45. Younger strong Democrats were either willing to put partisanship aside in order to vote for Jackson the outsider or they actually saw Jackson as a bearer of the Democratic standard in a way that older respondents did not. All told, support for Jackson was strongest among those 27 to 44 years of age. While the youngest cohort (18 to 26) was not a key component of Jackson's support, the important connections that Jackson established between this group and the larger electoral and political systems are sure to develop further and will demand our attention in the future.

The most significant thing about Jesse Jackson's success is that he not only kept the momentum going in black areas, he also intensified it. While many black leaders opposed him, the "new black voter" did not. To be sure, not all of these voters condoned some of his more insensitive and injudicious remarks, but just as white politicians have been forgiven, so Jackson's supporters expect the same for him. In addition, Jackson has inspired a large number of blacks to register and vote and has made them more conscious of their potential impact. He has opened the door for future black candidates; he has acted as a symbol of race pride; he has underscored the concerns of blacks and other minorities; he has pushed for a more peaceful world; and he has helped shape the Democratic agenda.

It should be clear by now that Harold Washington, Wilson Goode, and Jesse Jackson did not really start this movement; they are more the result than the cause. The current movement, while fueled by these black politicians, is larger than the personalities involved. The new black voter, driven by the search for fairness, justice, and more social equity, has transferred his energy from the civil rights movement to the electoral arena. It is not episodic and isolated: rather it is a patterned response to hostile conditions that threaten the self-esteem of a people.

These data suggest a number of interesting observations. First, Jackson received strong support from younger voters, but the people who really turned out to vote were the 27-to-44-year-old group. The problem is that while younger voters supported Jackson, they did not turn out in as large numbers as the 27–44 group did. Second, while Jackson did well with 44 + black voters, a large number of this group voted for Mondale. Part of the explanation is in the South. Some members of the black establishment urged their supporters to vote for Mondale, and this depressed the vote for Jackson. It also may be that older voters, possessing more political experience, did not believe Jackson could win and did not want to waste their votes.

Another interesting finding is that males voted in a higher proportion for

Jackson than did females. One might assume that since black females are more closely attached to the church than black males, they would be more supportive of Jesse Jackson, given his ministerial status. This did not happen. Since black females now out-vote black males, this could pose a problem for Jackson should he run again. Fourth, the non-South tended to vote more heavily for Jackson than the South. This may be a function of when the southern primaries are held or of support for Mondale by black politicians, or it may be that the Southern Crusade did not really attract as many voters as many had thought.

Finally, it should be noted that while Jackson could have done better, especially if more people had registered and if the young blacks who registered had actually voted, he did better than he or others expected. The important thing he did for the young is to get a large number of the disconnected to start thinking about politics and the fact that they can have an impact on the political system. The key is to begin converting the one-third of the 18–26 group who "would have voted for Jackson" into voters supportive of candidates sensitive to the needs and aspirations of the black community. Jackson's candidacy was successful with young voters to the extent that it began this conversion. Ultimately, he gave symbolic hope to a whole new generation of young potential and actual politicians.

One of the greatest compliments one can pay a politician is that he or she has inspired a large number of people to get involved in a process that will ultimately give them more influence over the decisions that affect their lives. Jesse Jackson most assuredly deserves such a compliment for his 1984 effort.

NOTES

1. This paper will use voting data from the NBC polls as well as data from a study done by a group of black scholars at the University of Michigan; see James S. Jackson, Shirley Hatchett, and Ron Brown, *National Black Election Study* (Ann Arbor: Institute of Social Research, University of Michigan, 1984). We would like to express our thanks to Ron Brown for permission to use these data.

2. Michael B. Preston, "The New Black Voter: Mobilization, Participation and Turnout in the Black Community" (paper prepared for a conference on "Where Have All the Voters Gone?," University of Chicago, April 26–28, 1984). The first two sections of the present essay draw heavily on this paper.

3. Charles V. Hamilton, "Introduction," in *The New Black Politics: The Search for Political Power*, ed. Michael B. Preston, Lenneal J. Henderson, Jr. and Paul Puryear (New York: Longman, 1982), XIX.

4. Thomas E. Cavanagh, *The Impact of the Black Electorate: Election '84*, Report #1 (Washington, D.C.: Joint Center for Political Studies, 1984).

5. *The Champaign-Urbana News Gazette*, April 25, 1983.

6. Ibid.

7. Ibid.

8. For a more detailed discussion of the main forms of political participation, social status, and participation, see Sidney Verba and Norman H. Nie, *Participation in America: Political Democracy and Social Equality* (New York: Harper and Row, 1972), pp. 157–58. For the thinking of another group of scholars who argue along similar lines, see Robert Erickson, Norman R. Luttberg, and Kent L. Tedin, *American Public Opinion: Its Origins, Content, and Impact,* 2nd ed. (New York: John Wiley and Sons, 1980).

9. Verba and Nie, *Participation in America,* pp. 157–60.

10. Norman H. Nie, Lutz Erbring, and Edward Hamburg, "Electoral Participation in America: Looking Back" (paper delivered at conference, "Where Have All the Voters Gone?"), pp. 10–11.

11. Verba and Nie, *Participation in America,* p. 157.

12. Ronald Terchek, "Incentives and Voter Participation: A Research Note," *Political Science Quarterly* 94 (Spring 1979):135–36. See also Penn Kimball, *The Disconnected* (New York: Columbia University Press, 1972), chapters 3 and 8. In addition, see Harlan Hahn, David Klingman, and Harry Pacton, "Cleavages, Coalitions, and the Black Candidate: The Los Angeles Mayoralty Elections of 1969 and 1973," *Western Political Quarterly* 29 (December 1976): 507.

13. Nie, Erbring, and Hamburg, "Electoral Participation in America," p. 22.

14. Thomas E. Cavanagh, "Black Mobilization and Partisanship: 1984 and Beyond" (paper presented at the Joint Center Conference on "The 1984 Elections and the Future of Black Politics," the Carnegie Endowment Conference Center, Washington, D.C., April 30, 1985).

15. Cavanagh's paper also points out that Jackson received strong support from younger blacks, ibid., p. 9.

16. *New York Times,* March 23, 1984.

17. *New York Times,* April 5, 1984.

18. I would like to thank my research assistant, Tom Murray, for his assistance on this section of the paper.

19. While Washington did not give Jackson all-out support, he did not actively oppose him.

## PART IV

The Party

A View from the Bottom: A Descriptive Analysis of the Jackson Platform Efforts

## 7

Curtina Moreland-Young

The drafting of platforms is a practice which developed as a natural outgrowth of the development of national parties. In fact, between 1789 and 1832 no party issued a platform.[1] As parties began the practice of national conventions, the drafting of party platforms had its genesis. In 1832 the Republicans became the first party to issue a platform. However, most experts agree that the serious practice of platform drafting began with the Democratic party of 1840.[2] Thereafter both parties often issued platforms, the practice becoming institutionalized in 1852.[3]

Though the platform process now is established practice, some scholars have minimized its importance. However, there is a body of literature which contradicts that argument, and some scholars have found that party platforms have a high incidence of influencing or becoming national plans.[4] In any event, most political candidates and their supporters are convinced of their import and invest vast amounts of time, money, and activity in trying to influence the platform process. In this regard, the 1984 presidential election was no exception as each candidate sought to make the platform process reflect his interests.

In 1984 I served as a member of the platform committee of the Democratic National Convention and as the leader of the Peace, Security and Freedom Task Force (sub-committee) for the Jackson preference from the state of Mississippi. This experience provides the basis of this essay—a descriptive analysis of the platform process from the perspective of a political scientist who was actively involved in these efforts. I am aware of the inherent problem of academic objectivity which may result when a participant observer becomes a full member of the group; however, I hope the unique circumstances of my involvement and professional training will somewhat ameliorate this concern.

Becoming a Member of the Platform Committee

Although I was a member of the Democratic National Committee during the summer of 1984, my actual quest for that position began in my home state in March and proceeded through a maze of precinct, county, district, and state caucuses which ended on May 1. Once the state caucuses ended, the final selection for the committee took place at a special meeting of national delegates from Mississippi.

Theoretically, one could be elected to one of the three national Democratic standing committees without participating in the caucus process, but it would have been difficult. The caucus process provided opportunities to lobby potential delegates and familiarize them with one's view on salient issues. Of course, I campaigned throughout with party leaders in the Jackson and Mondale camps. Since the prevailing belief was that standing committee members would be chosen at large by all the national delegates, I mailed a position letter to all the state's delegates before the party held a general meeting for them. On a warm Saturday morning in June, all of the national delegates met in Jackson to choose members for the platform, rules, and credentials committees of the national Democratic party.

By the time the national delegates met, it was abundantly clear to me that selection had become as much a matter of protecting state party unity and accord as of having qualified representation on the committee. In fact, an ad hoc group had been meeting prior to the beginning of the caucuses.[5] The sole purpose of this group—composed of party leaders and leaders of the Hart, Jackson, and Mondale preferences—was to guard against issues which might cause discord. The members of the ad hoc group felt that an at-large election might also exacerbate strong feeling which many Jackson delegates already held against both at-large elections and the caucus system.

As a result, the ad hoc group proposed a plan, which the party leadership accepted, giving each preference group (Hart, Jackson, Mondale) the standing committee membership it felt most beneficial. Moreover, each preference group would be allowed to select their own representatives, who would serve as members of a particular standing committee representing the state. Under this arrangement the Hart preference opted for the rules and credentials slots, the Mondale preference selected platform and credentials, and the Jackson preference chose platform and rules.

State and national leaders of the Jackson campaign felt that the platform committee would be an excellent forum in which to raise and debate issues. We believed that our participation might influence national policy if the Democrats won the presidency. And having representation on the rules committee was also deemed important to the Jackson cause. During the primary campaign Rev. Jackson charged repeatedly that the 1984 rules advanced mainstream candidates and unfairly disadvantaged long-shot candidates such as himself. Obviously Jackson wanted to have an impact on reforming the rules for 1988.

Each preference group assembled and chose its two standing committee members. Even though members were now being elected by their respective preference group, I still had to compete. Fortunately, I had been in contact with all of the Jackson delegates from the beginning; therefore, it was easy for me to ask two Jackson delegates, both of whom were highly respected, to make nominating and seconding speeches on my behalf. Mayor Olivia Violet Leggette gave my nominating speech and Dr. Leslie Burl McLemore seconded my candidacy.[6] My opponent was Victor McTeer, a well-known civil rights attorney who was also an elected national delegate from Greenville. McTeer was a major proponent of the view that abolition of second primaries should be the litmus test for Democrats who professed belief in equitable political participation. However, Jackson campaign leaders and supporters genuinely believed that one of the major purposes of Jackson's campaign was to widen the base of opportunity for activism. To this end, effort was made to spread around the "plums" of activism. McTeer had already received a "plum"— of his selection to be a delegate. Since I was not a delegate, I surmised that this factor would weigh in my favor for election to the platform committee. Apparently it did: when the secret ballots were counted, I was chosen for the platform committee, to serve as one of two elected members from Mississippi.

Drafting the Platform

Soon after my election to the platform committee, the national campaign office informed me that the committee would meet in Washington to look at the first draft of the platform, written by a committee composed of members representing all of the candidates. Knowing that in the past in both parties the platform was usually virtually unchanged after the drafting, I began to wonder if my going to Washington would be superfluous. However, I was assured by Prof. Ronald Walters, the major issues person for the Jackson campaign, that there would be work to do.

When I arrived in Washington and began work, I realized that the platform committee was, ironically, a microcosm of the national campaign: Mondale's people were firmly in control of the platform process, and Jackson's preference group seemed underrepresented in both resources and personnel.

During the presidential campaign Rev. Jackson had complained that the rules gave unfair advantage to a mainstream candidate. This perception appeared accurate in reference to the platform committee. Almost to a person, we of the Jackson preference felt that the staff persons who clearly determined procedures and voting order were not Jackson people. Although there was at least one Jackson platform co-chair and at least two identifiable Jackson supporters on the drafting committee, which consisted of 21 persons, the committee was numerically dominated by non-Jackson forces. When one remembers that the platform process began months before the meeting of the full committee, the fact that Jackson was not in control of the appointive process becomes particularly telling. By and large appointive members were party regulars, which, at least in the state of Mississippi, meant that they were Mondale people.[7] Since the Mondale forces controlled the drafting, when the full committee arrived, they had a document written to Mondale specifications.

In contrast, the Jackson platform delegation was greatly outmanned. Of the approximately 185 members of the platform committee, thirty-three were black; a little more than half of these were Jackson people. Many of these people had devised ingenious plans to become members of the committee. Some of the members, such as William Garling of Washington and state representative Polly Williams of Indiana, came officially committed to other candidates but were in truth Jackson people; they switched once they came to the platform meetings.

In a letter from Jackson Headquarters, we were asked to arrive in Washington in time to attend meetings in the late afternoon prior to our first official meeting as platform committee members. We arrived at the meeting around 6:30 P.M., and we left around 2:00 A.M.. (The Mondale group held social gatherings that evening.) During this time we were instructed in procedures and directed to participate in the drafting of a Jackson platform. As I glanced around the meeting, I was impressed with the diverse kinds of persons in the room. The team of experts and platform members present were old-style liberals, neoliberals, civil rights workers, antinuclear activists, pan-Africanists, gay activists, Arab activists, Jewish activists, and just people who believed in Rev. Jackson. Ethnically, we were a "rainbow" also. Later, we would find that our diversity would be a source of our ineffectiveness as well as our efficacy.

Although I had worried that our role would be the insignificant one of endorsing an already developed document, I was soon made aware that we would make a more substantive contribution. Ronald Walters, the overseer of Jackson's platform efforts, assured the group that we would be revising the initial document to conform as much as possible to a Jackson perspective. He gave us each a draft of the Jackson platform and the draft of the Democratic platform.

Walters informed us that on the first day of meetings of the full group we would be divided into three task forces, or subcommittees: growth and prosperity; justice; and peace, security and freedom. He then suggested that, on the basis of our own interest and expertise, we divide ourselves into three corresponding groups. Each task force then went into separate quarters with experts to revise, rewrite, improve, or sanction our portions of the drafts. I opted for the peace, security and freedom task force.

Each task force selected three administrators: a leader, a whip, and a secretary. The leader would be a point person, emissary, lobbier, debater, and assigner. The whip would keep track of how persons in our delegation felt on an issue. The secretary would keep track of the order of the votes, keep position papers in order, and stay abreast of the revision in the planks. All of us were to make arguments, engage in debates, and watch for cracks in either our opponent's or our own committee strengths. When the peace and security task force assembled, I was selected as the leader.

The Jackson peace and security platform task force was ethnically, geographically, racially, sexually, and ideologically diverse. There were two white males, two black females and two black males. We were from each portion of the country and neophytes to the platform process. All of us had been politically and civically active, although not necessarily as party activists. We ranged in age from young adult (in our twenties) to senior citizen (in our sixties).

Although much of the national debate, at least in the press, was over domestic issues, in the platform committee the most contentious debates were in the peace, security and freedom task force. All the task forces were to begin at 9:00 A.M. and end in the early evening, in time to attend a reception; the other task forces completed their work around the expected time. Our task force was involved in a twelve-hour session which broke only forty-five minutes for lunch.

The heated debates were triggered by the Jackson view of what the peace and security platform should be. Outsiders who didn't understand the global concerns of the Jackson campaign were surprised, and in some respects this surprise represented a subtle racism and sexism: the Jackson effort provided a forum for the discussion of foreign policy by persons who are not traditionally a part of the foreign policy debate in either party.

The peace and security task force first addressed the platform plank on defense. The Jackson group agreed on general points, such as the language concerning the mutual pull-back of battlefield nuclear weaponry on the front lines. However, contention arose over two major points: the Jackson position of "no first use" of nuclear weapons as a policy and a bilateral "quick freeze."

Despite much heated, but civil, debate over the "no first use" of nuclear weaponry, we failed to get that language into the platform. However, we won enough backing from the Hart people and some Mondale representatives to have the language adopted as a minority report. In fact, we received enough support on this issue to send a minority report from the general session to be voted on during the full convention.

The following Jackson platform on defense spending also received significant support:

> The Democratic Party understands that excessive military spending endangers our National Security, just as inadequate spending does. Today, our cities look as if a war has already occurred. Tens of thousands are homeless; millions without jobs. We cannot undertake vitally needed domestic initiatives unless military spending is reduced. Defense is not at issue; we spend far more than what is required for

strong defense. By eliminating wasteful procurement policies and unnecessary weapons system, by cutting back our inventionary forces, by negotiating a nuclear freeze, and by ensuring that our allies—now our economic rivals—bear their fair share of the military burden, we can gain substantial real reductions in military spending over the next five years.[8]

As with the previously discussed position we were able to garner sufficient support in the task force and among the platform committee members to send this plank to the full convention as a minority report.

The influence of the Jackson campaign on defense language in the platform was directly related to the extent that our ideas were within the mainstream and coincided with those of a group of Hart and Mondale delegates who were likewise concerned about the threat of nuclear war and the burgeoning military budget. In fact, when we discussed issues such as Africa and, to some extent, Central America, we were able to coalesce with these Hart or Mondale delegates and have an impact on the platform. However, when we pushed other than mainstream agenda views for defense or foreign policy, we encountered much more difficulty.

While the Democratic (Mondale) platform and the Jackson New Directions Platform had obvious points of commonality, there were also major differences. These differences were reflected vividly in the opening paragraphs of the two documents. The Democratic document reads:

> The purpose of foreign policy is to attain a strong and secure United States and a world of peace, freedom and justice. On a planet threatened by dictatorships on the left and right, what is at stake may be freedom itself. On a planet shadowed by the threat of a nuclear holocaust, what is at stake may be nothing less than human survival.

In contrast, the Jackson document reads:

> The Democratic Party must reverse the militarization of our foreign policy and establish the clear priority of human rights and development over intervention, the sale of weapons and other forms of military assistance. This must be the guiding principle in our relations toward the Third World and the developed nations alike.[9]

The Jackson platform stated that a new direction in U.S. foreign policy must emphasize the interrelatedness and relationship of all peoples in order to achieve world peace. The Mondale, subsequently the Democratic, platform emphasized "a strong and secure" United States. While the Jackson platform drafters were concerned with exploitation and subjugation of the Third World, the party-line drafters evidenced a concern with the East/West dimensions of foreign policy. Therein, of course, lay the difference: the Jackson approach to foreign policy could more closely be couched in terms of the North/South dialogue.

Nowhere were the views of the majority of the committee and the majority of the Jackson supporters more divergent than on the direction of U.S. foreign policy in the Middle East. The following chart provides an illustration.

Jackson Position	*Mondale Position*
1. Opposes movement of U.S. embassy from Tel Aviv to Jerusalem	1. Supports movement of U.S. embassy from Tel Aviv to Jerusalem
2. Calls for the establishment of a Palestinian homeland	2. Calls for resolution of the Palestian issue
3. Supports the official status of Jerusalem as an international city	3. Supports established status as international city. (See No. 1)
4. Calls for readjustment of relationships in Middle East to more "balanced" proportions	4. Supports the fundamental principle of peace in the area centered around continued strong U.S. support of Israel
5. Supports the security of Israel within internationally recognized boundaries	5. Supports the existence of Israel with secure and defensible boarders

The debates on these issues were the most emotional and dramatic of the evening. When the U.S. foreign policy was labeled inadequate and reprehensible in the Jackson platform, many pro-Israeli supporters were visibly angered. The Mondale spokesman announced that if the Jackson plank were adopted Mondale would not support the platform nor run on the ticket.[10]

The arguments over the Middle East had a disruptive effect on the ranks of Jackson representatives also. One of our members refused to support the plank outright and voted with the Mondale preference. Moreover, when it became clear that the Africa plank would not be passed if the Middle-East issue were pushed, some black members became disgruntled. As one of them stated, "I know Jesse is concerned about the Rainbow Coalition and he feels he must represent a broad spectrum of oppressed people, but he *is* black and the black community is most concerned about the Africa plank." As expected, the Jackson Middle-East plank failed overwhelmingly; the next day it was introduced in full session, where it again was easily defeated.[11]

The African plank, about which there was so much consensus on the part of the general body, also failed. It failed because of the Middle-East stance. There were enough people in favor of our position on Africa who were going to vote positively before we introduced the Middle-East plank. But when we did not withdraw that plank, the Mondale people carried out their threat and voted against our position on Africa. After the vote, some black Mondale delegates admitted that it hurt them to vote negatively on the African plank. One black woman, with tears in her eyes, tried to explain to me her vote by saying that she had a "political career to consider."

Overall, the Jackson group saw first-hand the strategic advantages of being in control of the process. Had we been able to dictate the voting order, we would never have debated the Middle-East plank before debating Africa. If the

Jackson campaign had been in control of the party machinery, people could not have been influenced to vote against their convictions because of the threat of retaliation. But, of course, the Mondale people undoubtedly realized this also and acted accordingly.

In truth, however, the African plank was an issue that the majority of the delegates were disposed to support, and the reasons for its failure in the subcommittee were clearly tactical and political. When we met in the general session the next day, the Africa plank was introduced and passed with a groundswell of support: persons from all factions were willing to speak in favor of its adoption. In fact, the language on Africa in the Democratic platform is virtually the Jackson plank. Some important specific proposals were to:

1. exert maximum pressure on South Africa to hasten the establishment of a democratic unitary political system.
2. ban all new loans, sale or transfer of sophisticated computer and nuclear technology.
3. withdraw landing rights to South African aircraft.
4. progressively increase sanction against South Africa until it grants independence to Namibia.
5. develop mutual economic strategies, commodities pricing and other treaties of international trade with nations on the African continent.

The adopted text condemned South Africa for "unjustly holding political prisoners." It further stated: "Soviet harassment of the Sakarovs is identical to South African house arrests of political opponents of the South African regime. Specifically, the detention of Nelson Mandela, leader of the African National Congress, and Winnie Mandela must be brought to the world attention and we demand the immediate release of all other political prisoners in South Africa."

When we met in full session the next day, we knew we would present four amendments to the platform. They would concern no first use of nuclear weapons, defense policy, the Middle East, and Africa. Of the four, two became minority reports, one was adopted as text, and one was resoundingly defeated.

On the day of the general session we again faced a gruelling schedule. All members of the Jackson task forces gathered at 6:00 A.M. for a final drafting and caucus meeting. This was especially difficult for the peace and security task force members, since we did not arrive at our hotels until after 1:00 A.M. At this early meeting we determined who would speak on the various drafts and the time allotment each would have. We had no trouble finding prominent Jackson supporters to speak for the amendments on "no first use," defense, or Africa. However, no prominent Jackson supporter would speak on the Middle-East plank in the full session, since it would be televised and public. One person frankly said that "it would be a political kiss of death."

In the end, as chair of the Jackson foreign policy section, I was asked to inform the full committee of the Jackson position on the Middle East, as well as on the other planks. After my presentation a number of persons, particularly black Mondale and Hart delegates, indicated to me, informally but clearly, that Jackson's defense and foreign policy positions did indeed represent their personal positions, but not their public or political positions.[12]

The Platform Efforts as a Microcosm

As mentioned earlier, the efforts of Jackson's supporters to influence the platform process may be viewed as a microcosm of the national Jackson campaign. We were outsiders trying to influence a process, the outcome of which was largely predetermined by others.

The tradition of the outsider is well documented.[13] The most useful description is perhaps that of Huitt, who characterized the outsider as unconcerned with traditions of behavior or folkways, nonaccommodating, and catering to "his contituents and ideological allies across the nation." Additionally, he tells us:

> The Outsider feels impelled to stand for principle absolutely, preferring defeat on those terms to half-a-loaf. He likes to tell people what they should and frequently do not want to hear. He is never confident of the soundness of his opinions as when he holds them alone. He is as comfortable alone against the crowd as the Senate type is in the bosom of the club; indeed, he is probably happiest when he stands by himself against powerful and wrong-headed foes. As a consequence few people, in the body or outside, are lukewarm about him; they tend to like him or dislike him strongly.

The outsider's role may be understood as an alternative, not a "deviant" one. It is this context that we may view the Jackson platform efforts. Although Huitt found that the role of the outsider is "functional for protest groups seeking a spokesman, dysfunctional for groups needing leverage inside," such was not the case with the Jackson preference group. The inclusion of the African plank in the 1984 platform is certainly related to the force and the influence of the Jackson candidacy and the presence of Jackson people on the committee. Although Africa was discussed in the Democratic platform of 1980, it did not receive the central setting it won in the 1984 campaign. The Jackson efforts brought a concern for Africa in general and South Africa in particular to the platform committee. Jackson people wrote the African Plank and marshalled the favorable sentiment about Africa among the platform committee members so that when the plank was presented it was accepted.

In contrast, when the Jackson views were "deviant," or outside of the accepted philosophy of the majority—such as the Jackson views on the Middle

East, Cuba, or military spending—the ideas were not incorporated into the final document.

Some might view our participation in the platform process as largely symbolic—more symbolic than substantive. But symbols are important.[14] And the fact that we did participate may also be seen as expanding avenues of access for women, blacks, latinos, and other groups who have not, traditionally and substantively, been a part of policy process. I have stated that the great diversity which was our strength was also our weakness. One of the missions of the Jackson campaign was to provide a forum for all groups no matter how small and politically insignificant; we internalized this mission on the platform committee. In many ways our effort to represent all peoples and all issues drained our mental and economic resources, but I'm not sure that the Jackson campaign would have been "THE JACKSON CAMPAIGN" without these efforts.

As a result of participation on the committee, many of us felt, as Linda Grice of South Carolina put it, "We have to come back; we now know the process." The building of expertise and experience in national party politics among the locked out was one of the goals of the Jackson campaign. I believe that our participation and work on the platform committee furthered this goal.

NOTES

1. Thomas Hudson McKee, *The National Conventions and Platforms of All Political Parties, 1789–1905* (New York: AMS Press, Inc., 1971), pp. 1–26.

2. Ibid.

3. Donald B. Johnson and Kirk H. Porter, *National Party Platforms, 1840–1972* (Urbana: University of Illinois Press, 1971).

4. Paul T. David, "Party Platforms as National Plans," *Public Administration Review* 8 (May–June 1971).

5. Interview with Ed Cole, Executive Vice Chair State Democratic Executive Committee (Jackson, August, 1985).

6. Mayor Leggette was from the same area of the state as my opponent. She holds myriad political appointments, including membership on the Democratic National Committee. Leslie Burl McLemore is a former candidate for Congress and chairperson of the Hinds County Democratic Executive Committee.

7. The Mondale appointee was the black mayor of Mayersville, Mississippi, Unita Blackwell. The other member of the platform committee from Mississippi was Mondale supporter and former congressman David Bowen.

8. All quotes on the Jackson planks are from the final draft of the Jackson New Directions Platform.

9. "Two Mississippi Democrats Tugged over Party Platform," *Clarion-Ledger*, June 25, 1984, B-2.

10. Ibid.

11. Introducing this plank again was debated, in the end we were advised by one of the consultants that it had to be introduced because of its symbolic importance.

12. Of course I believe that most of the Mondale persons who expressed a positive reaction to the speech were expressing a respect for an opposing point of view.

13. Ralph K. Huitt, "The Outsider in the Senate—An Alternative Role," *American Political Science Review* 55 (1961): 566–75; Donald R. Matthews, *U.S. Senators and Their World* (New York: Random, 1960); Craig R. Ducat and Victor E. Flango, "The Outsider on the Court," *Journal of Politics* 47, no. 1 (1985): 283–89.

14. Murray Edelman, *The Symbolic Use of Politics* (Urbana: University of Illinois Press, 1967; rpt. 1985).

The "Naive" and the "Unwashed": The Challenge of the Jackson Campaign at the Democratic Party National Convention

8

Robert G. Newby

The 1984 Democratic National Convention was marked by two events which demonstrated a major division among blacks over the candidacy of Jesse Jackson. The events in question were the expressions of ridicule directed toward Mayor Andrew Young of Atlanta and Coretta Scott King: Young was booed as he attempted to address the convention in opposition to a minority plank offered by the Jackson campaign and in support of the Mondale position on the problem of dual primaries; Mrs. King, at the Black Delegate Caucus the next day as she attempted to chastise those who had booed Young. In many ways these circumstances were reminiscent of the 1964 "Goldwater Convention" of the Republican party in which the conservatives of that convention showed their outright contempt for Nelson Rockefeller by booing him to the extent that he found it difficult to finish his speech to the convention.[1]

For many, these expressions were moments of shame and embarrassment: Mayor Young and the widow of Nobel Laureate Dr. Martin Luther King are expected to be honored and revered rather than scorned. Not understanding how persons of such high esteem could be so crudely treated, the news media suggested that the problem was one of naiveté on the part of the Jackson delegates, who were perceived as inexperienced politically, lacking the seasoning of the other convention delegates. Andrew Young went one step further, suggesting that the Jackson delegates were "a bit unwashed."[2] In this regard, there was no consideration that Jackson's call for a "new direction" for the Democratic party was, in reality, outside the pragmatic politics of the party and much more a social movement being expressed within the electoral arena.

It is the purpose of this essay to provide an understanding of the set of convention dynamics described above—specifically, to examine the treatment of Andrew Young and Coretta Scott King to ascertain the extent to which the assertions that the Jackson delegates were either "naive" or "unwashed" are valid or whether some alternative explanation is more likely. The examination will be based primarily on comparative profiles of the delegates. These profiles will focus on both social characteristics of the delegates and their orientations toward various issues relative to the overall political campaign. The delegate profiles are based on polls of the delegates performed by the *Los Angeles Times* in June of 1984 and a similar joint effort on the part of ABC and the *Washington Post* prior to the San Francisco convention. In addition to these polls, other data sources such as convention proceedings, newspaper reports, and personal observations by the author (a Jackson delegate at the convention) will be utilized.

At Issue: The Family Feud

The booing of Andrew Young by the Jackson delegates and the subsequent treatment of Coretta Scott King may, at first glance, appear trivial. Yet, while the treatment of Young was usually reported—an indication that the action was at least newsworthy—these reports more often than not placed the event in the context of a minor platform skirmish. Such a perspective misses several important points. This feud surfaced as a platform fight. The first point here is that the issues or "planks" in the party's platform should not be considered minor; the platform frames the content of what the party stands for. Many argue that such an exercise is not important, since candidates do not abide by that document once the convention is over and certainly not after one is elected. Of course, the point is moot for the loser, except in cases like that of George McGovern, whose platform, or at least that of his party in 1972, led to a certain and overwhelming defeat. Although in the rush to package conventions for television,[3] platforms have been trivialized, the platform is the last vestige of making the parties democratic and something more than a personality contest.

A second point is that, in spite of the deep-seated emotional commitment to the issue being debated, the context of events tended to obscure the reaction to Young's remarks. After all, the public booing of one of the stature of Andrew Young, when juxtaposed to the Reverend Jackson's prime time "political sermon," pales by comparison. In the context of the "moral high ground" to which Jackson took the convention and the nation on that Tuesday evening, the debate on the platform issues, even the "dirty" fight, was of lesser importance. The coverage by the *San Francisco Chronicle* exemplified this difference: the front page banner line emblazoned "Jackson 'Peace' Speech" in a three-inch heading.[4] Such competition obscured the importance of the platform struggle on the voting rights of blacks in the South.

Thirdly, and most importantly, the issue which was being debated is in large measure crucial to a continuing pretext of democracy within the party and for the nation as a whole. The issue in this case is central to whether or not "democracy" in the South can accommodate blacks. At the time of this writing there are twenty-two blacks in Congress. With the exception of William Ford of Memphis, Tennessee, and "Mickey" Leland of Houston, Texas, all of the black congresspersons are from the North and West. Yet more than half of the black population resides in the South. A variety of schemes, including dual primaries and gerrymandering, minimize the impact of black political power. Twenty more black congresspersons could make a major impact on Congress, particularly since the Congressional Black Caucus consistently provides the most progressive leadership in the Congress. Also, since blacks comprise in the neighborhood of 10 percent of the nation's population, twenty more congresspersons would more closely approximate a proportional representation in Congress. The denial of these seats, by whatever means, is a denial of democracy. This denial was central to the Jackson campaign.

Fourthly, and directly related to the third point, the essence of the Jackson candidacy centered on the platform. In fact, the real stuff of the Jackson campaign was not in the nomination of Jesse Jackson to be the party's standard bearer, but in whether the issues of his campaign could provide a new direction for the party. In this light, the platform became a central focus of the campaign and represented the real challenge to the party.

Finally, whether the larger society thinks that crass treatment of eminent black citizens is of importance or not, the analysis of such events is crucial to understanding the relationship of "the family" to the larger body politic. In other words, the black leadership needs to know its limits within its constituency, and the larger society needs to know the extent to which it can enlist blacks to act against the interests and aspirations of the black community as a whole.

Setting the Stage

It is not possible to understand the hostility and invective directed toward Andrew Young and, subsequently, Coretta Scott King without placing these events in the context of the whole nomination process. The Democratic party rules leading up to the Convention had been grossly unfair to candidacies such as Jesse Jackson's. In the July issue of *Harper's*, an article authored by Walter Karp and entitled "Playing Politics" argued that the traditional leaders of the Democratic party wanted to return control of the nomination process to its "rightful owners," the party bosses, including the leadership of organized labor.[5] Karp argued that, following the 1968 Chicago convention, the nomination process had become too democratic. The result of this "democracy" had been the nomination of George McGovern in 1972, which much of the party did not support, and of an "outsider," Jimmy Carter, in 1976, to the chagrin of the labor leadership. Even more, in 1980 labor leadership and other party bosses encouraged Ted Kennedy to challenge Jimmy Carter, a seated Democratic president, in the presidential primaries. In response to this circumstance, Karp argued, the party concentrated on rules changes that would allow the leadership to regain control of the nomination and its various facets.[5]

This control, including the selection of Mondale and public endorsement by the leadership, was well-established even before the first primary was held. In sum, the exclusion of anyone, including a Jesse Jackson, not selected by the party's leadership was paramount. Needless to say, this meant that the Jackson delegation was very much embattled at every stage of the process long before they reached San Francisco.[6] Furthermore, this control continued through to the convention floor. As evidenced by presidential nomination votes on Wednesday of the convention, Mondale had 2,191 delegate votes compared to 1,200.5 for Hart and 465.5 for Jackson. Of Mondale's more than 2,000 delegates, 700 were floor whips. The rationale for approximately one in three delegates being in a "leadership" capacity is best articulated by one of the Mondale organizers, who stated, "You can hold onto delegates you give titles to."[7] Organization such as this caused many liberal delegates to vote in opposition to a "no first use" (of nuclear weapons) minority plank offered by the Jackson campaign. For example, a young, liberal lawyer—a Mondale delegate who favored the "no first use" principle—felt compelled to vote against the plank because he had to set an example for the eight other Mondale delegates he was "in charge of."

An examination of the votes on the minority planks, with one exception, shows very little deviation on the part of the Mondale delegates from the position put forward by the platform committee.[8] Nowhere was such organization more apparent than on the issue of defense spending. While Mr. Mondale, the candidate, forged a position which called for a slight increase in defense spending to "ensure effective American strength at an affordable cost," the Jackson campaign offered a minority plank which called for "substantial, real reductions in military spending over the next five years."[9] The vote on this plank showed a very similar profile on a state-by-state basis to the votes cast for Mondale state by state.[10] Yet, according to the *Los Angeles Times* data, such a vote did not reflect how the delegates felt about the issue. Table 1 shows that 92 percent of the Mondale delegates supported a cut in defense spending rather than an increase. Even if some of the Mondale delegates considered "substantial" too drastic, it is not unreasonable to assume that the 39 percent who wanted to spend "a good deal less" would not have found "substantial reductions" objectionable. Yet what support Jackson did get for this plank came almost totally from his own delegates and those of Gary Hart; the plank received 1,127.5 votes in support and 2,591.5 in opposition, or slightly more than the nearly 2,200 votes committed to Mondale.[11]

In addition to the "rigged" primary process and the heavily managed con-

Table 1. Delegate views about how much should be spent on national defense by presidential candidate preference

How much should be spent on national defense	President candidate preference		
	Mondale	Hart	Jackson
A good deal more	1%	0%	0%
Somewhat more	7	5	0
Somewhat less	53	52	34
A good deal less	39	43	66
Total %	100	100	100
# of responses	(N = 1684)	(N = 1104)	(N = 302)

Source: *Los Angeles Times* Delegate Survey

vention delegates who were committed to Mondale, the managers of the podium, in an attempt to discredit the issues put forth as minority planks, brought forth opposition speakers whose credentials on their respective issues seemed to be beyond reproach.[12] The first such example was the debate on the issue of "no first use" of nuclear weapons. The major speaker in opposition to the inclusion of this plank in the platform was none other than one of the Senate's major proponents of peace, Michigan Senator Carl Levin. Representative Barbara Kennely was employed similarly. As a member of the House Ways and Means Committee, she has been an outspoken opponent of spending for the MX missile, aid to the Nicaraguan Contras, and similar issues. She was called upon to speak in opposition to the plank calling for "substantial reductions" in defense spending.

The antagonism toward Andrew Young must be understood within this context of discrediting challenges to the platform by using opposition speakers in what might be considered "role reversals." The Jackson minority plank argued that depriving about half of the black population of proper representation was a violation of the Voting Rights Act. While the Mondale platform called for "a serious in-depth study" of the problem, the Jackson campaign's plank sought "the adoption of strong measures to enforce the Voting Rights Act."[13] By supporting a study, a classic maneuver for inaction and maintenance of the status quo, Andrew Young betrayed the very essence of the Jackson campaign—to challenge the fact that blacks usually "put the Democratic Party first while the Party puts blacks last," as was argued by Malcolm X.[14]

Jackson's campaign director of Michigan, one of the many Jackson delegates to boo Andrew Young, stated that Young "had it coming. . . . To run Andy up as the foil on Jesse was wrong. He shouldn't allow himself to be used. . . . From your opponents you expect that kind of talk. But you don't expect it from your friends."[15] Andrew Young's response to the heckling was to say:

"I think some of those who booed don't know what democracy is all about.
. . . I've been fighting for their rights for years, and then they come here and
don't let me speak. . . . This is what you expect from new voters or people
new to the movement." [16] Young's comments, which suggest that those booing
him were not aware of his contributions, are consistent with the "naive" and
"unwashed" thesis offered as an explanation for the manner in which he was
treated.

The next day, when Coretta Scott King addressed a meeting of the Black
Delegate Caucus, she seemed to be operating on the same set of assumptions
about the Jackson delegates. Invoking the "spirit of Martin Luther King, Jr.,"
her twenty-nine years of struggle in the civil rights movement, and the fact that
Andrew Young had "paid dues" for all of us, she chastised those delegates of
"lesser" credentials. It was precisely as a result of this patronizing attitude and
criticism of the delegates' treatment of Andrew Young that she and the "spirit
of Martin Luther King, Jr.," were booed to the extent that she had to leave the
podium in tears.

The assumption that the delegates' response to Andrew Young and Coretta
Scott King was simply a matter of inexperience or gracelessness needs to be
examined. To what extent can it be claimed that these actions were based on the
naiveté of the Jackson delegates as opposed to some alternative explanation?

The Delegates

An examination of the Jackson delegates in comparison to the delegates of Hart
and Mondale will place in perspective the extent to which the assertion that
the Jackson delegates were inexperienced is valid. A number of characteristics
indicate the experience and likely sophistication of the delegates.

Social Characteristic Profiles

One such issue is the age of the delegates. An examination of table 2 shows
that the Jackson delegates did tend to be younger than the Mondale delegates.
Almost 40 percent of the Mondale delegates were fifty years of age or older,
compared to about one quarter of the Jackson delegates. On the other hand,
noting the mean age of the delegates by personal preference shows more than
a ten-year difference between the Hart delegates at almost thirty-seven and the
delegates who preferred Mondale, whose mean age was almost forty-seven.

Another characteristic directly related to the question of political experience
is that of the number of political conventions previously attended. Table 3
shows that, for a large percentage of the delegates, the San Francisco convention was their first national convention. While it is true that Mondale tended
to have more people who had previously attended a national convention, the
difference between Mondale and Jackson delegates does not appear to be that

Table 2. Age of delegates by candidate preference

| | Candidate preference | | |
Age of delegates	Mondale	Hart	Jackson
18–29	4%	17%	8%
30–39	25	39	33
40–49	32	25	35
50–59	25	13	17
60+	14	6	7
Total %	100	100	100
# of responses	(N = 1697)	(N = 1110)	(N = 302)
$\overline{X}$	46.88	36.69	42.96

Source: *Los Angeles Times* Delegate Survey

Table 3. Previous convention participation by candidate preference

| Number of national conventions | Candidate preference | | |
previously attended	Mondale	Hart	Jackson
None	67%	83%	79%
One	17	9	12
Two	8	4	4
Three	4	2	3
Four or more	4	2	2
Total %	100	100	100
# of responses	(N = 1743)	(N = 1133)	(N = 311)

Source: *Los Angeles Times* Delegate Survey

great. Slightly more than one fifth of the Jackson delegates had attended conventions previously, compared to about one third of the Mondale delegates. Gary Hart's delegates were the least experienced, which is consistent with his delegates also being the youngest. Given the millions of Democrats nationwide, it should not be surprising that a quadrennial convention, for which fewer than 4,000 members are selected, makes for rather stiff competition, and chances to repeat are difficult. Consequently, while nearly 80 percent of the Jackson delegates were first-timers, similar levels of inexperience were the case for both Mondale (almost 70 percent) and Hart (more than 80 percent).

Another characteristic which might serve as an indicator of sophistication, if not direct experience, is educational attainment. In this area Jackson delegates rank favorably when compared to the Hart and Mondale delegates. As shown in table 4, nearly 80 percent of the Jackson delegates were college graduates, whereas among Mondale delegates this category was nearer to 65 percent.

Table 4. Educational attainment of delegates by candidate preference

Educational attainment	Candidate preference		
	Mondale	Hart	Jackson
Less than high school	1%	0%	1%
High school grad	17	5	4
Some college	18	16	17
College grad	23	32	31
Master's degree	21	20	26
Doctorate	4	5	9
Medical degree	0	0	1
Law degree	15	21	10
Other degree	1	0	1
Total %	100	100	100
# of responses	(N = 1745)	(N = 1132)	(N = 311)

Source: *Los Angeles Times* Delegate Survey

Jackson delegates had about twice as many academic doctorates—at 9 percent —as either Mondale or Hart delegates, at 4 percent and 5 percent respectively. If educational attainment gives sophistication, the Jackson delegates were not naive.

The occupations of the delegates should also indicate the experience of the delegates. Overall, the occupational profile of the delegates for the three candidates for the nomination appears to be very similar. The most marked differences were that among Jackson and Hart delegates only 1 percent were "labor leaders" compared to 15 percent for Mondale. Among "other professionals" Mondale had 7 percent compared to almost 20 percent, or one in five, for Jackson. The proportion of government employees and teachers was about the same for all three candidates, except that Hart had a smaller percentage of teachers than Jackson and Mondale.

Related to the occupations of the delegates are their incomes. The family incomes of the delegates for each candidate were very similar, particularly at the middle income levels of $20,000 to $70,000. Between $20,000 and $50,000 annual income, the percentage distributions were almost identical for the delegates of all three candidates. At the highest category of more than $75,000, the percentage of Mondale delegates (24 percent) was somewhat greater than that of the Hart delegates (19 percent) and almost double the percentage rate for the Jackson delegates (12 percent). The percentage rate of delegates with lower family incomes, less than $20,000, was in double figures for both Hart (13 percent) and Jackson (16 percent) compared to Mondale's 8 percent.

Summing up, the social profiles of the delegates do not seem to show

Table 5. Occupations of delegates by candidate preference

Occupation of delegates	Candidate preference		
	Mondale	Hart	Jackson
Business	10%	17%	15%
Law	26	21	21
Teacher	15	9	16
Housewife	4	5	3
Labor Leader	15	1	1
Student	0	5	4
Other professional	7	15	18
White collar	5	6	7
Blue collar	5	1	3
Farmer	1	1	0
Retired	3	1	2
Total %	100	100	100
# of responses	(N = 1740)	(N = 1125)	(N = 311)

Source: *Los Angeles Times* Delegate Survey

Table 6. Annual household incomes of delegates by candidate preference

Annual household incomes of delegates in thousands	Candidate preference		
	Mondale	Hart	Jackson
Less than 8	1%	2%	2%
8 to 12	1	2	3
12 to 20	6	9	11
20 to 30	16	17	16
30 to 50	32	31	32
50 to 75	21	20	25
75 +	24	19	12
Total %	100	100	100
# of responses	(N = 1610)	(N = 1068)	(N = 293)

Source: *Los Angeles Times* Delegate Survey

that the Jackson delegates were particularly likely to be any more naive or inexperienced than the other delegates. Educationally, Jackson had a higher percentage of college graduates than either Hart or Mondale. While the Jackson delegates tended to be somewhat younger than those who supported Mondale, they were, on the average, a full seven years older than those delegates who supported Gary Hart. Occupationally, the differences were not that great. More directly related to the question of experience was the number of previous

Table 7. Political ideology of delegates by candidate preference

Political ideology of delegates	Candidate preference		
	Mondale	Hart	Jackson
Very liberal	15%	19%	38%
Somewhat liberal	49	52	38
Moderate	29	23	19
Somewhat conservative	6	5	5
Very conservative	1	1	0
Total %	100	100	100
# of responses	(N = 1714)	(N = 1103)	(N = 298)

Source: *Los Angeles Times* Delegate Survey

national conventions attended. On this issue, clearly, most delegates, even Mondale's, were first timers.

Ideological and Issue Profiles

An examination of the ideological orientation of the delegates and their attitudes toward the issues of the campaign should also provide some evidence as to whether or not the problem was one of their being novices to "the struggle." A cursory look at table 7 shows that about 40 percent of the Jackson delegates identified themselves as being "very liberal" as compared to only 15 percent of the Mondale delegates and about 20 percent of the Hart delegates. On the other hand, more than one third of the Mondale delegates considered themselves to be either middle of the road or conservative. Given the absolute number of Mondale delegates, his one third is a considerable number, particularly when compared to the less than one fourth of the approximately 300 Jackson delegates who were respondants.

This "liberalism" of the Jackson delegation is exemplified in their desire to spend more on health care; nearly two thirds of them felt that "a good deal more" should be spent. Delegates for the other two candidates tended to be considerably more conservative on this issue. Less than one half, or about 40 percent, of Mondale delegates favored spending "a good deal more" on health care. As to government spending for public service, the breakdown of the delegates by candidate shows a pattern similar to that on health care. The Jackson delegates were about twice as likely as other delegates to favor spending "a good deal more" on public service. The position of the Jackson delegates on these issues places them to the left of the other delegates on the whole.

In this same regard, how one views the state of the nation's economy is likely to have an effect on one's selection of political alternatives. The Jackson

Table 8. Delegate views on how much should be spent on health care and public
service by candidate preference

	Candidate preference		
	Mondale	Hart	Jackson
Delegate views on health care spending			
A good deal more	38%	31%	63%
Somewhat more	54	56	34
Somewhat less	7	12	3
A good deal less	1	1	0
Total %	100	100	100
# of responses	(N = 1620)	(N = 1028)	(N = 301)
Delegate views on public service spending			
A good deal more	35%	25%	59%
Somewhat more	58	62	39
Somewhat less	6	10	2
A good deal less	1	3	0
Total %	100	100	100
# of responses	(N = 1627)	(N = 1034)	(N = 302)

Source: *Los Angeles Times* Delegate Survey

delegates tended to be much more pessimistic about the condition of the
nation's economy. While the bulk of the Mondale and Hart delegates felt that
the nation's economy was "in between" rather than bad or good, nearly 60
percent of the Jackson delegates felt the economy to be in "bad shape." Such
a response on the part of a substantial majority of Jackson's delegates certainly
suggests a perception that the nation is in a state of crisis. For the delegates of
both Mondale and Hart, the same perceived urgency did not exist.

Another indication of the ideological distance between the Jackson contingent and that of the other delegates is their respective perceptions of the
Muslim minister Rev. Louis Farrakhan. As table 10 shows, while more than
a quarter of the Jackson delegates had a "very favorable" impression of Rev.
Farrakhan, none of the Hart or Mondale delegates were so impressed. Only 5
percent of the Mondale delegates and 3 percent of the Hart delegates were at
all favorable in their impression of Mr. Farrakhan. For the Jackson delegates,
on the other hand, nearly two thirds, or 65 percent, were favorable in their
impression of Farrakhan. Needless to say, the gap here is considerable and in
many ways marks the vast ideological differences that separated the Jackson
candidacy from that of the more mainstream candidates.

The divergence on the part of the Jackson delegates from the views of the

Table 9. Delegate views about the state of the nation's economy by candidate preference

Delegate views on the economy	Candidate preference		
	Mondale	Hart	Jackson
Good	4%	6%	2%
In-between	51	59	39
Bad	45	35	59
Total %	100	100	100
# of responses	(N = 1734)	(N = 1126)	(N = 308)

Source: *Los Angeles Times* Delegate Survey

Table 10. Delegate views of Muslim Minister Louis Farrakhan by candidate preference

Views on Farrakahn	Candidate preference		
	Mondale	Hart	Jackson
Very favorable	0%	0%	27%
Somewhat favorable	5	3	38
Somewhat unfavorable	16	22	14
Very unfavorable	56	58	8
Not aware of him	23	17	13
Total %	100	100	100
# of responses	(N = 1699)	(N = 1111)	(N = 305)

Source: *Los Angeles Times* Delegate Survey

other delegates on Mr. Farrakhan surfaces again in some related campaign issues. The ideological affinity with Farrakhan no doubt lies in his alienation from and disdain for "the system," a system he perceives to be conspiring against blacks in general and, in this case, Jesse Jackson in particular.[17] One example of this "conspiracy" was the attempt to label Jesse Jackson as anti-Semitic. As shown in table 11, hardly any Jackson delegates perceived Jesse Jackson to be anti-Semitic, while approximately one third of both Mondale and Hart delegates felt that he was. Two other issues which bore directly on this systemic discrimination are the delegates' views on the fairness of the party's rules and the implementation of affirmative action programs. Almost all of the Jackson delegates thought Jackson to be right on the systematic discrimination inherent in the party's rules. Because their candidate was similarly affected, four out of five Hart delegates felt the same way. On the other hand, 70 percent of the Mondale delegates thought Jackson to be wrong in his criticism of the rules. Another example of the division between the Jackson delegates and the party generally was how to compensate for past practices of discrimination.

Table 11. Delegate views on selected issues by candidate preference

Delegate views on selected issues	Candidate preference		
	Mondale	Hart	Jackson
Jackson anti-Semitic			
Yes	33%	31%	1%
No	67	69	99
Jackson on rules			
Right	30	80	99
Wrong	70	20	1
Affirmative Action			
Yes, Quotas	39	36	73
Yes, No Quotas	56	61	26
No	5	3	1

Source: *Los Angeles Times* Delegate Survey

Almost three fourths of the Jackson delegates favored the use of quotas in the application of affirmative action guidelines. Only about one half of that proportion of delegates for Hart and Mondale felt similarly. The fact that about 30 percent of the Mondale delegates were blacks, who were more likely to support quotas, makes the gap between Jackson's delegates and the other delegates even more striking.

The most telling ideological difference, however, is shown in how the Jackson delegates rated themselves and their perceptions of Walter Mondale on a liberal-to-conservative scale. An inspection of table 12 shows a considerable difference in how they rated Mr. Mondale in comparison to themselves. The relative proportional frequencies show that the distribution for Mondale tended to be a "normal" distribution. In contrast, the distribution for the delegates tended to be bi-modal with about 20 percent (.196) near the middle, as would be expected, but also about 18 percent (.184) at the liberal extreme. Their ratings of Mondale were far to the "right" or considerably more conservative. The Kolmogorov-Smirnov two-sample test shows the difference of distribution between how the delegates rated themselves and Walter Mondale to be statistically significant. The statistics suggest the perceived political gap between themselves and Mondale to be so wide that the difference is not likely to be a matter of chance but real. This degree of difference between themselves and Mondale, including his control of the convention, was the real basis for the level of alienation the Jackson delegates felt toward the convention and its norms.

This chapter has examined the relationship of the Jackson delegation to the 1984 Democratic Party National Convention by exploring the hypothesized

Table 12. Kolmogorov-Smirnov Two-Sample Test comparing the political ideologies of the Jackson delegates and Walter F. Mondale

Political ideology ratings by Jackson delegates	Liberal to Conservative Cumulative frequencies*										
	0	1	2	3	4	5	6	7	8	9	10
themselves ($S1_{248}$)	.184	.263	.391	.541	.661	.857	.908	.955	.995	.998	1.0
	(.184)	(.079)	(.128)	(.150)	(.120)	(.196)	(.051)	(.047)	(.040)	(.003)	(.010)
Mondale ($S2_{248}$)	.011	.020	.048	.109	.242	.569	.714	.870	.947	.971	1.0
	(.011)	(.009)	(.028)	(.061)	(.133)	(.327)	(.145)	(.156)	(.077)	(.024)	(.029)
$[S1_x - S2_x]$	.173	.243	.343	.432	.419	.288	.194	.085	.048	.027	

Maximum D = .432 x^2 = 106.30 at 2 df p < .001 (two-tailed)

Source: ABC/*Washington Post* Delegate Survey

*Relative adjusted frequencies in parentheses.

explanations of the derision heaped upon Mayor Andrew Young and Coretta Scott King during the convention—that the Jackson delegates tended to be naive and inexperienced or simply uncouth. The preceding delegate profiles provide strong evidence that neither hypothesis is correct.

The profile of social characteristics shows little difference between the Jackson delegates and those of Mondale and Hart. The Jackson delegates, in fact, were on the whole, better educated than those of Mondale and Hart. While there was some difference in family incomes at the extreme high as well as at the extreme low end of the scale, the delegates seemed to be very similar on this characteristic as well. On the issues of occupations and convention experience, the similarities seemed to be greater than the differences. The average convention expense of about $2,000, to a large extent, restricted who could be a delegate.

The major distinction between the Jackson delegation and the party as a whole was an ideological difference: the Jackson delegates were twice as likely as the delegates of both Hart and Mondale to consider themselves to be "very liberal," and on the ABC/*Washington Post* Poll nearly 20 percent of the Jackson delegates rated themselves to be at the most extreme "liberal" point. The consistency in these self-ratings on the *Los Angeles Times* and ABC/*Washington Post* polls suggests the ideological differences between the Jackson delegates and the rest of the party to be real. This difference in political ideology is the difference between mainstream, status quo politics and the politics of change, or "movement politics," with its attendant ideology.

Jackson's delegates were adherents to his movement for a new direction for the Democratic party and American politics on behalf of black Americans and other progressive forces considered to be a part of the Rainbow Coalition. The Democratic party establishment, which had regained control of the party for the first time since 1968, was in no mood to have its authority challenged to any serious degree. Oberschall describes opposition to the status quo in this context:

> Discontents and Conflicts resul[t] from the illegitimate exercise of power by ruling groups resisting the attempts to crowd them off the center of the historical stage. . . . Political stability becomes precarious, and a crisis of legitimacy develops when the status of major conservative institutions is threatened during a period of social change. Common ways in which ruling groups seek to block change, and which then become occasion for organized opposition and social turmoil, are staging rigged elections, preventing fair elections, [etc.].[18]

Jackson's position on the rules and his delegates' endorsement of his position no doubt led to a "crisis of legitimacy" at the Mondale-controlled convention. Consequently, the "continued denial of political and civil rights, [and] discrimination . . . of negatively privileged groups becomes intolerable and leads to movements of collective protest and opposition."[19]

As movement adherents, with their oppositional ideology framed, the Jackson delegates challenged the ruling group instead of acquiescing to the status quo.

For the embattled Jackson delegates the convention had long since lost its legitimacy. Therefore, when Andrew Young spoke out on the Voting Rights Act in opposition to "the movement" and in support of a set of rulers who had stolen the full impact of the Jackson appeal, he was viewed as a "collaborationist" with "the enemy." The same could be said for Coretta Scott King for both her support of Andrew Young and her long effort to undermine the Jackson candidacy in support of Mondale. The responses to Young and King were not matters of naiveté, inexperience, or uncouthness. Instead, attempts by Young and King as "collaborators" to *impose* their "highly respected" status on "the movement" were rebuked by "the movement's" adherents, the Jackson delegation, spurred by their "sense of urgency" in addressing the problems facing "the left out," which included blacks, women, workers, and other facets of the Rainbow Coalition, and unconcerned with keeping the peace and presenting a good image for the satisfaction of the traditional party bosses.

NOTES

1. See *New York Times,* July 14, 1964, p. 1, and *Time,* July 24, 1964, p. 22.

2. This suggestion is not name-calling as such but Rev. Andrew Young's reference to a biblical term meaning the unbaptized. See Acts 22:16, also John 3:4–5.

3. Lack of television packaging was another problem for the McGovern candidacy. Convention *democracy* delayed his acceptance speech to 3 A.M. in the Eastern time zone. For a full flavor of this convention, see *Time,* July 24, 1972.

4. *San Francisco Chronicle,* July 18, 1984, A-1.

5. Walter Karp, "Playing Politics," *Harper's,* July 1984, pp. 51–60.

6. *Detroit Free Press,* March 16, 1984, p. 3.

7. *San Francisco Chronicle,* July 18, 1984, p. 7.

8. Official Proceedings of the 1984 Democratic Convention (see Appendixes).

9. "The Report of the Platform Committee to the 1984 Democratic National Convention" Democratic National Committee, Washington, D.C.; "Minority Report 4," p. 55.

10. Official Proceedings of the 1984 Democratic Convention, Appendix III, p. 500, Democratic National Committee, Washington, D.C.

11. Ibid., Appendix II, p. 498.

12. On the rigged primary process, see Karp "Playing Politics"; "Suit Seeks to Block Caucuses," *Detroit Free Press,* March 10, 1984.

13. *Report of the Platform Committee . . .* , p. 33; "Minority Report #2," Ibid, p. 55.

14. Malcolm X, "Ballots or Bullets," in *Malcolm X Speaks,* ed. George Breitman (New York: Meritt, 1965).

15. *Detroit Free Press,* July 18, 1984, p. 9.

16. Ibid.

17. Minister Louis Farrakhan espouses the traditional Black Muslim line, which expresses an extreme condemnation of whites and their system. See C. Eric Lincoln, *The Black Muslims of America* (Boston: Beacon Press, 1961).

18. Anthony Oberschall, *Social Conflicts and Social Movements* (Englewood Cliffs, N.J.: Prentice-Hall, 1973), pp. 46–47.

19. Ibid., p. 46.

PART V

The Impact

Traditional Democratic Party Politics and the 1984 Maryland Jackson Presidential Campaign: A Case Study

9

Alvin Thornton
and Frederick C. Hutchinson

The Jackson campaign has been viewed from a number of perspectives. However, considerably less attention has been devoted to rigorous case studies that focus on how the Jackson presidential campaign fared in particular states. Our concern in the present research is with such a case study. Here we offer a detailed analysis and commentary on the nature, development, and dynamics of the Jackson campaign in Maryland. This study is informed both by our research as political scientists and by information and insights gained from our own participation in and observation of the Jackson campaign and its impact on subsequent developments in state and local politics in Maryland.*

Jackson's campaign in Maryland was really a statewide effort. By the end of the presidential primary election day (May 8, 1984), Jesse Louis Jackson had captured 129,387, or 25 percent, of the 517,852 votes cast and 11 of 42, or 26 percent, of the contested congressional-district-level delegate positions in the Maryland Democratic presidential primary.[1] Jackson finished second in a field of three—truly a remarkable feat considering that this was the first time in modern state political history that blacks purposefully and aggressively participated in the presidential nominating process and that they were hampered by a set of rules designed, as we will show, to compromise their effective participation. The Maryland Committee for Jesse Jackson fielded delegate slates in five of the state's eight congressional districts, engaged in intensive voter registration, raised over $70,000 in campaign funds, effectively targeted campaign mailings to strategic precincts throughout the state, set up telephone

---

*Alvin Thornton was chairman of the Maryland Jackson campaign issues committee and a member of the Democratic National Convention's platform committee. Frederick Hutchinson was a member of the issues committee and a key organizer in Prince George's County.

banks in the targeted congressional districts, and even distributed food to pollworkers across the entire state on election day.

In short, Jackson's was a full-fledged and sophisticated political campaign and the most unified rank-and-file black electoral activity in the state's history. And as a result of this effort, he swept the contested delegate and alternate positions in Maryland's fifth and seventh congressional districts, and he won the popular vote in Baltimore City (7th) and in Prince George's County (5th). Jackson also secured four additional at-large delegates and, overall, placed his campaign committee in a position to demand a fair share of the pledged and unpledged delegate and alternate slots reserved for the state's party and elected officials.

Moreover, Jackson's campaign had brought together a rather diverse group of individuals and politicians. His official delegate candidates covered the gamut, ranging from elected officials, both black and white, to persons whose political background and experiences might be described as "militant" and "radical"—from the white mayor of the city of Takoma Park to former members of the Black Panther Party who were official Jackson delegates from the fourth congressional district.

There were two salient dimensions to the Jackson campaign in the state of Maryland. On one dimension the campaign provided a forum for the articulation of frustration with the then-current state of affairs in American politics. On another dimension the campaign served as a trial balloon to test potential electoral strength in strategic intrastate political jurisdictions in preparation for future efforts aimed at broadening the base of black political representation at the state and local levels. Success on both dimensions required a well-organized and coordinated campaign effort coupled with a solid electoral performance from the candidate.

Perhaps the most useful and appropriate theoretical framework for this study is that provided by Professor Mack Jones, who demands that theoretical work in the field of black politics transcend symbolic and general trappings of power and focus directly on the actual bases of power.[2] Jones suggests that in order to determine the nature and level of development of black political activity one must examine the "character of political organizations and other supportive structures developed within black communities; the recruitment of black leadership; voting behavior of the rank and file—both black and white; and the response of entrenched white economic and political leadership to the changing circumstances."[3] This framework uniquely characterizes the nature and scope of the Jackson effort in both state and local contexts. It demands a detailed examination of the statewide campaign organization and of the ways both black leadership and rank and file at the local level related to the campaign. It also demands an examination and assessment of the campaign's efforts to recruit new and independent black leadership at the local level. It demands a survey of voting patterns in key political jurisdictions within the state. And finally it demands that this study chronicle, in significant detail, the conflict between the campaign organization and entrenched white political leadership.

This case study of Jackson's campaign in Maryland is organized into several, mainly chronological, sections. First we give an overview of the political-social context of the election campaign. Here we outline state and local demographic characteristics relevant to the election campaign and outcome, including population mix, the state's political traditions, important counties and cities, and other socioeconomic factors. Second, we discuss Jackson's campaign organization in Maryland. Here we describe how Jackson's organization was started, who was instrumental in its formation, and the nature of the organizational structure that evolved. An important part of this section is a discussion of the relationship of the Jackson organization to already established political organizations and elites.

In the third part of the paper we look at the nature of the primary campaign and election. This section focuses on major issues of the campaign and describes in some detail the battle over delegate selection rules and the actual selection and distribution of delegates. Our next section focuses on Jackson's Maryland delegation at the 1984 Democratic National Convention. It includes a description of the behavior and activity of Jackson's Maryland delegates in context of the overall Maryland state delegation and the national convention process generally. We then give attention to the period immediately after the national convention and assess how Jackson's Maryland supporters fared during the presidential election. We also give follow-up discussion on what has happened to Jackson's Rainbow Coalition in Maryland since the presidential primary and the 1984 presidential election. In a final section we offer some concluding observations with respect to the effects and impact of the Jackson candidacy and campaign on Maryland politics.

Social and Political Context

Maryland is a state of approximately 4.5 million people. These people live throughout its twenty-four constant political subdivisions (twenty-three counties and Baltimore City) and span the ethnic, ideological, and occupational spectra. In Maryland there is a heterogeneous population mix including blacks and whites, liberals and conservatives, civil servants and migrant workers, as well as urban blue-collar Chesapeake Bay watermen. This population diversity is almost evenly spread out across the state's two urban areas, Baltimore City and Annapolis; the state's four major suburban areas, Baltimore, Howard, Prince George's, and Montgomery counties; and the state's remaining nineteen rural counties.

Maryland is also a southern state with a political history not dissimilar in many respects to the more celebrated states further south. Maryland was a slave state and joined with Florida, North Carolina, Arkansas, Oklahoma, and Texas in 1954 to argue before the Supreme Court in defense of its dual system of public education.[4] Like other southern states Maryland has a strong tradition of conservative politics within the Democratic party, evidenced by the 69-percent Democratic registration of its citizens and its unpredictable behavior in presidential elections. In 1968 George Wallace won the state's Democratic party presidential primary, and the Ku Klux Klan still has a very visible presence in the state, especially in the outer suburban and rural areas. Yet, in spite of this conservative tradition, Maryland is capable of a liberal politics in those areas where there are high concentrations of black people.

Of Maryland's 4.5 million people, slightly over three million are of voting age. By the end of 1982 there were 1,968,498 registered voters in the state (45 percent of the state's population). Of these 1,968,498 voters, 1,360,233, or 69 percent, were registered Democrats; 463,761, or 24 percent, were registered as either independents or as affiliates of other political parties.[5]

As these voter registration numbers would suggest, the state Democratic party effectively controls state and local politics. Six of the state's eight congressional representatives are Democrat, and one of the two U.S. senators is a Democrat. At the state and local level almost all the elected offices are held by Democrats.

Blacks comprise 22 percent of the state's population, and the overwhelming majority of them are Democrat. However, in 1982 only 61.4 percent of the voting age black population in the state was registered to vote—a lower percentage than that of Mississippi, a central battleground for challenges to the enforcement of the Voting Rights Act. The remaining 38.6 percent of the black population that was not registered to vote translated into 256,119 persons. The *National Black Leadership Roundtable Voter Registration Plan, 1983–84*, prepared by the Congressional Black Caucus Brain Trust on Black Voter Participation and the National Black Leadership Roundtable, targeted Maryland for a 25 percent increase in black voter registration (64,029). But the actual increase in the number of registered black voters approximated 33 percent or 84,519. This target was set because President Reagan had lost the state in the 1980 election by only 45,555 votes. It was hoped that the increase in registered black voters would protect the state from eroding into the Republican column in the 1984 general election.[6]

Historically, black political activity has been confined almost exclusively to the two major areas of black population in the state, Baltimore City and Prince George's County. In fact, with one exception—a county councilman in Howard County—all of the state's black elected officials are, and have been in recent years, from these jurisdictions. During the Jackson campaign, these jurisdictions remained the major focus of political activity, and all of Jackson's congressional district-level delegates ultimately came from these jurisdictions as well.

But the Jackson presidential candidacy also took hold in other Maryland counties which had significant concentrations of black people. Aside from Baltimore City (62 percent black) and Prince George's County (40 percent black), significant campaign activity also took place in Anne Arundel County (21 percent black), Montgomery County (17 percent black), and Howard County (15 percent black). Lesser activity took place in Baltimore and Charles counties, but the activity in Baltimore County was a function of the Howard County organization, and the Charles County activity was blunted due to the nature of its congressional district.[6] The most significant characteristic about black Marylanders during the Jackson campaign was the dissimilar political circumstances which engendered their participation.

In Baltimore City there is a very visible black elected official presence in city and state political offices: six city councilpersons (18 total), two state senators (11 total), fourteen state delegates (43 total), a chairperson of the city council, a state's attorney, as well as the dean of the state's black elected officials, Congressman Parren Mitchell. For the most part, these black elected officials have relationships of convenience with the state Democratic party structure and, therefore, initially did not move to endorse the Jackson candidacy. Instead, they opted to parlay for positions within the Mondale and then Hart organizations, hoping to pick up delegate and alternate slots to the Democratic convention through the implementation of the state's affirmative action component of the delegate selection rules. Once it became clear that extra-electoral forces within the black community had begun to develop political momentum and that there were not enough "spoils of association" to go around, a few of the black elected officials allied themselves with the Maryland Jackson campaign.[7] Thus the backbone of the Baltimore contingent in the Jackson campaign was comprised of forces external to the city and state Democratic party structure.

In Prince George's County, the candidacy incorporated a significant portion of the county's black elected official contingent even though they had very visible and significant ties to the politically dominant white Democratic party structure, which supported Vice President Mondale. Both black county council members, the county's only black state senator, and one of the county's four black state delegates were delegate candidates representing the Jackson candidacy. The Jackson candidacy in Prince George's County was also fueled by a large contingent of politically disaffected civic and community leaders and activists who have been struggling in opposition to the county's Democratic party structure for years. This unlikely marriage of potentially conflicting forces within the black community was probably conditioned by two factors.

First, the state headquarters for the Jackson candidacy was located in the middle of the state's twenty-fourth legislative district, the heart of the county's black community. Second, because the nature of the political base of these local elected officials was tenuous at best—due in large part to the fact that three of the four participating officials were first term incumbents—attaching themselves in a visible manner to a political phenomenon which had already gained significant legitimacy in the black community could only serve to enhance their own legitimacy in that same community. Another, less significant contributing factor was the leadership void among local black elected officials which resulted from the felony conviction of the dean of the county's cadre of black elected officials, the generally recognized broker for the county's black community. This prevented most of them from playing politics as usual.

Anne Arundel County, a very small portion of Howard County (eight precincts), and thirty southern precincts in Prince George's County comprise Maryland's Fourth Congressional District. In the state legislature this congressional district is dominated by conservative Democrats, as is evidenced by their overwhelming electoral majority, and the entrenched congressional fixture of conservative Republican congresswoman Marjorie Holt. Until the 1985 general election, when Congressman Clarence Long was defeated in Baltimore County, Congresswoman Holt was the only Republican congressional representative in the state of Maryland. The major pockets of black people in this congressional district are in the southern portion of Prince George's County and in the city of Annapolis, the core of Anne Arundel County's black population.

The majority of the Fourth Congressional District's delegate candidates came from the Annapolis area. These candidates were the most unique of the Maryland Jackson campaign's delegate slates in that they had no previous formal or informal relationship with either the city of Annapolis or the Anne Arundel County Democratic party organizations. As a delegation they had the most militant and potentially radical background of any of the state's county contingents. Perhaps their most substantive interaction with the Annapolis Democratic party structure was the recent successful effort to change the representation structure in the city from an at-large system to a district system. On the other hand, the two delegate candidates representing southern Prince George's County had a history of negotiating a relationship (sometimes successfully and sometimes not) with the Prince George's County Democratic party structure. They viewed Jackson's candidacy as an opportunity to register new black voters and thus up the ante in their ongoing negotiations with the party structure.

Howard and Montgomery counties have the most affluent black populations in the state of Maryland. One of the most significant contributions to the Jackson campaign by the organizations in Howard and Montgomery counties was financial; the two counties contributed the lion's share to the campaign's finances. These counties are almost exclusively suburban which helps to explain the relatively low percentage of blacks living in the respective counties.

The 15 percent black population in Howard County is highly and visibly political. The unique feature of the black participation in the Jackson candidacy is that it was spearheaded for the most part by professional women who have had a history of coalescing with liberal white groups. Undoubtedly, the issue of parity between the sexes was a major impetus for their enthusiastic participation.

In Howard County, there is only one black elected official—a county councilperson, who did not run as a Jackson delegate candidate in the primary contest. However, toward the end of the campaign, he did come out visibly in support of the candidacy. Throughout the primary season he provided logistical information for the state campaign committee as it was needed. He was chosen as a bonus delegate from the category of pledged elected official delegates as per the Maryland state Democratic party rules.

In Montgomery County the Jackson campaign fielded its only progressive white elected official delegate candidate, Takoma Park mayor Sam Abbott. But for the most part black politics in the county is in its embryonic stages. Aside from the county NAACP, no visible county-wide black political organization exists for the purpose of cultivating black political power. The major political issues of concern to blacks in Montgomery County center around quality education for their children, incidents of police brutality against black persons, and a general hate campaign by right-wing groups directed against racial, ethnic, and religious groups. Generally, the NAACP is the vehicle through which blacks express opposition to such acts.

Given the diversity of demographic and political characteristics among the various county jurisdictions, there had to be a thread that could unite the diversity of purpose into a unified and spirited statewide campaign. This thread emerged with the formal challenge of the state delegate selection rules by the formal state campaign organization, the Maryland Jackson for President Committee. This challenge began in February 1984 and was pursued at every turn until the last member of the three permanent committees of the Democratic National Convention (rules, credentials, and platform committees) had been elected by the Maryland delegates to the convention. In this context procedural concerns become the substantive basis for challenging Democratic party political dominance over the various pockets of the black population in each of the participating political jurisdictions. Furthermore, the nature and the duration of this challenge on the local level was, and is, a reflection of the stage of black political development within each particular jurisdiction. The delicacy of the task at hand is to articulate an analysis of the Jackson candidacy in the state of Maryland without compromising the thrusts of various local efforts.

Figure 1. Maryland Jesse Jackson presidential campaign organization

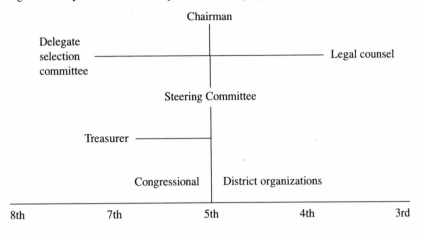

Source: Maryland Jackson for President Committee.

The Jackson Organization in Maryland:
Its Beginning and Development

The Maryland Jackson campaign organization evolved into a complex operation with functioning chapters in five of the state's eight congressional districts. In each of the five districts the campaigns were initiated by individuals with a history of active community involvement. For the most part they were not elected officials, although some elected officials played an important role in the early development of the Jackson campaign. The organization started to come together immediately after Jackson announced his decision to seek the presidency. By late November 1983 small groups of individuals had assembled as Jackson committees in the third, fourth, fifth, seventh, and eighth congressional districts (see figure 1).

It is very important to note that each of the congressional districts had a particular local political situation that produced significant dissatisfaction among many voters, especially blacks. This dissatisfaction stemmed from such long-held grievances as inequities in political representation for blacks and women, declining public education systems, economic disparities, and discriminatory at-large voting districts. As a result, the development of the Maryland Jackson campaign was as much a response to these concerns as to the idea of a black running for president on an attractive platform.

The Primary Campaign and Election

The primary campaign was to determine which Democratic party presidential candidate would win the support of Maryland's ninety-nine pledged and un-

Figure 2. Maryland's delegate allocation

Total Delegate votes 74					
Pledged delegates (62)			Unpledged delegates (12)		
Total base delegates (56)					
District Level	At-Large	10% Add-on	State & Vice Chairs	Add-on for Party & elected	Additional Add-on
42	14	6	2	8	2
Alternates 25					
Total Delegation size 99					

pledged delegates and alternates to the 1984 Democratic National Convention. A process that had been traditionally without much conflict became the focus of major challenges from the Jackson committee. The state's allocation factor resulted in the following distribution of delegates and alternates:[8]
The electoral contest in Maryland, then, was over forty-two district levels and fourteen at-large pledged delegates to the Democratic National Convention.

The approach of the Maryland Committee for Jesse Jackson to the delegate selection process was conditioned by the concerns being raised by the national Jackson campaign about the general Democratic party delegate selection rules. Jackson argued that at the national level many aspects of the rules were unfair, especially the 20 percent threshold requirement. In addition, he was concerned about the enforcement of the affirmative action requirement in the national rules.

The Jackson campaign took advantage of opportunities offered by the "rules of the game" by challenging the rules themselves—in this case the guidelines governing the selection of delegates to the 1984 Democratic party convention in San Francisco. Since 1964 the primary issues involving the selection of delegates to the Democratic National Convention have centered on providing equal opportunity to participate in the process, ensuring a role for party officials and holders of public office, ending winner-take-all primaries, improving the timeliness of the selection process, printing explicit state party rules, notifying the public of delegate selection meetings, and strictly limiting delegate fees. Perennial conflicts over these issues have generally occurred over attempts to expand the base of the Democratic party and, thereby, keep it more in tune with and representative of its varied constituent groups. In fact, Jackson's initial challenge to Democratic party rules injected into the campaign concepts of fairness and justice ignored by the other seven candidates in the primary.[9]

In this way procedural issues took on substantive significance. Consider, for example, Jackson's claim that the 20-percent threshold rule and run-off primaries were unfair and that failure to implement affirmative action plans was unjust. Issues such as these were important to Jackson's state committees, who needed substantive ways to interact with their regular state and local party structures. All of this activity, however, would not have been possible without the reforms (guidelines) initiated in 1969 by the McGovern-Fraser Commission. The McGovern-Fraser Commission created eighteen guidelines which, although more wide-ranging, focused on nonprimary states. These reforms or guidelines were actually "moderate, programmatic compromises designed to revive a party that had been fractured by the 1968 convention and by the impact of the Vietnam War." [10] But the McGovern-Fraser reforms were in turn revised by the Hunt Commission following President Carter's defeat in 1980. Nevertheless, in Maryland in 1984 the guidelines would serve the Jackson committee well. The Maryland Jackson committee wanted to know the contours of the road on which it was traveling.

The commission was chaired by former Governor James B. Hunt of North Carolina. Although the Hunt Commission required the Democratic party to engage in voter registration campaigns—potentially a democratizing action—the net effect of the commission's rules was to blunt the reforms allowed under the McGovern-Fraser rules. It has been suggested that the purpose of the Hunt Commission was to "protect the Democratic Party against newcomers." [11] This charge was based on suggested changes that (1) conceded to states the option of reserving delegate slots for senior elected officials and party chairpersons; (2) restored the "loophole" primary in which voters cast ballots for convention delegates and not directly for candidates (beauty contests); (3) removed the bind on delegates that required them to vote on the initial ballot for the candidate for whom they were elected; and (4) provided incentives to states to encourage them to hold caucuses rather than primaries (this was viewed as being good for the party building). [12]

Overall, the Democratic party delegate selection rules made factional mobilization rather than coalition building the key to the nominating process. Only first choices would count in primary elections or caucuses. Thus, as some put it, "the only game in town is to try . . . to mobilize one's own voters, to activate a faction, and hope for the best." [13] This operating principle as well as other rules of the game were clearly understood by the Maryland Jackson campaign committee, and this knowledge served the Jackson committee well.

The Maryland Democratic party delegate selection plan was adopted by the Maryland Democratic party in late January of 1983. It divided the forty-two congressional-district-level delegates and alternates as shown in table 1. [14]

The at-large delegates were apportioned only to those candidates who met the 20-percent threshold requirement. [15] In Maryland, Jackson and Mondale met this requirement. (The actual distribution of delegates and alternates among Hart, Jackson, and Mondale will be analyzed later.) The 20-percent

Table 1. Delegate Distribution

Congressional district	Delegates	Alternates
1	5	1
2	5	2
3	6	2
4	5	2
5	5	2
6	4	1
7	6	2
8	6	2

threshold rule and the lack of implementation of the Maryland delegate selection plan were the primary points of focus of the Maryland Jackson committee's procedural challenge. For those concerned with the traditional politics of exclusion, the question was, how do you control the Jackson phenomenon while giving the impression that there is procedural justice in the process used to select delegates? Historically, this had always been accomplished in Maryland with little opposition. But Jackson's Rainbow Coalition brought about some change to this situation.

The Jackson campaign committee raised several concerns about the Maryland Democratic party central committee's implementation of the delegate selection rules. They included: (1) lack of timeliness in the application of the rules; (2) failure to implement the affirmative action requirements of the Democratic National Committee (DNC); (3) the unrepresentativeness of the "minority representational goal" for the state and the 20-percent threshold requirement of the DNC delegate selection rules.

The Jackson committee charged that "the [delegate selection] process has been replete with tardiness and exclusion of important elements of the Party to the point where effective participation by minorities, women, and low-income people have been compromised." On January 24, 1984, the Maryland Jackson for President Committee sent a letter to the Maryland Democratic central committee expressing serious concern about the process.[16]

Another concern for the Jackson committee was the extent to which the affirmative action requirements of the Democratic National Committee were carried out. The central provision where affirmative action is concerned is that "the state delegate selection and affirmation action plans must be submitted to the Compliance Review Commission (CRC) for approval on or before April 15, 1983, and [that] the Compliance Review Commission should act on the plans in no case later than September 15, 1983, or 90 days preceding the first step in the state's delegate selection process, whichever is earlier." [17] The Maryland plan was not approved by CRC until January 19, 1984, which gave little time for the candidates and their delegates to organize campaigns consistent with state and party regulations.

Significant elements of the procedural equality question centered around issues related to affirmative action, the 20-percent threshold rule, official slates, and citizen education. "The time, dates, places, and rules for the conduct of all caucuses, conventions, and meetings, and other events involved in the delegate selection process," according to DNC rules, "shall be effectively publicized, bilingually where necessary, to encourage the participation of minority groups." [18] However, the party organized very limited publicity on network or public television or in the print media regarding such meetings, caucuses, or conventions.

Additionally, the Maryland Jackson committee raised the issue of the 20 percent threshold requirement and asserted that it "effectively undermines the principle of one person one vote." [19] Maryland's 20 percent threshold provides that "at-large delegates and alternates [twenty-one positions in Maryland] shall be allocated according to the division of preference among district level delegates at the time of the district level selection providing that a 20 percent threshold is met." [20]

Another important consideration for the Maryland Jackson campaign was the "minority representational goal" for the state. Representational goals were established by the Maryland Democratic central committee.[21] The primary concern of the Jackson committee was that the representational goals were structured around "an inappropriate base in that the goals should have been based upon the percentage of blacks and other minorities within the Democratic Party and the sustained loyalty of these groups to the Democratic Party." [22]

The Jackson committee also focused on two other issues of procedural equality and delegate selection. Given the constituency base of the Jackson campaign, voter registration and mobilization was very important. Realizing this, the Jackson campaign demanded that the Hunt Commission rules requiring the allocation funds for voter registration be implemented. In Maryland the Democratic party provided no funds for voter registration, notwithstanding the fact that in 1980 Reagan almost carried the state.[23]

The second issue concerned the Jackson committee's belief that the representational goals, established in the state party's affirmative action plan, should have been applied to the at-large delegate and alternate category, including party and elected officials, as well as to the base delegation. This concern was raised because most of the state's highest ranking Democratic officials had announced support for Walter Mondale long before the Maryland delegate selection process begun. In light of this, the Jackson committee argued that such officials "should be appointed as delegates via the provision calling for six pledged party and elected official delegates as opposed to the provision allowing for the selection of 12 unpledged party and elected official delegates." [24] The provision allowing twelve unpledged party and elected official delegates was designed to give party and elected officials greater influence both in the delegate selection process and at the convention, where as unpledged delegates they would be in a position to consider the larger interests of the Democratic party. However, the early endorsement of presidential candidates by individuals who were subsequently selected as unpledged delegates compromised this goal. In general, the Jackson committee believed that the Democratic central committee's implementation of the delegate selection rules and the content of the rules threatened its ability to effectively participate in the delegate selection process.

While it is difficult to define the specific causes of this maladministration, several "notions" may be suggested. Possibly, the party was simply doing business as usual—i.e., in an environment where there is limited political and ideological challenge to the pre-ordained nominee of party regulars, there is little need to focus on efficient application of party rules. To some degree, the Jackson factor broke this tradition and posed basic electoral, procedural, and ideological challenges to the Maryland Democratic party. Another contending conception is that by January 19, 1984, the Jackson campaign in Maryland had become a major inconvenience to the Mondale campaign and therefore had to be contained. If this view is acceptable, then the maladministration of the rules was an extension of the containment strategy. The final view is that the county level Democratic central committee in the state of Maryland is not structured or designed to effectively implement party rules and regulations. In fact, the local central committees are the first ring of the party patronage network with little responsibility for rule administration and adjudication.

In Maryland, party central committee organizations are better suited for service and mobilization activities than for political persuasion.[25] The issue development and articulation function is traditionally carried out by incumbent elected officials who have the finances and staff unavailable to the central committees. The primary role of these committees is recommending candidates to the state governor to fill vacant positions. Secondarily, they organize candidate slate literature for distribution during the general election.

The issues associated with the debate over the delegate selection rules become very important in the state election. However, they were not the only major issues that concerned the Jackson committee. The committee endorsed the major elements of the national Jackson platform: reduced military spending, a more rational foreign policy toward Africa, enforcement of the Voting Rights Act, elimination of run-off primaries, equal rights for women, a more rational Latin America and Carribean policy, and restoration of the "social safety net." The particulars of these issues were important to the Rainbow

Coalition constituency in Maryland. This was true notwithstanding the demographic and political traditions of the areas where the Jackson committee contested for delegate positions.

Although these issues were very important for the Jackson committee, they were not as salient as concerns that were more specific to the state of Maryland and to particular political subdivisions. The examples of Prince George's County and Baltimore City are instructive. In Prince George's County the Jackson committee focused on the issue of power sharing among blacks and whites and the need for politically mature and independent black politics. In addition, the election of a black to a state circuit court position and the modification of a limitation on the county's taxing authority (TRIM-Tax Reform in Maryland) were important concerns around which the Jackson committee mobilized voters to participate in the primary and general elections. The black judge was nominated in the primary and won in the general election, and TRIM was modified in the general election.

The situation in Baltimore was similar to the one in Prince George's County. There was a general concern about the level of political equality between blacks and whites in the city. The national Jackson platform also played an important role in the mobilization of the Rainbow constituency. As in Prince George's County, local issues were very important. Two issues were significant in Baltimore. The Rainbow Coalition supported legislation that would provide for an elected school board and change the multi-member city council districts to single-member districts. Neither of these efforts was successful.

Jesse Jackson, Walter Mondale, and Gary Hart did very little campaigning in the state. Jackson came to the state twice during the campaign, visiting the University of Maryland at College Park (a predominantly white 40,000-plus student university), two churches in black communities in Prince George's County, and a major church in the black community of Baltimore. His visits attracted large crowds and attention from the media. They also helped increase the name recognition of leaders of the Jackson campaign committee. Mondale and Hart did not campaign in the state. Mondale had key campaign figures in the state—Senator Paul Sarbanes, Congressman Michael Barnes, Congresswoman Barbara Milkuski, and Congressman Parren Mitchell—and might have felt it unnecessary to campaign in a late primary state that usually goes with the wishes of traditional party elites. Hart had only a minor organization in the state, although he did receive the endorsement of a small number of state and local elected officials.

In the Maryland Democratic party primary, 517,852 individuals voted—a 36.1 percent turnout of the 1,435,794 registered voters. A breakdown of the vote distribution by congressional district is provided in table 2. Jackson won 25 percent, Mondale 41 percent, and Hart 24 percent of the primary vote.

Jackson got the largest share of his votes from the fifth and seventh congres-

Table 2. 1984 Democratic party primary vote by congressional district

Congressional district/county		Registered voters	Total voted	% voted	Jackson	Hart	Mondale	Others
1st		154,451	45,873	29.7	6,979	15,289	17,967	
2nd		198,801	62,895	31.6	4,466	19,409	31,370	
3rd	Baltimore City	147,060	53,149	36.1	8,267	10,056	29,738	
	Baltimore County	67,639	23,040	34.1	1,977	5,975	13,040	
	Howard County	20,008	8,098	40.5	2,497	2,152	2,889	
	Total	234,707	84,287	35.9	12,741	18,183	45,667	
4th	Anne Arundel	101,353	35,768	35.3	4,762	11,399	15,732	
	Howard	5,060	1,707	33.7	362	593	599	
	Prince George's	38,279	16,078	42.0	8,507	2,133	4,155	
	Total	144,692	53,553	37.0	13,631	14,125	20,486	
5th	Prince George's	149,919	66,021	44.0	26,180	13,348	20,668	90
6th		132,954	43,686	32.9	3,361	16,492	10,047	
7th	Baltimore City	220,509	82,596	37.5	48,019	4,237	23,118	
	Baltimore County	21,716	7,616	35.1	2,796	1,293	2,866	
	Total	242,225	90,212	37.2	50,815	5,530	25,984	
8th	Montgomery	178,045	71,325	40.1	11,214	20,989	34,033	
Total		1,435,794	517,852	36.1	129,387	123,365	215,222	38,912

Source: State Administrative Board of Elections, *Primary Election Returns and Voter Turnout Statistics*, Annapolis, Maryland, May 1, 1984.

Table 3. 1980 and 1984 Maryland Democratic presidential primary vote totals* by congressional districts

Districts	1980	1984	Difference 1984 over 1980
1	47,557	45,873	− 1,684
2	73,675	62,875	− 10,780
3	59,262	84,287	+ 25,025
4	35,812	53,552	+ 17,740
5	44,615	66,021	+ 21,406˙
6	52,141	43,686	− 8,455
7	49,323	90,212	+ 40,889
8	59,560	71,325	+ 14,765
Totals	421,945	517,852	+ 104,907

Source: State Administrative Board of Elections, *Primary Election Returns and Voter Turnout and Statistics*, Annapolis, Maryland.
*Totals for 1980 do not include the votes for two minor candidates and those who voted "other."

sional districts—20 percent and 39 percent respectively. These are the areas of the state with the largest concentration of black voters. He also got 11 percent of his votes from the fourth congressional district, which has two large black population centers. Polls taken prior to the election projected Jackson to capture no more than 10 percent of the vote.

Mondale received a large number of votes from all sections of the state. The largest share came from the eighth and third congressional districts. The eighth is largely Montgomery County, a suburb of Washington, D.C., and the third is mostly the white precincts of Baltimore City and parts of Baltimore and Howard counties.

Hart was able to beat Jackson and come in second to Mondale in all the districts except the seventh and fifth, where Jackson beat him by a wide margin. Hart's showing in Baltimore City, 5,530 votes, was very weak when compared to the 50,815 and 25,984 votes for Jackson and Mondale respectively.

Chapters of the National Coalition on Black Voter Participation ("Operation Big Vote") and other organizations engaged in an aggressive voter registration and get-out-the vote campaign, particularly in the fifth, seventh, and part of the fourth (Prince George's) districts. The campaign might have been the cause of the relatively high voting percentage in these districts, which were among the highest in the state. Table 3 contains data showing the 1980 and 1984 Maryland presidential primary vote totals by congressional districts. These data suggest that the "Jackson factor" was one factor that resulted in a dramatic increase in voter turnout, particularly in districts three, four, five, and seven.

As a result of the primary vote, Jackson was awarded eleven delegates and four alternates at the congressional district level, and Mondale and Hart received twenty-seven delegates and ten alternates, and three delegates and no alternates, respectively, at this level. One person was elected to go as an uncommitted delegate. In Prince George's County (Fifth Congressional District), Jackson won all the delegate and alternate slots. In Baltimore City (Seventh Congressional District) Jackson won all the slots (six delegates and two alternates). A total of forty-two delegates and fourteen alternates (fifty-six positions or the base delegation) was selected on May 8, 1984. At this point the 20 percent threshold rule came into effect.[26] Jackson won 26 percent of the forty-two district level delegates and 25 percent of the popular vote. Jackson's delegates, therefore, were not negatively affected by the 20 percent threshold rule.

Having successfully participated in the primary portion of the delegate selection process, the Jackson committee proceeded to the stage where at-large delegates and alternates would be selected with a view toward making sure that the Jackson factor would not be compromised by traditional considerations that shape decisions about who goes to the Democratic National Convention from Maryland. The at-large delegates and alternates (forty-three) were selected by the state Democratic central committee at a June 12, 1984, meeting.[27] Twenty-one of the forty-three positions were delegate and alternate at-large slots (fourteen delegates and seven alternates). Twenty-two of them were for party and elected officials (twelve unpledged delegates, six pledged delegates, and four unpledged alternates).[28] The Jackson committee argued that it should receive no less than 25 percent of the at-large positions. It reasoned that it should receive the following distribution of delegates and alternates:

Category	Allocation Proposed	Actual	Source
1	11	11	Congressional district level delegates
2	4	4	Congressional district level alternates
3	6	6	At-Large delegates and alternates (4 delegates and 2 alternates)
4	2	2	Party and elected officials delegates
5	2	0	Unpledged party and elected officials delegates
Total	25	23	

Categories 1, 2, 3, and 4 were guaranteed to the Jackson committee. The committee understood that the persons in category 5 were unpledged and therefore would not reflect a candidate preference. The committee also knew that in Maryland Democratic party politics, even unpledged delegates are pledged. Category 5 was the only area in which the Jackson committee was unsuccessful: none of the persons selected in the category had a preference for Jackson;

each had indicated preference for Mondale. Since the state central committee was dominated by Mondale supporters, the Jackson Committee could do little about this. Overall, however, the Jackson committee accomplished its goals in the delegate allocation process.

But the Jackson committee in Maryland was less successful in the selection of permanent members of the party's standing committees—rules, platform, and credentials. The Jackson committee recommended that the election of permanent members to the standing committees take place within five days of the primary election. This recommendation was based on a desire to have actual state presidential preferences reflected on the committees—especially the platform committee—as soon as possible. Maryland's delay in selecting permanent committee members (the primary was held on May 8th and members elected by the state party central committee more than a month later and after the platform committee's hearings) appeared to be unreasonable. In fact, in testimony before the temporary state platform committee the Jackson committee made a formal appeal to the party to modify the selection schedule.[29] The basis of the appeal was that Maryland's permanent committee members would not be selected until after most of the platform committee's work had been completed. The month delay caused Jackson's platform committee member to miss one major public hearing. This issue was not a cause for concern for the Mondale campaign because it was sure that two of the temporary members on each of the standing committees would remain as permanent members. Eventually, three nonparty regulars who were nominated by the Jackson committee were elected by the Maryland Democratic party delegates to the convention to sit on the three standing committees.

Jackson's Maryland Delegation: Convention and Postconvention Activities

The Maryland delegation was led by a U.S. senator (Paul Sarbanes), the secretary of state (Lorraine Sheehan), and a labor leader (Edward Lemon)—all Mondale supporters—and the state chair of the Rainbow Coalition (Bennie Thayer), and a county councilperson (Hilda Pemberton)—both Jackson delegates. There was a minor problem related to whether a Jackson delegate should be vice-chair of the Maryland delegation, with full powers of the chair in his absence. As it was finally resolved, the chair was a Mondale delegate, the vice-chair a Jackson delegate, and co-secretary positions were assigned to two Mondale and one Jackson supporters.

Entering the convention process, the Jackson delegation had several objectives in mind. The delegation wanted to remain structured as a distinct entity within the general Maryland delegation. Only two of the Jackson delegates had attended a convention in the role of delegate; this lack of convention experience and the fact they were Jackson delegates contributed to their desire to remain a distinct entity. The delegation also wanted to be an informed contributor to the national Jackson delegation. To facilitate this, the delegation held daily morning and late-night caucuses to discuss developments at the convention. Representatives of the delegation were dispatched to all informational caucuses called by the Jackson campaign and the Maryland general delegation. The delegation also wanted to get support for the Jackson minority planks from members of the Maryland delegation. We comment on this point later in this section. Two objectives that were not specific to the convention were important to the Jackson delegation: it wanted to bargain for revisions in the way the Maryland Democratic party conducts general elections and to make a contribution to the institutionalization of the Rainbow Coalition in Maryland.

To some extent all of these objectives were reflected in a proposal developed at the convention by a committee chosen from the Maryland Jackson delegation and composed of representatives of the various congressional districts where Jackson won delegates. The proposal included seven major areas: respect, money, programs, political development, job training in the political arena, and fairness.[30] We have reproduced below the specifics of these proposals and outlined the reaction they received from the Mondale campaign and the leadership of the Maryland Democratic party.

I. *Respect*

The basic principle is that the Maryland Rainbow Coalition should be recognized as a viable element of the Democratic Party in Maryland. Several things must happen if this principle is to be realized. They are:

   A. The Rainbow Coalition (R) must participate in the structuring of the Maryland Mondale campaign.
   B. Campaign positions should be allocated on an equitable basis to all constituency groups that constitute the Maryland Democratic Party. Highest level positions like co-chairpersons, deputy campaign managers should be included in this allocation scheme.
   C. The Rainbow Coalition should be included as part of all policy-making decisions taken by the Mondale campaign.
   D. After we have won the Fall election, the RC should be included as part of voter registration by providing for voter registration at the presidential transition team.

It is necessary for the Rainbow Coalition to make these points very clear to the Mondale Campaign and the Party because historically the Democratic Party in Maryland has not adhered to most of them.

II. *Money*

The basic principle is that *all* monies should be distributed on an equitable basis to all Democratic Party constituency groups throughout the campaign. Several things must happen if this principle is to be realized. They are:

A. A voter registration and mobilization position (Director) should be allocated to a representative from the RC as part of the Maryland Mondale Campaign.

B. No less than 50 percent of the voter registration and mobilization monies should be allocated to this office.

C. Black, female and other minority businesses should be used on an equitable basis by the Mondale campaign in Maryland. Such services as polling, banking, vending, public relations, and speech writing are examples of what we have in mind.

III. *Programs*

The basic principle is that the Maryland Democratic Party should commit itself to a platform of full employment, peace, and freedom. This principle is not sufficiently reflected in the 1984 Democratic Party Platform. The Maryland Democratic Party can help to realize this principle by doing the following:

— Supporting legislation, on a statewide basis, that will facilitate voter registration by providing for voter registration at Motor Vehicle Administration offices, Social Services and Health Department facilities.

IV. *Political Empowerment*

The basic principle is that the Maryland Democratic Party should reinforce the RC's efforts at political empowerment. To accomplish this principle, several things must happen.

— The Maryland Democratic Party should support the RC's participation in the structuring of slates for state and local elections. It should also seriously consider persons recommended by the RC for appointment to state and local judgeships, and other elected and appointed positions.

V. *Job Training in the Political Arena*

The basic principle is that the Party should equitably make available jobs in the Fall campaign and in the Party, generally, to youth and young adults of the RC.

VI. *Minority Planks*

The basic principle is that the Party should support the four minority planks to the 1984 Platform dealing with civil rights, affirmative action, military spending, and no first use of nuclear weapons.

VII. *Fairness*

The basic principle is that the Maryland Democratic Party should commit itself to being fair and open to all elements of the population that supports the Party's philosophy and objectives. To operationalize this principle, the Party should:

A. Support the naming of the Fairness Commission as the Jesse L. Jackson Fairness Commission.
B. Support a minority or a woman (i.e. Sharon Pratt Dixon) for the chairperson of the Democratic National Committee.
C. Support the Honorable Maynard Jackson to be chair of the Fairness Commission.
D. Select a Maryland representative to the Fairness Commission that reflects the RC contributions to the success of the Democratic Party in Maryland.
E. Support the establishment of a study commission to propose solutions to irregularities in Maryland's Democratic Party's delegate selection regulations.
F. Support the establishment of an open door policy for voter registration forms and activities related to voter registration, in general. No limitations on the number of forms and registrars should be supported by the Maryland Democratic Party.
G. Support the elimination of at-large elections, which are discriminatory, and other irregularities in the electoral process. RC leaders should be involved in the Attorney General's audit of local election procedures.

Although the Maryland Mondale campaign and the Democratic party expressed an interest in working with the Jackson committee to enact the proposal, as it developed, most of what was proposed was never acted upon or even given serious attention. Some of the proposals, particularly those related to "respect" and "political empowerment," could not be easily implemented. In addition, after the Democratic convention many important individuals in the Maryland Rainbow Coalition refused to actively support the implementation of the proposals. In this context the Baltimore Rainbow Coalition refused to endorse the Mondale-Ferrarro ticket in the general election. The black elected officials from Baltimore who were part of the Jackson campaign did endorse the Democratic party ticket. Their relationship with the state and local Democratic party was not primarily an extension of their participation in the Jackson campaign; they had a political party base to return to. However, for most of the Baltimore Rainbow Coalition members, who were not traditional Democratic party members, there were insufficient reasons to support the Mondale-Ferrarro tickets. They selected to focus on local issues that, in their opinion, were more important to the Rainbow constituency.

Rainbow Coalition members did participate in the structuring of the Maryland Mondale campaign—to the extent that there was a structured campaign. Considering the fact that Carter carried the state in 1980 and almost all of the state's elected leadership is Democratic, many experts automatically placed Maryland in the Democratic column. Therefore, Mondale's national campaign allocated little money and staff to Maryland. Responsibility for organizing the general election fell to the central committees. In selected jurisdictions Rainbow Coalition members were made temporary co-chairs of the central committees for the duration of the general election. This was done in Prince George's, Howard, and Anne Arundel counties, and Baltimore City—areas where Jackson made a strong showing.

Although the Democratic party of Maryland and the Mondale campaign re-affirmed their support for a platform of full employment, peace, and freedom as requested by the Jackson campaign, they did not endorse the idea of legislation that would provide voter registration at Motor Vehicle Administration offices, Social Services, and Health Department facilities. In fact, no group organized voter registration and mobilization and no voter registration monies were appropriated for the campaign.

The Prince George's County central committee made an effort to involve minority businesses in contracts for services from the Mondale-Ferraro campaign; it gave minor printing contract to a black female-owned small business. No other Democratic central committees made any effort along these lines.

The Mondale-Ferraro campaign and leaders of the Maryland Democratic party gave no response to the proposal relating to political empowerment. There was no identifiable participation of Rainbow members in jobs created by the general election campaign.

The Maryland delegation, the Maryland Democratic party leadership, and leaders of the Mondale-Ferraro campaign did not support the minority planks endorsed by the Rainbow Coalition. The differences over the minority plans clouded the relationship between the Jackson and Mondale camps during the general election. Mondale supporters felt that the minority planks would make the party platform unacceptable to the general electorate, and Jackson's supporters viewed them as essential to the presentation of real alternative to policies of the Reagan administration.

None of the items under the Fairness category was acted upon by the Democratic party or the Mondale-Ferraro campaign.

The Jackson committee's concern with an open Democratic party was reflected in its fight over the rules for delegate selection and was carried over into the convention and general election.[31] The demands made by the Jackson committee on the party clearly went beyond issues that could be dealt with at the national convention. Issues related to the general election, slate-making in the state, voter registration, etc., went beyond the purposes and goals of the convention. The demands were pressed primarily by those in the Jackson delegation who had had minor or no formal association with the party—in the main, persons attracted to the campaign by the fact that a black man was challenging for the U.S. presidency, articulating issues not traditionally discussed in presidential campaigns, and providing a campaign structure to which leadership and other resources could be devoted. Through this structure they were able to do what they had been unable to do at the state and local levels —organize a campaign, and challenge and defeat the traditional Democratic party structure. They saw the campaign (primary, convention, and general election) as a mechanism to expand the base of the Maryland Democratic party in preparation for the 1986 federal, state, and local elections and, as a consequence, further the black political agenda.

Demands on the Maryland Democratic party and the general objectives of the Jackson Committee were clearly an effort to get the spoils of victory. Even though Jackson came in second to Mondale in the state, the leadership of the Mondale-Ferraro campaign clearly understood that they needed the Rainbow Coalition's support in the general election. The demands and objectives went beyond traditional black/white relations within the Maryland Democratic party. To the extent that they did, they caused some tension within the Jackson delegation—some divisions over the appropriateness of raising the demands, some discomfort with the projected institutionalization of the Rainbow Coalition in Maryland. This was especially true of several incumbent elected officials who apparently viewed the Rainbow Coalition as unworkable beyond the presidential campaign or as a threat to their existing district organizations. In addition, some people in the Jackson delegation also wanted to begin the "healing" process and repair damaged relations with the party leadership. Of course, such divisions were major impediments to the institutionalization of the Rainbow Coalition in Maryland.

To the extent that the Rainbow Coalition remained inside the Maryland Democratic party, it retained the support of most black elected officials. Where the electoral interests of blacks in Maryland are concerned, the Democratic party operates a kind of "structured incrementalism" that preserves white incumbents and restrains black and female political advancement and the articulation of progressive ideas. To the degree that the Rainbow Coalition engaged in issue-based politics, the participation of black elected officials waivered. Factions within the Rainbow Coalition may openly clash in the future, as in important electoral contests in 1986, especially in Prince George's County, Maryland, where blacks are 38 percent of the population but have only minor political power.[32] Under such circumstances some Jackson supporters might well decide to rejoin the traditional party slates and forgo the kind of political independence manifested in the Maryland Jackson campaign. On the other hand, where the black population is significant, other Jackson supporters are likely to build upon the raised expectations of blacks, the campaign experience gained, and the increased voter registration roles in an effort to elect slates independent of traditional party leadership.

Some of these divisions within the Jackson committee became evident when it tried to implement the convention-based demands upon its return to Maryland. With few exceptions the implementation of these demands was left to those who held no prior or current official role in the Democratic party or in public office. Most of the individuals who had been elected to office as Democrats resumed their normal responsibilities and routines. Indeed, some in the Jackson committee saw the need to reintegrate themselves into the Democratic party and help defeat Ronald Reagan, but others were more concerned with building the Rainbow Coalition and positioning it as the voice of disenfranchised segments of the population. And the indecisiveness of the national Jackson campaign Committee exacerbated this division. During much of the general election campaign Jackson's national campaign committee, and Jackson himself, did not seem to know whether or not to support the national Democratic ticket.

In Maryland, the response to the Democratic ticket by the various chapters of the Rainbow was mixed. The Baltimore chapter refused to endorse it; Prince George's and other chapters endorsed it with conditions. particularly in Prince George's County these conditions were a result of efforts to realize the convention-based demands to further the black agenda. In Prince George's County and Baltimore City, where most of Maryland's blacks live, the electoral machinery that had been developed during the primary was placed in the service of local ballot questions that were of interest to the Rainbow Coalition: In Prince George's County, electing sitting judges who were opposed by a candidate the Rainbow felt was racist and "law-and-order" oriented, passing a measure that would lift the cap on funds that could be collected from property taxes, and electing blacks to the school board; in Baltimore City, legislating single-member districts and amending the city charter to provide for elected school board members. The Jackson campaign committee also opposed the so-called "Broadwater Amendment," which was designed to require persons holding public office to be registered voters. This development pointed to the potential of the Rainbow Coalition in these jurisdictions to be an independent participant in the state, county, and local political processes.

The Essential Impact of the Jackson Candidacy on Politics in Maryland

There are many different perspectives from which to view the effects of the Jackson presidential candidacy—for example, exclusively in terms of the national politics associated with the recruitment and nomination of a presidential candidate or from the perspective of its impact on local politics. We have elected to discuss the Jackson phenomenon as it influenced the development of black politics of the state and local levels. Although the returns are far from final, the important consequences of the Jackson candidacy clearly will be felt for some time at the state and local levels. In Maryland, especially in Prince George's County and Baltimore City, the Jackson candidacy provided an issue framework and a media context for the emergence of latent conflicts rooted in local Democratic party politics.

Presidential politics involving the recruitment and nomination of candidates usually does not arouse political issues based in local political and social relations. The issues are usually framed in national and international terms and debated at a level that requires only passive participation by the average citizen. The Maryland Jackson campaign sought to change this arrangement. The "politics of exclusion" practiced by the local leadership of the Maryland

Democratic party became the most important issue addressed by the Maryland Jackson campaign. Because of the Maryland Jackson committee's approach, the idea of being "locked out" ceased to be a primary or general election question and became an issue continuously debated in Maryland politics long after the presidential election. It is very unlikely that such local party issue conflicts would have been opened and discussed to the point they have but for Jesse Jackson's candidacy.

The real effect of Jackson's presidential effort in Maryland must not be measured only by the primary and general election vote totals or the success or failure of the bargaining process at the Democratic National Convention. It must also be evaluated in terms of the degree to which it facilitated organization, issue development, and expertise identification and utilization peculiar to state and local political empowerment objectives of the black community and other disenfranchised segments of Maryland. In these dimensions the Jackson campaign was largely successful and effective. Still some basic questions remain about the Jackson campaign in Maryland. Will electoral possibilities at the local level be advanced in the wake of the Jackson candidacy? To what extent did the Jackson candidacy inform and clarify the black agenda? Did the candidacy catalyze the formation of progressive organizations at the local level which, in turn, will facilitate the recruitment of future black leadership? How has and will entrenched white political leadership respond to the Jackson campaign and the Rainbow Coalition? Will the legacy of the Jackson campaign be sufficient to sustain the long-term interests and support of rank-and-file black people necessary to achieve the objectives sought?

Insofar as the politics of campaign finance, voter registration, voter education, voter mobilization, and campaign management are concerned, the Jackson campaign produced significant benefits. Jackson's supporters, many of whom had no previous experience in traditional politics, met with enviable success in fundraising, registering many new voters (mostly in Prince George's County), and developing an elaborate campaign organization. New electoral possibilites were clarified and opened up by the Jackson campaign as black leaders, party leaders, and others became aware of the response rank-and-file voters would give to a dynamic candidate who discusses issues of importance to them. No electoral effort in the past had ever so graphically clarified the potential voting strength in the black community and that of other disenfranchised constituencies in the state as did the Jackson campaign. Thus the furthering of the black agenda was an important consequence of the Jackson 1984 Maryland presidential campaign.

NOTES

1. State Administrative Board of Elections, *Primary Election Returns and Voter Turnout and Statistics,* Annapolis, Maryland.

2. Mack H. Jones, "Black Political Empowerment in Atlanta: Myth and Realty," *AAPSS* 439 (September 1978): 91.

3. Ibid., p. 92.

4. The Ad Hoc Committee on Quality Education in Prince George's County, "The Challenge to Achieve Quality Education in Prince George's County, Maryland" (Unpublished Manuscript, April 30, 1985), p. 4.

5. Congressional Black Caucus Brain Trust and the National Black Leadership Roundtable, *National Black Leadership Roundtable Voter Registration Plan, 1983–84*, June 11, 1983.

6. Charles County is part of Maryland's First Congressional District, which takes up all the counties on the state's eastern shore. Small pockets of black people are sparsely scattered in Charles, Wicomico, Dorchester, and Somerset counties.

7. Of the twenty-four black elected officials in Baltimore City, only six identified themselves with the Jackson candidacy, in spite of the fact that Jackson swept the contested delegate and alternate slots in his congressional district in the May 8 primary election.

8. Maryland's ninety-nine delegates were allocated by the Democratic National Committee in the following manner:

$$\text{National formula: } A = \frac{1}{2} \frac{(\text{SDV '72, '76, '80} = \text{SEV})}{(105, 484, 250, 538)}$$

A = Allocation factor; SDV = State Democratic Vote; SEV = State Electoral Vote. Maryland's allocation factor was .01873375
Preliminary Call For the 1984 Democratic National Convention, February 5, 1983.

9. Christopher Edley, Jr., has written: "Perhaps he should minimize his time spent on reforming the party and the attitudes of its officers and maximize the time spent on reforming policies and attitudes of the nation. If he inspires the public, party functionaries will pay homage enough." Edley also felt that a "brawl over rules is dangerously diverting." See "Jesse Jackson v. Party Rules," *Washington Post*, December 27, 1983, A-19.

10. The commission required that at least 75 percent of the delegates in nonprimary states be elected in open caucuses at the precinct, district, or other regional level and not at the state convention. All such meetings for the party were to be scheduled well in advance, held in easily accessible locations, and well publicized. It banned the proxy, the automatic delegate, and the unity rule. An affirmative action plan was also provided for. See *Mandate for Reform* (Washington, D.C.: Democratic National Committee, 1970), pp. 33–48.

11. See "Bring Back the Polls," *New Republic*, March 22, 1980, p. 8. Structuring in predictability of issue positions by delegates has been one of the primary objectives of party leaders. State delegations have had consistent issue focus over time. To a significant degree the process used to select delegates has reinforced this tendency. See Anne H. Costain, "An Analysis of Voting in American National Conventions, 1940–1976," *American Political Quarterly* 6., no. 1 (January 1978): 99.

12. Ibid.

13. Nelson W. Polsby, cited in David S. Broder, "Is Jesse Jackson. . . ?," *Washington Post*, December 14, 1983, A-23.

14. See the Maryland Democratic Central Committee, *Maryland Delegate Selection for the Democratic National Convention, 1984,* p. 1.

15. Maryland's adoption of the DNC's threshold requirement provided for the following: "At-large delegates and alternates shall be allocated according to the division of preference among district level delegates at the time of the district level selection, providing that a threshold of 20 percent is met. If no preference reaches the applicable level, the threshold shall be the highest percentage received minus 10 percent." Ibid., p. 5.

16. The leadership of the Maryland Jackson committee understood that the trust of the challenge had to be based on "the strength of all deprived and rejected constituencies using the moral force and political energy of the black movement." See Andrew Kopkind, "Black Power in the Age of Jackson," *The Nation,* November 26, 1983, p. 530.

17. Maryland Democratic Central Committee, *Delegate Selection Rules for the 1984 Democratic National Convention,* Paragraphs C and D of Rule 1. This requirement resulted from the work of the McGovern-Fraser Commission, which mandated that delegates were to be chosen through processes which "assure all Democratic voters full, timely, and equal opportunity to participate and include affirmative action programs to that end." This language was a compromise from stronger provisions that addressed the inclusion of various minorities in the nomination process by guaranteeing adequate representation of their views. Women, blacks, and liberal reformers saw affirmative action as being very important in 1974, and this concern was continued in the Maryland Jackson committee's charge that the Maryland Democratic party was not implementing its affirmative action plan. See Robert Blank, *Political Parties* (Englewood Cliffs, N.J.: Prentice-Hall, Inc., 1980), pp. 346–47, and *Mandate for Reform* (Washington, D.C.: Democratic National Committee,1970), pp. 33–48.

18. *Delegate Selection Rules,* Rule 6, Para D.

19. Maryland Jackson for President Committee to Maryland Democratic party, p. 3. See also David Broder and Milton Coleman, "Democratic Rules Pact Collapses," *Washington Post,* January 21, 1984, A-1, 4.

20. *Maryland Delegate Selection,* Section B, p. 5.

21. Ibid., p. 11.

22. Jackson for President Committee to Maryland Democratic party central committee, p. 3.

23. In 1980 Reagan lost the general election by only 45,555 votes; this notwithstanding the fact that Maryland is a one-party state controlled by Democrats. It is curious that the state party would make the money-based promises in its delegate selection rules when it knew that it lacked the funds to carry them out.

24. Jackson for President Committee to Maryland Democratic Party Central Committee, p. 4.

25. Paul Allen Beck, "Environment and Party: The Impact of Political and Demographic County Characteristics on Party Behavior," *American Political Science Review* 68 (September 1974): 1243.

26. The 20 percent threshold rule, which the Maryland Jackson committee strongly opposed, applied to the forty-two delegates. See note 4 for an explanation of this rule. The concern about the gap between the popular vote for Jackson and the number of

delegates allocated to him, as expressed in Jackson's May 19, 1985 letter to the Democratic National Committee, was not manifested in the Maryland campaign because Jackson's delegate and popular vote percentages were roughly the same. In fact, in Maryland Jackson received one percent more delegates than votes. See "Jackson Says a Floor Fight Might Be Waged Over Rules," *Washington Post,* May 20, 1984, A-4.

27. Although the rules are fairly specific about how at-large positions are to be allocated, there is some room for discretion by the central committee. See *Maryland Delegate Selection,* pp. 4, 5.

28. The party and elected official category resulted from the Hunt Commission's desire to partially structure party responsibility into the delegate selection process. In Maryland, and other states where most high-level party and elected officials are male and white, such a provision could be very exclusionary of the Democratic party's most loyal constituencies.

29. See the unpublished "Testimony of the Maryland Committee for Jesse Jackson" presented before the temporary state platform committee on June 5, 1984, in Forestville, Maryland, pp. 11–12.

30. See "Strategies for Improving Participation in The Maryland Democratic Party: A Winning Combination for the November 1984 General Election" (unpublished letter from the Jackson for President Committee to the Maryland Democratic Party) August 2, 1984.

31. The Jackson committee anticipated that the black vote would be crucial to the Mondale-Ferraro Maryland campaign. Discussion of the DNC-based demands were couched in that context. The data provided below indicate that this assumption was well founded.

Presidential elections in Maryland: percentage Democratic vote

1984 Rank	Subdivision	1984	1980	Diff.
1	Baltimore City	71.2	72.5	(-1.3)
2	Prince George's	58.6	50.9	$+7.7$
3	Montgomery	49.7	39.8	$+9.9$
4	Howard	41.7	40.1	$+1.6$
5	Calvert	39.4	43.7	(-4.3)
6	Charles	38.8	40.4	(-1.6)
7	Baltimore	38.1	43.3	(-5.2)
8	Kent	37.8	47.4	(-9.6)
9	St. Mary's	36.3	42.2	(-5.9)
10	Alleghany	35.7	38.6	(-2.9)
11	Somerset	35.0	48.2	(-13.2)
12	Cecil	33.6	42.1	(-7.5)
13	Wicomico	33.5	43.1	(-9.6)
14	Anne Arundel	33.4	38.6	(-5.2)
15	Washington	32.8	36.1	(-3.3)
16	Dorchester	31.7	46.5	(-14.8)

17	Worchester	31.4	41.0	(−9.6)
18	Hartford	31.4	39.3	(−7.9)
19	Frederick	31.1	34.8	(−3.8)
20	Caroline	31.0	41.9	(−10.9)
21	Queen Anne's	30.1	41.9	(−11.8)
22	Talbot	28.4	37.3	(−8.9)
23	Garrett	25.2	31.7	(−6.5)
24	Carroll	24.6	31.6	(−7.0)
Maryland		47.02	47.1	(−.98)

Source: "Campaign '84—Wrap Up Memorandum," prepared by John T. Willis for the Maryland Democratic Party, December 4, 1984.

32. Structured incrementation in Maryland politics is an issue for future research. The lag in black political empowerment in Baltimore City and Prince George's County partially can be explained by this phenomenon.

Did Jesse Jackson Cause a White Backlash against the Democrats? A Look at the 1984 Presidential Election

## 10

John F. Zipp

For over three decades social scientists have been concerned with the notion of white backlash against social, economic, and political gains by blacks. Research has focused on a variety of topics: voting behavior,[1] resistance to racial integration,[2] opposition to school desegregation,[3] reaction to the Voting Rights and Civil Rights acts,[4] and relatedly, white defection from the Democratic party as a result of Democratic support for these acts,[5] and support for George Wallace.[6] Essentially, at the base of this literature is the thesis that various groups of whites (e.g., southerners) will react to the real or perceived threat of black empowerment through increased racism or through conservative resistance to any changes in the status quo.

Jesse Jackson's campaign for the Democratic presidential nomination gave rise once again to this thesis. First and foremost, Jackson's candidacy had a tremendous substantive and symbolic effect on the politics of black Americans. As the first black to seriously compete for the presidential nomination on a majority party ticket, Jackson stirred the hopes of black Americans. However, his success also affected white Americans and revived arguments concerning "white fear." A number of experts contended simply that Jackson's success drove whites, especially southern ones, away from the Democratic party.[7] Although this argument may have some face validity, given the racial polarization in the 1984 election, this essay will test it empirically by specifically addressing two issues: (1) did Jackson's success spur white defections from the Democratic party in general; and (2) were defections, if any, concentrated among certain segments of the New Deal coalition?

Jesse Jackson, Race, and the 1984 Election

The 1984 election was marked by extreme racial polarization. According to the New York Times/CBS News national exit poll, while 90 percent of blacks voted for Mondale, only 34 percent of whites did. Southern whites were even less likely to support the Democratic nominee: only 28 percent voted for Mondale. For the first time in history, a majority of Southern whites did not identify themselves as Democrats.[8] Results like these led Senator Daniel Patrick Moynihan (D. N.Y.) to claim that, on the national level, the Democrats are seen as the party which appeals mainly to minority groups.[9]

Many saw the increasing black strength in the Democratic party in general and the success of Jesse Jackson in particular as part of the reason for the Democrat's poor performance among whites. Wilson Carey McWilliams noted that southern whites, already alarmed at black power in the Democratic party, were frightened even more by Jackson.[10] Ladd also assigned race a crucial role in driving southern whites away from Mondale in 1984.[11] Shoch perhaps said it best: "White Southern voters clearly defected from the Democrats in reaction to Jesse Jackson's sustained registration and mobilization of Southern black votes."[12]

There was some indirect evidence for these sorts of conclusions. From January 1983 to April 1984, over 183,000 new black voters were registered in just five states—Alabama, North and South Carolina, Georgia, and Louisiana.[13] Partly as a response to this, the Republicans engaged in a massive voter registration drive and indeed registered more new voters than did the Democrats in the South.[14] At least partially due to the emergent strength of Jesse Jackson, in Louisiana political officials attempted to cancel the primary and urged citizens to boycott it. Finally, the failure of two blacks to win congressional seats in predominantly black districts in Mississippi and South Carolina, an event that black congressman Walter Fauntroy feared would result from a black presidential candidacy, was linked to Jackson.[15]

This evidence for a white backlash against Jesse Jackson is, at the risk of understatement, far from overwhelming. Yet it has been widely accepted —so much so that future directions for the Democratic party are based on this conclusion. Right after the 1984 election, then national Democratic party chair Charles Manatt said that, among other things, the Democrats have to go after the "blue collar vote." (The obvious interpretation is that, despite labor's strong and early support for Mondale, there are some aspects of the Democrats' message—e.g., support for racial justice—that blue-collar workers don't find appealing.) In party discussions about their future, Democrats have deliberately started to gear their appeals more to "middle America," even at the risk of alienating some groups, especially blacks.[16]

Thus the existence of white backlash against Jesse Jackson apparently has both scholarly and practical implications, and therefore its presence should be ascertained by solid empirical testing.

Data and Methods

The data for this analysis primarily comes from the 1984 American National Election Study (ANES) conducted by the University of Michigan. It is a multistage area probability sample, with a total sample size of 2,257. These are high quality data familiar to anyone working in the area of electoral behavior. The ANES contains information on voting in the presidential election, along with other attitudinal, social, and demographic variables. As such, it allows for a careful examination of voting preferences in the 1984 presidential election. It does not, however, have any direct information on our central hypothesis —namely, whether white voting in the presidential election was partially a function of Jesse Jackson's success in the primaries. For this information we had to turn elsewhere.

Many studies of white reaction to black empowerment, especially in the South, have found an association between white racism, fear, and backlash and black demographic concentration in the immediate political environment. Perhaps the classic work in this tradition is V. O. Key's *Southern Politics,* in which Key argued that white racism was greater in areas in which blacks were more concentrated. In these areas whites were much more threatened by blacks. Given the historical importance of the county as a political unit, typically the county was used as the unit of analysis; concentration usually has been measured by the percentage of county residents who were black. This "concentration" hypothesis has received a good deal of empirical support.[17]

We propose to adopt a similar strategy here; however, instead of using black demographic concentration to measure the black "threat" to whites, we shall use the support that Jackson received in the primary. The argument here is that if white fear caused white defections from the Democratic party, then we might expect that these defections occurred at a rate proportional to blacks' political success, measured by Jackson's showing in the primary. Thus, where Jackson did well in the primary, white fear should be high, and this would be reflected in low support for the Democrats in the subsequent presidential election. Conversely, if voting by whites was largely unrelated to Jackson's strength, then the white fear hypothesis would not be supported.

This analytical strategy required us to collect information on Jackson's performance in the various states at the county level and then to match this information to respondents in the ANES survey. The ANES includes a code for all respondents, listing their states and counties of residence, and we used these codes for matching. Because no one agency collected information in performance in the primaries at the county level for all the states, we gathered this ourselves.

We initially hoped to get Jackson's share of the primary vote (at the county level) in each state that held a primary and Jackson's share of delegates (at the county level) in each state that held a caucus. Although it is easy to argue how the former is the relevant reference group for white fear, it is not so easy to do so for the latter, for a number of reasons. First, the state Democratic parties run the caucuses, and they differ widely in their operation. Second, the caucuses often are not conducted at the county level (e.g., in Missouri where townships and wards are used), or results are not reported at the county level (e.g., Washington), or counties are buried in larger districts (e.g., one district in Kansas includes eighty-five counties). Because of these, we decided that in caucus states information on county support was not a reliable indicator of Jackson's "threat." Thus, data at the county level were analyzed only for the states included in the ANES which conducted primary elections.[18]

This strategy meant that we would not include in our analyses respondents who lived in states which held presidential caucuses.[19] We felt that our results would be more generalizeable if we could include them. Thus, in addition to measuring white fear by Jackson's success at the county level, we also calculated it as Jackson's success at the state level. These figures were widely reported and certainly can serve as a reference level for voters. It also is worth noting that at least one researcher examining the concentration hypothesis found black demographic concentration at the state level to have more explanatory ability than concentration at the county level.[20]

In our analyses, then, we will seek to determine if there is any systematic relationship between Jackson's performance in gathering support both at the county (primary only states) and the state (both primary and caucus states) levels and Democratic voting for president.

Results

We felt it would be best to begin by presenting some basic information on the range of support for Jesse Jackson in the counties and states under study. In table 1 we have listed the percentage of support, rounded to the nearest integer, that Jackson received in the primary. At the county level Jackson's share of the vote ranged from 2 percent to 39 percent. At the state level Jackson got from 0 to 27 percent of the vote or delegates.[21]

Having described our measures of Jesse Jackson's threat to whites, we now can test to see if these are related to voting for Walter Mondale in the 1984 presidential election. Since our dependent variable (voting for Mondale vs. Reagan) was dichotomous, we chose to use logistic regression to analyze these issues. Essentially we have conducted separate logistic regression equations of Mondale voting on Jackson's support in the primaries at the county level and at the state level. Instead of presenting the logistic coefficients themselves, we felt that our results would be more accessible if we graphed the estimated probabilities of voting for Mondale across levels of Jackson's support.[22] In each

Table 1. Jesse Jackson's support among white voters in the primaries at the county and state levels

County			State	
%	N		%	N
2	(14)		0	(78)
3	(63)		1	(50)
4	(74)		2	(54)
5	(18)		3	(96)
6	(13)		4	(37)
7	(29)		5	(69)
8	(139)		7	(71)
9	(5)		9	(58)
10	(195)		10	(52)
11	(79)		12	(120)
12	(4)		14	(47)
13	(64)		16	(143)
14	(10)		17	(278)
16	(47)		18	(25)
17	(43)		20	(303)
18	(17)		21	(97)
19	(13)		24	(58)
20	(73)		25	(155)
21	(65)		26	(161)
22	(7)		27	(26)
23	(15)		Total	(1968)
26	(22)			
28	(79)			
30	(9)			
31	(40)			
33	(50)			
35	(4)			
38	(6)			
39	(4)			
Total	(1201)			

Source: State Election Boards and State Democratic Parties
Note: Percentages are rounded to nearest integer. This table's entries are to be interpreted as follows: taking the county variable, the first entry in this column means that 14 white voters lived in counties where Jackson got 2 percent of the votes in the primary. State figures are similarly interpreted.

case, the results for the county level are represented by a solid line and those for the state level by a dashed line. When we refer to a statistically significant effect, we mean that the variable was significant in the logistic analysis.

In figure 1 we have plotted the Democratic presidential vote as a function of Jackson's primary vote at the county level and at the state level. With respect to the former, quite surprisingly there is a positive, though nonsignificant, relationship between Jackson's support and Democratic voting. In counties where Jackson did worst, Mondale got 34 percent of the vote. In counties where Jackson did the best, Mondale received 41 percent of the vote. At the state level, there is a clearer pattern—a significant decline in Democratic voting as Jackson strength increases. In states in which Jackson fared the poorest, Mondale received 43 percent of the vote; where Jackson ran the best, Mondale received 32 percent. Although this decline is statistically significant, it is not that great in magnitude. Thus, there is some support at the state, but not the county, level for the hypothesis that Jackson weakened the Democratic allegiance among white voters.

Although there may be a weak association between Jackson's strength and Democratic voting among all white voters, a more careful examination of the hypothesis requires more precise testing. The hypothesis implies that Jackson's threat drove white voters who *normally*—i.e., in the absence of a black candidate—would have voted Democratic to vote Republican. Without interviewing people both before and after Jackson's candidacy, it is impossible to assess this directly; however, we attempted to address it indirectly. To do this, we needed groups of people who might be expected to vote Democratic under normal circumstances. We first thought of Democratic party identifiers, given the long-standing association between party identification and normal voting.[23] The problem with this is that the same forces which could have led one to vote Republican also could have caused a switch in party identification, and thus using Democrats only might miss the effects of Jackson.[24] A second strategy was to examine the behavior of traditional Democrats—groups that comprised the New Deal coalition and that over the years have provided the core support for Democratic candidates. In our case, these groups were white southerners, Catholics, union members, blue-collar workers, and low income families.[25] We thus will replicate the analyses reported in Figure 1 for each of the groups in the New Deal coalition.

Figure 2 contains the results for blue-collar workers. Jackson's strength at the county and state levels had opposite effects on Democratic voting. At the county level there was a (nonsignificant) positive relationship between Jackson's and Mondale's vote among blue-collar workers. Where Jackson did best, Mondale did well also, and vice versa. At the state level there was a (nonsignificant) negative relationship between these two variables. Since neither is statistically significant and since they conflict, overall there is little

Figure 1. Mondale vote by Jackson share of the primary vote

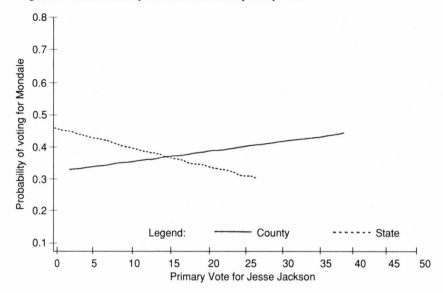

Figure 2. Mondale vote by Jackson share of the primary vote: Blue collar workers

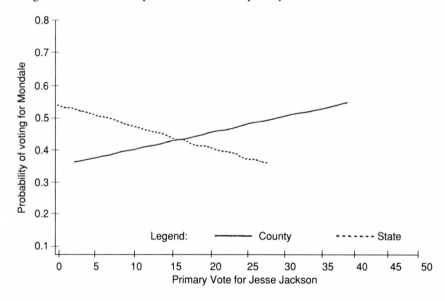

Source: 1984 American National Election Study, State Election Boards,
and State Democratic Parties

evidence on which to base the claim that blue-collar workers defected from voting Democratic as a result of white fear.

We have plotted the results for union members in figure 3. In each instance there was a negative relationship between Mondale's and Jackson's vote. Mondale's share of the two-party vote decreased slightly with Jackson's support at the county level. At the state level, however, the results are much different. Voting for Mondale declines serially as a function of the state's support for Jackson in the nomination process. Where Jackson fared most poorly, Mondale got 74 percent of the votes of union members; conversely, where Jackson gathered the most support, Mondale registered his worst showing, getting only 36 percent of the votes of unionists. This, then, is solid evidence which backs the thesis that some groups of white voters rejected the Democrats due to Jesse Jackson.

Figure 4 contains the results for Catholics. Catholic voting for Mondale vs. Reagan exhibit a slight decline as Jackson's showing at the county level increases. Forty-four percent of Catholics who lived in counties where Jackson ran the worst voted Democratic, while only 34 percent who lived in counties where Jackson ran well did the same. Jackson's performance at the state level had a similar, though significant, negative relationship with Democratic voting among Catholics, with the latter declining from 57 percent to 35 percent across Jackson's support. Taken together, this represents additional evidence that Catholics defected from the Democrats in response to Jesse Jackson.

The analyses for low-income respondents are plotted in figure 5. Jackson's performance at the county level had a positive, though not statistically significant, impact on Democratic voting among those with low income. At the state level just the reverse occurred, as there was a negative nonsignificant relationship between Mondale's support and Jackson's. Thus, there is not very much support for the white fear hypothesis among low-income groups.

Figure 6 contains the plot of Democratic voting by Jesse Jackson's vote among southerners. Again the results for the county and state levels are in opposite directions, although neither is statistically significant. At the county level there is a general negative relationship between these two variables, with Mondale's support reaching its zenith among southerners who lived in counties where Jackson polled the fewest votes. In contrast, there is a very weak relationship between voting Democratic and state support for Jackson among southerners. Mondale's support ranged only from 36 percent to 30 percent across levels of Jackson's performance. Overall, then, there is not much evidence for the white fear hypothesis among white southerners.

What can we conclude from these results? Jackson's performance was significantly related to voting Democratic in three of twelve instances: among all white voters, among the union members and among Catholic subsamples. In each case Jackson's support, measured at the state level, reduced voting for

Figure 3. Mondale vote by Jackson share of the primary vote: Union members

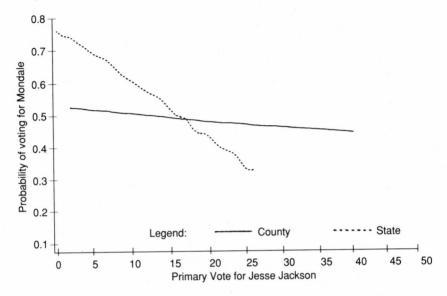

Figure 4. Mondale vote by Jackson share of the primary vote: Catholics

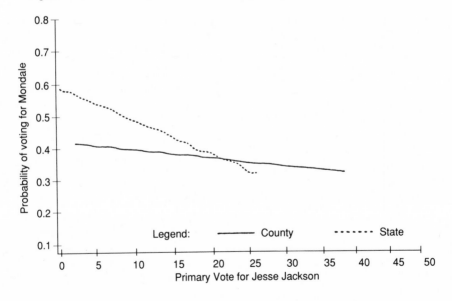

Source: 1984 American National Election Study, State Election Boards,
and State Democratic Parties

Figure 5. Mondale vote by Jackson share of the primary vote: Low income respondents

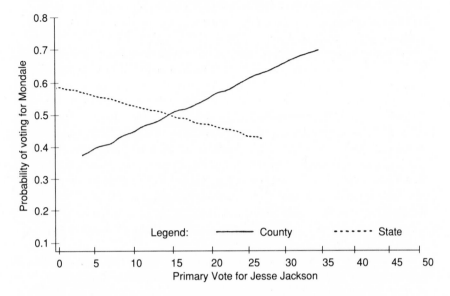

Figure 6. Mondale vote by Jackson share of the primary vote: Southerners

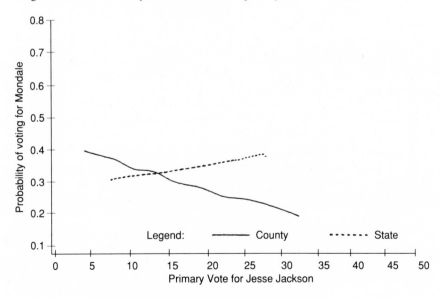

Source: 1984 American National Election Study, State Election Boards,
and State Democratic Parties

Mondale. Of the nonsignificant relationships five were in the same negative direction and four were positive. Although it can hardly be said that there is an overwhelming amount of support for the white backlash hypothesis, the evidence presented here should not be dismissed lightly, especially since any errors in measurement would attenuate the observed relationships and perhaps prompt us to fail to reject an erroneous null hypothesis. Thus, even modest evidence of white backlash to Jesse Jackson may be substantively significant.

To place a greater degree of faith in the presence of white backlash against Jackson, we conducted a similar set of logistic regression analyses. The logic of using Jackson's primary showing as an index of black threat was based on the substantial literature which used some form of black demographic concentration to measure black threat. Since black concentration and Jackson's support may be positively related, white voters who rejected the Democrats may have reacted not to Jackson but rather to the sheer percentage of blacks in the geographical area. And since black demographic concentration precedes Jackson's support in a causal sequence, the relationship between voting for Jackson and for Mondale may be spurious.

Given this, we have replicated the logistic regressions, this time including the percentage of blacks (at either the county or state level, whichever is appropriate) as another independent variable. In these analyses we want to assess whether Jackson had an independent effect, over and above that of black demographic concentration, on Democratic presidential voting. Once again we have plotted these results, and they are contained in figures 7–12. Because in logistic regression the effect of Jackson's vote on Mondale's vote is not constant across levels of black population concentration, plotting required us to "fix" the value of the latter. It is customary to do so at the mean, and thus all our subsequent plots exhibit the estimated probability of voting for Mondale across levels of Jackson's support with black concentration held at its mean value.

Figure 7 contains these results for all white voters. Controlling for the effects of black concentration in the county, Jackson's performance in the primary has a statistically significant, positive impact on voting Democratic. A similar, though not statistically significant, relationship exists at the state level, as Jackson's and Mondale's support increases together. In both cases black demographic concentration has a significant negative effect on voting for Mondale (results not reported). Thus, white fear operated more as a response to black population density than to Jesse Jackson.

In figures 8, 9, and 10 we have reported the results for the subsamples of blue-collar workers, union members, and Catholics, respectively. In all these groups and at both levels there is no significant relationship between Jackson's support and voting Democratic in the presidential election. The trends for blue-collar workers and union members are positive, while Catholics exhibit

Figure 7. Mondale vote by Jackson share of the primary vote: White voters

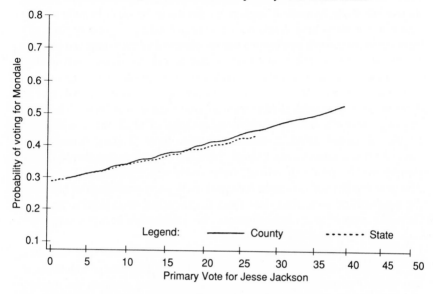

Figure 8. Mondale vote by Jackson share of the primary vote: Blue collar workers

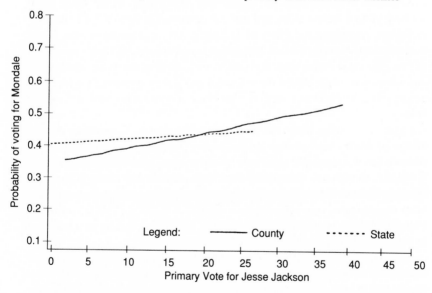

Source: 1984 American National Election Study, State Election Boards,
    and State Democratic Parties, and 1980 U. S. Census of Population

Figure 9. Mondale vote by Jackson share of the primary vote: Union members

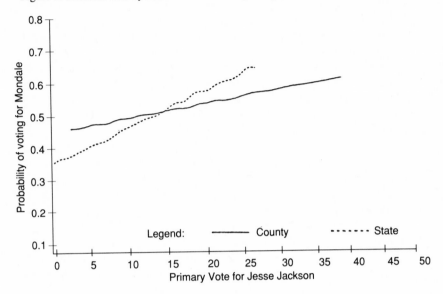

Figure 10. Mondale vote by Jackson share of the primary vote: Catholics

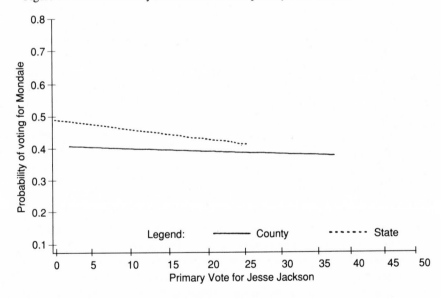

Source: 1984 American National Election Study, State Election Boards,
and State Democratic Parties, and 1980 U. S. Census of Population

only the slightest negative effects. Only among union members does black concentration have a significant effect, and at both the county and state levels increased black concentration is related to decreased Democratic voting.

The results for low-income families and for southerners are plotted in figures 11 and 12. Among both groups at both levels there is a positive relationship between Jackson's performance in the primary and Mondale's in the presidential election. This relationship is significant only among low-income families at the county level and among southerners at the state level. Finally, except for the county results for southerners, black concentration has a significant impact on voting for Mondale.

Taken in total, the findings graphed in figures 7 through 12 present no evidence for the argument that Jesse Jackson caused a white backlash against the Democratic party. If anything, once the black population concentration is taken into consideration, Jackson's showing was modestly related to increased Democratic voting among whites.

In general terms, we have not found very much support for the claim that white voters rejected the Democratic party because of the success of Jesse Jackson. In twelve bivariate comparisons (figures 1–6) there were only three instances in which there was a statistically significant negative relationship between support for Jesse Jackson and voting for Mondale in the presidential election. When black population concentration was included in our analyses (see figures 7–12), Jackson's showing was positively related to Democratic voting in three of twelve instances. Thus it appears, based on these analyses, that white backlash against Jesse Jackson probably did not play a major role in the 1984 election.

Before discussing this further, we must note several limitations of our findings. First, although we have not found evidence for a white backlash to Jackson, we did find that, in seven of twelve possible cases, black demographic concentration had a significant negative relation to Democratic voting among whites. Although further examination of this is required, this tentatively shows the existence of white fear. It could also mean that Jackson, just by being a serious candidate, fanned the fires of this fear and that white backlash surfaced, not necessarily where Jackson did well, but where blacks were demographically concentrated.

Second, white backlash against Jackson could have existed in certain instances, such as the congressional races in Mississippi and South Carolina, which were beyond the scope of this analysis. Our results certainly do not preclude this. Third, our measure of Jackson's threat—his performance at the county and state levels in the primary—assumes that it is the relative amount of support Jackson received in the particular geographical area in which one resides that causes consternation about black empowerment. It could be that

Figure 11. Mondale vote by Jackson share of the primary vote: Low income respondents

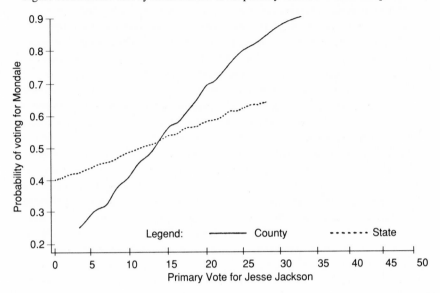

Figure 12. Mondale vote by Jackson share of the primary vote: Southerners

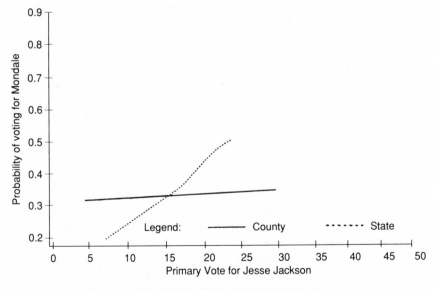

Source: 1984 American National Election Study, State Election Boards,
    and State Democratic Parties, and 1980 U. S. Census of Population

Jackson's success *anywhere* led to white defections from the Democrats. Although similar measures of black concentration have been used frequently in the past in testing the white fear hypothesis, any weakness in it as a measure of white fear would attenuate the relationship between it and voting Democratic. This then would make us somewhat less likely to reject the null hypothesis of no relationship between Jackson's support and Democrat voting. Although we have no way of unequivocally ruling out this possibility, the facts that concentration measures have proved successful in previous research and that we obtained markedly similar results in examining this relationship in a variety of social groups lead us to believe that it is not a serious problem. Regardless, the reader should be advised to temper our conclusions with the above caveats.

This having been said, speculations about Jackson's role in driving away white voters needs to be placed in a broader framework. Perhaps the best place to start is by noting that the New Deal coalition, which was the bedrock of Democratic support, has been withering away for the past two decades. Although Carter briefly revived it in 1976, a number of analysts are now debating whether or not we are undergoing a new partisan realignment.[26] Our purpose is not to enter this debate but rather to note that the demise of the New Deal coalition's traditional voting allegiances began before Jesse Jackson was a political candidate, with the most recent break-up beginning between 1976 and 1980. Indeed, although racial polarization was substantial in 1984, with only 34 percent of white voters and 90 percent of black voters voting Democratic, often overlooked is the fact that in 1980 only 38 percent of whites and fully 85 percent of blacks voted for Carter.[27] Furthermore, as Pomper observed, only 10 percent of voters switched their preferences between the 1980 and 1984 presidential elections, and among the groups we analyzed, the only significant changes were among white southerners.[28] Thus, Jackson could have a minimal impact on all but white southerners, and as we have seen here, he had no consistent effect on their voting behavior. Scholars, therefore, should turn their attention to explaining the 1976–80 changes rather than focusing on Jesse Jackson.

In terms of the real world of politics, although Jackson's candidacy did not cause much of a white threat at the mass level, it may have done so at an elite level. As a number of scholars have noted, three major distinct groups now comprise the Democratic party, and each had a major candidate in the 1984 presidential nominating campaign.[29] Mondale represented the old New Deal Democrats—union members, working- and lower-middle-class families, etc.—and his calls were directed at the interests of these groups—traditional liberalism, the revival of basic industry, and so forth. Gary Hart represented one of two alternatives to this. He found his support among more affluent, socially liberal, yet fiscally conservative Democrats who tied themselves more to the growing sectors of the economy. Hart's economic solutions were geared much more to advances in high-tech industries rather than to a revival of the basic goods-producing ones. Jackson represented the second alternative to the traditional Democrats. He found his support among the more marginal groups in society—blacks, Hispanics, and so forth. Jackson's programs were aimed at the problems of these groups—increased social spending, equality, etc.

Mondale's sizeable defeat in 1984 means that the traditional liberal center (usually referred to as the "left") of the Democratic party has been severely weakened. Although there may be attempts to revive it, the struggle could be between the neo-liberals like Hart, Senator Bill Bradley (D. N.J.), and others, and people like Jesse Jackson. If Jackson is seen as pushing white voters to the Republican party, then power will fall more easily into the hands of the neo-liberals. In policy terms, it will be easier then for Democratic candidates to let concern for social justice fall by the wayside: it could more easily be seen as a political albatross, weighing heavily on the necks of any major political candidate. This, then, may be the real backlash which has resulted from Jackson's candidacy. Perhaps the figures here will help to undercut the thesis on which this is based and also undermine any possible changes based on it.

NOTES

1. V. O. Key, Jr., *Southern Politics* (New York: Knopf, 1949); Donald R. Matthews and James W. Prothro, "Social and Economic Factors and Negro Voter Registration in the South," *American Political Science Review* 57 (March 1963): 24–44.

2. Thomas F. Pettigrew, "Regional Variations on Anti-Negro Prejudice," *Journal of Abnormal Psychology* 59 (July 1959): 28–36; "Demographic Correlates of Border-State Desegregation," *American Sociological Review* 22 (December 1957): 683–89.

3. Lillian B. Rubin, *Busing and Backlash* (Berkeley: University of California Press, 1972).

4. Donald L. Davidson, "The Political Consequences of the Voting Rights Act of 1965" (Ph.D. dissertation, Washington University, 1985).

5. Norman H. Nie, Sydney Verba, and John Petrocik, *The Changing American Voter* (Cambridge: Harvard University Press, 1976).

6. Robert A. Schoenberger and David R. Segal, "The Ecology of Dissent: The Southern Wallace Vote in 1958," *Midwest Journal of Political Science* 15 (August 1971): 583–86.

7. Dennis Altman, "A New Barbarism," *Socialist Review* 16 (January–February 1985): 7–12; David S. Broder and Milton Coleman, "The South Is Solid Again-For the GOP," *Washington Post National Weekly Edition,* November 12, 1984, p. 14; Allen Hunter, "What Explains the Conservative Shift?," *Socialist Review* 16 (January–February 1985): 29–33; Everett Carl Ladd, "On Mandates, Realignments, and the 1984 Presidential Election," *Political Science Quarterly* 100 (Spring 1985): 1–25; Wilson Carey McWilliams, "The Meaning of the Election," in *The Election of 1984,*

ed. Gerald M. Pomper (Chatham, N.J.: Chatham House, 1985), pp. 157–83; Jim Shoch, "Politics in Post-Industrial America: The 1984 Presidential Campaign," *Socialist Review* 14 (September–October 1984): 7–31; Ronald Smothers, "Election Results Troubling Blacks," *New York Times,* November 9, 1984, A-20.

8. Ladd, "On Mandates, Realignments, and the 1984 Presidential Election," 21–22.

9. John Herbers, "Party Looks Inward for Ways to Regain Majority," *New York Times,* November 8, 1984, A-24.

10. McWilliams, "The Meaning of the Election," 174.

11. Ladd, "On Mandates, Realignments, and the 1984 Presidential Election," 13.

12. Shoch, "Politics in Post-Industrial America," 39.

13. Manning Marable, "Jackson and the Rise of the Rainbow Coalition," *New Left Review* 149 (January–February 1985): 3–44.

14. Gerald M. Pomper, "The Presidential Election," in *The Election of 1984,* Ed. Pomper, pp. 1–34.

15. Marable, "Jackson and the Rise of the Rainbow Coalition," 10; Smothers, "Election Results Troubling Blacks."

16. Phil Gailey, "Democratic Group, On Trip, Seeks Political Mainstream," *New York Times,* May 19, 1985, 13; "Slouching toward the Center (Post-Reagan)," *New York Times,* September 18, 1985, 18.

17. For a summary, see Gerald C. Wright, Jr., "Contextual Models of Electoral Behavior: The Southern Wallace Vote," *American Political Science Review* 71 (June 1977): 497–508.

18. These were Alabama, California, Connecticut, Florida, Georgia, Illinois, Indiana, Maryland, Massachusetts, New Hampshire, New Jersey, New York, North Carolina, Ohio, Oregon, Pennsylvania, Tennessee, and West Virginia.

19. The caucus states included in the 1984 ANES were Arkansas, Colorado, Iowa, Kansas, Michigan, Minnesota, Missouri, Texas, Virginia, Washington, Wisconsin, and Wyoming.

20. Wright, "Contextual Models of Electoral Behavior."

21. In no state included in this survey did Jackson get 0 percent of the votes or delegates. In Wyoming Jackson received .4 percent of the delegates, and this was rounded down to 0 percent.

22. The calculation of these probabilities is rather straightforward. See Eric A. Hanushek and John E. Jackson, *Statistical Methods for Social Scientists* (New York: Academic Press, 1977).

23. Philip E. Converse, "The Concept of a Normal Vote," in *Elections and the Political Order,* ed. Angus Campbell, Philip E. Converse, Warren E. Miller, and Donald E. Stokes (New York: Wiley, 1966), pp. 9–39.

24. Ladd, "On Mandates, Realignments, and the 1984 Presidential Election."

25. We have not looked at two other core New Deal groups, Jews and Hispanics, due to their small sample size in the ANES survey.

26. Paul R. Abramson, John H. Aldrich, and David W. Rohde, *Change and Continuity in the 1980 Elections,* rev. ed. (Washington, D.C.: CQ Press, 1983); Russell J. Dalton, Scott Flanagan, and Paul Allen Beck, eds., *Electoral Change in Advanced*

Industrial Democracies. (Princeton: Princeton University Press, 1984); Ladd, "On Mandates, Realignments, and the 1984 Presidential Election"; John R. Petrocik, *Party Coalitions* (Chicago: University of Chicago Press, 1981); James L. Sundquist, *Dynamics of the Party System,* rev. ed. (Washington, D.C.: Brookings Institute, 1983).

27. New York Times/CBS News exit poll.

28. Pomper, *The Election of 1984*, p. 83.

29. Martin Carnoy and Manuel Castells, "After the Crisis," *World Policy Journal* (Spring 1984); 495–515.

The Coalition at the End of the Rainbow: The 1984 Jackson Campaign

11

*Lorenzo Morris
and Linda F. Williams*

Without a doubt one of the single most significant elements of the presidential campaign of 1984 was Jesse Jackson's candidacy for the Democratic presidential nomination. The 1984 election would hardly have been interesting without it. Other leading candidates in the race tread well-known ground. By 1984 Ronald Reagan, his campaign style, themes, targeted constituencies, and policy priorities and orientations were well known. The Mondale campaign, too, offered few surprises. Typical of the party out of power, Walter Mondale was closer to the traditional kind of Democratic party candidate than other recent nominees. Indeed, it is a commentary on how far we have changed from the traditional party epoch that Mondale was criticized as "the candidate of special interests" because he tried to put the New Deal coalition back together. Gary Hart, while far less of a household name than other leading candidates in 1984, also seized upon the increasingly typical political style. For all his talk of "new ideas," Hart was closest in style to Ronald Reagan in 1984 and appealed heavily to conservative independents.

What made the Jackson campaign new and distinct to American voters was not simply or even primarily his racial identity nor the fact that he had never held political office, but most especially that he sought to mobilize the support of the historically dispossessed, a "rainbow coalition" of blacks, hispanics, women, young people, lower-income whites, and activists from various liberal causes. Historically, most of these groups have voted at far lower rates than affluent and middle-income whites. Typically they have been referred to as marginal voters—groups far more difficult to mobilize in large numbers.[1]

This essay examines why Jackson chose to mobilize these groups, his success in this effort, the constraints he faced, and implications of the 1984 attempt for the future of the Rainbow Coalition.

The Decision to Seek Multi-Ethnic Support

With the decision to run for president, Jackson, like every other candidate, had to decide on his key objectives, his programmatic concerns, and his chief potential constituencies. In determining the constituency toward which his campaign would be primarily directed, Jackson faced three choices.

First, he could seek black votes only—a kind of "blacks alone for black development strategy." If he selected this option, his candidacy would be a "protest," raising issues in the interest of blacks but giving up from the start all hope of securing a large block of votes. Running a protest campaign could have met several of Jackson's objectives: increasing black registration and voting, allowing Jackson to speak out on issues of great concern to blacks, and perhaps curtailing the rightward drift of the Democratic party.

What a "blacks alone" protest strategy could not do, however, was garner enough votes outside the black community to make Jackson and his supporters a central bargaining bloc within the Democratic party through which the interests he represented might have a critical impact on convention proceedings including the fashioning of the platform and the selection of the eventual nominee. Nor, given the small size of the black electorate, could Jackson be perceived as a serious contender for the nomination if he appealed only to blacks. If Jackson had not presented himself as a serious candidate, he and his representatives would not have been allocated places in the major party convention committees. They would not have been included in National Democratic mailings and fundraisers and appeared in Democratic party presidential debates. If he were not a serious candidate, he would have been denied much-needed media exposure. The perception of Jackson as a serious contender rested on his repeated insistence that he was in the campaign to win and to win by attracting a constituency far wider than blacks alone, a majority constituency.

Given a decision to appeal to a majority constituency, two other strategy alternatives remained. He could attempt to develop a coalition of blacks and middle-class whites with a vague emphasis on "progress" and a low emphasis on economic justice issues. Such a strategy had been demonstrated successfully by black mayoral candidates Andrew Young and Wilson Goode.[2] Alternatively, he could seek to align blacks with low-status whites and other minority groups in an interracial coalition emphasizing economic justice.

To have chosen the middle-class coalition approach, even if successful, would have negated Jackson's concerns for a fairer and more humane domestic and foreign policy agenda. Moreover, he would have found it difficult to differentiate himself from other Democratic contenders, especially Mondale, and he would have lost some, if not most, of his appeal to his nearly guaranteed voter base, blacks. Thus Jackson was largely compelled to choose the economic justice strategy. It had the potential of achieving all of the objectives of a protest candidacy plus providing Jackson with enough relevancy to other constituencies to be perceived as a serious candidate.

In an effort to coordinate black protest objectives with a wider constituency, Jackson in his announcement speech declared:

> This candidacy is not for blacks only. This is a national campaign growing out of the black experience and seen through the eyes of the black perspective—which is the experience and perspective of the rejected. Because of this experience, I can empathize with the plight of Appalachia because I have known poverty. I know the pain of anti-Semitism because I have felt the humiliation of discrimination. I know first hand the shame of breadlines and the horror of hopelessness and despair because my life has been dedicated to empowering the world's rejected to become respected. Thus, our perspective encompasses and includes more of the American people and their respective interests than do most other experiences.[3]

To attract people with diverse interests, Jackson sought to identify key issues which he could use to assemble a Rainbow Coalition. The roots of his issues agenda were in the Great Society and the poor and minority groups it had helped to politicize. Hence, his early proposals included a massive public employment program and renewed federal spending on social services. To appeal to antiwar activists whose political orientations had been formed in the 1960s, Jackson's foreign policy centered on the third world and on his pledge to reduce defense spending and secure the nuclear freeze. To attract women voters, from the start he argued that political tickets should be "balanced" sexually and racially, not simply regionally or on the liberal-conservative continuum. To win the support of American Indians, Jackson said he recognized the right of Indian people to represent nations, not just reservations, and that he would take the money that now goes to the Bureau of Indian Affairs and give it directly to the tribes. To appeal to farmers, he attacked the Reagan administration's farm policies, particularly the payment-in-kind program (PIK), which he described as a "pickpocket program" benefiting large and wealthy farmers. Jackson promised genuine programs of reform to improve the plight of farmers. To win the Hispanic vote, Jackson discussed the common interests of blacks and Hispanics and pledged programs to end the additional discrimination Hispanics suffer due to the language barrier. On the basis of these key issues Jackson promised not only to run himself but to field 10,000 Rainbow candidates for office at every level. The achievements and limitations of Jackson's economic justice strategy can be evaluated on the basis of this agenda.

Giving Rainbow Dimensions to the Campaign

Clearly Jackson got overwhelming black support. Estimates of Jackson's black support range from 59 percent of all blacks in the JCPS/Gallup survey to 85 percent in an internal Jackson campaign memo based upon CBS/*New York*

Table 1. Profile of Jackson's black support

	% Jackson	% Mondale	% Hart
Age			
18–29	68	18	6
30–49	62	29	3
50+	29	46	18
Region			
East	57	31	4
Midwest	55	34	4
South	61	29	4
West	56	24	6
Education			
Not high school graduate	49	41	2
High school graduate	67	22	3
College	59	25	10
Three most important campaign issues			
Unemployment	66	73	44
Help poor	47	47	24
Civil rights	41	34	34
Support/oppose affirmative action			
Support	55	41	37
Oppose	25	29	47
Compared with 5 years ago is the situation of black people better, worse, or about the same?			
Better	33	41	44
Worse	33	25	27
Same	33	31	27
Most white people want blacks to get a better break, keep blacks down, or don't care either way			
Get break	19	32	35
Keep down	44	30	38
Don't care	31	31	20
Pace of black rights gains			
Just right	12	27	30
Too fast	4	5	8
Too slow	81	66	58
Family financial situation compared to 4 years ago			
Better	27	35	41
Worse	49	37	25
Same	22	26	32

Source: JCPS/Gallup Poll, Summer 1984.

Table 2. Group support for candidates in the 1984 Democratic primaries

	Share of Primary Electorate	% Mondale	% Hart	% Jackson
Age				
18–29	17	26	39	26
30–44	30	30	38	23
45–59	24	41	34	18
60 and over	28	52	31	10
Education				
Less than high school	14	51	26	18
High school graduate	33	43	34	16
Some college	27	33	38	21
College grad	26	31	41	20
Ideology				
Liberal	27	34	36	25
Moderate	47	41	37	15
Conservative	21	37	34	16
Party				
Democrat	74	42	33	20
Independent	20	28	44	16
Race				
White	78	42	43	5
Black	18	19	3	77
Sex				
Male	46	38	36	17
Female	54	39	35	20
Union household	33	45	31	19

Source: Adam Clymer, "The 1984 National Primary," *Public Opinion*, August-September 1984, 53. Clymer's table combines data from exit polls in twenty-four states plus vote totals from secretaries of state.

Times polls.[4] Jackson did well especially among younger, southern, financially strapped, and more highly educated blacks. It also appears that racial consciousness spurred Jackson's support. Jackson did better with those blacks who listed civil rights as one of the three most important issues of the 1984 campaign, those who supported affirmative action, those who believed the situation of blacks was worse in 1984 than five years prior, those who believed whites want to keep blacks down, and those who thought that racial progress was moving too slowly. (see table 1).

Analysts from the *New York Times* combined the results from exit polls in twenty-four separate primaries into a single survey as if there had been one

Table 3. Jackson's support from nonblacks: Selected states

State	Total vote for Jackson	Total votes for Jackson from nonblacks	% Jackson's Total Votes from nonblacks
Alabama	83,943	1,624	1.9
California	544,953	266,777	50.0
Georgia	143,754	6,655	4.6
Illinois	348,479	62,726	18.0
Indiana	98,223	27,777	28.3
Maryland	129,256	31,484	24.4
Massachusetts	31,548	22,031	69.8
New York	355,315	115,426	32.5
Ohio	236,947	45,240	19.1
Pennsylvania	265,007	64,344	24.3

Source: Estimates were calculated from data in *Congressional Quarterly Weekly Report*, June 16, 1984, p. 1443, and U.S. Census Bureau, *Current Population Reports*, Series P-20.

extended national primary election (see table 2). This analysis shows that in terms of age and education Jackson and Hart voters were similar; i.e., support for Hart and Jackson dwindled with increasing age and increased with higher education while Mondale attracted older and less educated voters. The central distinguishing factor, however, between Jackson and Hart voters was race. While in this analysis Jackson won 77 percent of the black vote but only 5 percent of the white vote, Hart, by contrast, carried the white vote in all but seven states yet won only 3 percent of the black vote.

Because Jackson received only 5 percent of the white vote, most analysts concluded that no interracial hue was added to the basic black of Jackson's Rainbow. While this conclusion is reasonable, it has been overstated. An examination of the proportion of Jackson's total votes from nonblacks provides a clearer picture of the campaign's diverse support. While Jackson won only 5 percent of the white electorate, white votes accounted for 22 percent, or approximately 788,000, of Jackson's total 3.4 million votes nationwide.[5] In fact, the proportion of Jackson's total votes from nonblacks was substantial in every non-Deep South state, ranging from lows of 18 percent and 19 percent of Jackson's total vote in Illinois and Ohio respectively to highs of 33 percent, 50 percent, and 70 percent of Jackson's total vote in New York, California, and Massachusetts respectively (see table 3). Clearly Jackson's showing in the various state primaries was importantly affected by his ability to win votes from ethnic and racial groups other than blacks.

Jackson's nonblack support came from all ethnic groups: Hispanics, Asians, and whites. In California and New York, where Hispanics are concentrated,

Table 4. Ethnic vote for Jackson in selected states

Region and State	% Black	% Hispanic	% White	% Jewish	% Asian
South/Central					
Alabama	50	—	4	—	—
Georgia	61	—	1	—	—
North Carolina	84	—	3	—	—
Maryland	83	—	5	—	—
Florida	62	—	2	2	—
Northeast					
New York	78	33	8	5	—
Pennsylvania	77	33	4	8	—
Massachusetts	51	—	3	2	—
Connecticut	69	—	4	5	—
Midwest					
Illinois	79	—	4	10	—
Ohio	81	—	5	—	—
Indiana	71	—	3	—	—
Wisconsin	70	—	7	—	—
West					
California	78	14	9	8	16

Source: CBS/*New York Times* and NBC News exit polls

Jackson won 14 percent and 33 percent respectively of the total Hispanic vote. Jackson also received 16 percent of the Asian vote in California (see table 4). Without votes from these ethnic groups and white voters, he would have received only one-half as many votes in California and two-thirds as many votes in New York, his top two vote-getting states.

Finally, Jackson's achievements in winning Rainbow support cannot be fully measured by public opinion polling data. One must also take into account the inroads he made in winning support from leaders of nonblack ethnic groups. For example, in California Jackson was supported by Mario Obledo. Obledo served as a cabinet member under former Governor Jerry Brown and was then president of the League of United Latin American Citizens (LULAC), the nation's largest Hispanic organization. Obledo said he encouraged Jackson to run "because he seems to be the only candidate addressing the issues basic to the Hispanic community."[6] As a reaction to the Jackson campaign, Cesar Chavez, the farm labor leader, sought to forge a statewide Hispanic-black coalition to press a "Hispanic-black agenda" before the Democratic National Convention's 1984 platform committee. Virginia Reade, another of the Chavez group's organizers, vigorously worked in the Jackson campaign. Similarly,

Tony Bonilla, the past president of LUCLAC, endorsed Jackson and was critical to his campaign in Texas. Bonilla became Hispanic desk coordinator for the Jackson campaign. Other Rainbow Coalition staff included Barbara Honegger, formerly an official at the Justice Department, who concentrated on women's issues; Redbird, a Wisconsin Chippewa and formerly an activist with the American Indian Movement, who directed native American efforts; Marisa Tamari, formerly with the Arab-American Anti-Discrimination Committee, who served as coordinator of efforts among Arab-Americans, and Ann Gyorgy, formerly of Ralph Nader's Critical Mass Energy Project, who coordinated efforts to attract environmentalists.

Additionally, ethnic groups formed their own associations. For example, in New York, a latinos for Jackson organization was started in December of 1983, and Bill Chong, a 27-year-old tenant organizer in New York's Chinatown formed Asian-Americans for Jackson. Similarly, prominent members of the American Agriculture Movement, such as Darrell Ringer, supported Jackson.

The gay community, in Washington and New York especially, were also strong Jackson supporters. Throughout much of New York City, especially in Greenwich Village, white leafleteers could be found outside polling places asking passers-by to vote for Jackson. In Washington gays raised funds for Jackson at bars and house parties and dispatched motorcades mounted with loudspeakers through neighborhood streets, exhorting residents to register and vote. Many of the nonblack supporters empathized with blacks who felt locked out of the political process or in other ways estranged from the majority. Their motivations for supporting Jackson largely centered around a class-conscious sympathy for the disadvantaged.[7]

In the absence of sufficient data, an analysis of the full demographic characteristics of Jackson's nonblack support is impossible. Analysis of CBS/*New York Times* exit poll data of voters in the New York and Pennsylvania primaries, however, infers that Jackson's white voters were more likely to be liberals, independents, voters for John Anderson in 1980, and college graduates. Their second choice for the Democratic presidential nomination was Hart. Similarly, more white working women tended to support Jackson than white men or women in the aggregate (see table 5). Data from the JCPS/Gallup survey support these conclusions. These data reveal that Jackson did better with whites who were part of the 1960s generation (30 to 49 year olds) and college graduates. As compared to Mondale's and Hart's white voters, white voters who supported Jackson were much more likely to believe that the pace of black progress was too slow and much less likely to oppose affirmative action. They were also more likely to favor increasing spending on social programs and say that their family financial situation had worsened in the last four years (see table 6).

Table 5. Profile of Jackson's white support in two states

	% New York	% Pennsylvania
Sex		
Men	6	5
Women	6	4
Working Women	9	6
Age		
18–29	8	5
30–44	6	7
45–59	7	3
60+	4	3
Party ID		
Democrat	4	4
Independent	14	8
Political orientation		
Liberal	8	6
Moderate	4	4
Conservative	5	5
Family Financial situation		
Better	4	6
Worse	6	5
Same	7	4
1980 Presidential vote		
Carter	4	3
Reagan	5	5
Anderson	11	12
1983 Family Income (in thousands of dollars)		
Under 12.5	5	4
12.5–24.9	7	5
25–34.9	8	5
35–50	5	4
Over 50	4	8
Education		
Not high school graduate	1	3
High school graduate	4	3
Some college, not graduate	5	4
College graduate	9	10

Source: CBS/*New York Times* exit polls.

Table 6. Selected issue preferences of white voters

Issues	% Jackson	% Mondale	% Hart
Spend more/less on social programs			
Less	21	25	28
More	64	56	51
Support/oppose affirmative action			
Support	18	11	8
Oppose	59	72	75
Family financial situation compared to 4 years ago			
Better	39	34	44
Worse	41	34	30
Same	20	31	25
Satisfied with the way things are going in United States			
Satisfied	26	32	39
Dissatisfied	64	57	45

Source: JCPS/Gallup Survey, Summer 1984

In sum, while Jackson won only a small percentage of the votes of other ethnic groups, he was not engaging in mere wishful thinking about the potential for a rainbow coalition. While no full rainbow was visible, the campaign did exhibit a rainbow glow—certainly more than Hart's campaign, which won an even smaller proportion of blacks than Jackson won of whites. No one seriously expected overnight success in building the rainbow, but the inspirational effect of the campaign on blacks and other minority groups was massive.

The Racial Factor

Although Jackson's presidential campaign was by far the most successful ever attempted by a black candidate in terms of the votes received and delegates elected, the rainbow's impact on the national election was relatively marginal. First, the Rainbow Coalition did not significantly influence the platform and outcome of the Democratic convention (most if not all of Jackson's minority planks were rejected). Second, his votes were not transferable to other black candidates running for offices at higher levels of government. For example, six of the congressional districts won by Jackson were won by white congressional opponents of black candidates. Moreover, black candidates (who were not incumbents or running in open seats in majority black districts) were generally unsuccessful in competing for state legislative seats. Third, the dissatisfaction with the performance of the Reagan administration, which Jackson reinforced, was far from sufficient to prevent a Reagan landslide at the polls. For the results to have been different in each instance, the size of black turnout needed to be larger and a much bigger and more inclusive Rainbow Coalition created. Historical patterns and population size easily explain the limitations of the black vote but not the weakness of the coalition. What happened to the coalition?

The most obvious external cause of Jackson's failure to attract a larger segment of a rainbow coalition can be traced to the history of racism in the United States. Various ethnic groups encountered prejudice when they settled in the United States. Yet with the exception of Native Americans, no group has consistently experienced problems comparable to those of blacks. While progress has been made in recent years, the old dormant forms of unvarnished white male supremacy have resurfaced among extreme Reaganites in their attempts to redefine racism, discrimination, and civil rights in ways which limit black mobility. The bitter controversies in the last four years over administration-supported tax breaks for segregated academies, the administration's reluctance to support the Voting Rights Act and the King holiday bill, the Justice Department's refusal to enforce long-established civil rights policies such as busing and affirmative action; the partisan nature of the Civil Rights Commission and its propaganda war against civil rights, and Reagan's old stump speeches about "welfare queens" and "young bucks" with food stamps have revived an ugly legacy. In the context of this resurgent racism it is phenomenal that a black candidate secured as many votes from whites as Jackson did.

The bandwagon effect of American political campaigns makes Jackson's white vote achievement even more significant.[8] Interestingly, Jackson's profile among whites was surprisingly positive, and comparable to Mondale's in most respects. Whites in the aggregate found the two Democrats to be about equally hard-working and compassionate; they gave Jackson the edge in being exciting, getting things done, owing fewer favors, representing a new way of thinking, and being a strong leader. The differences that whites saw between the two men were just as noteworthy, however: Jackson was considered not only less knowledgeable, but also less fair, less likely to "care about people like me" (i.e., other whites), and far more prejudiced (see table 7). This pattern of white reactions to a black candidate has ample precedent: whites commonly fear that "powerful blacks in high office will prove antiwhite and will openly discriminate against whites in jobs, services, and taxes."[9] Additionally, in poll after poll, few whites indicated that they believed a black man in general, or Jesse Jackson in particular, had a chance to become president in 1984. Most white voters concluded that the nation "was not ready for a black president."[10] Skepticism about Jackson's candidacy was not limited to white voters, the press, and Democratic party leaders. Black leaders, as well, did much to reinforce the preconceived notion that Jackson could not win.[11] That so many voters would cast their votes for a candidate with no chance to win

Table 7. White perceptions of Jackson and Mondale

	% Jackson	% Mondale
Knowledgeable	58	74
Prejudiced	56	17
Hard-working	78	77
Exciting	53	16
Can get things done	49	37
Compassionate	57	58
Owes a lot of political favors	34	49
Cares about people like me	37	49
Clear on issues	37	49
Would be too quick to use military force	15	10
Represents a new way of thinking	62	30
Fair	46	66
A strong leader	45	32

Source: JCPS/Gallup survey

shows both the extraordinary vote-getting ability of Jackson and the still more extraordinary reorientation of many Americans toward the voting alternatives.

Yet racism was a critical factor in limiting Jackson's nonblack support. However circumspect reporters may have been, racial issues were daily fare in the media. While the media was definitive about Jackson's right to enter the presidential race and while Jackson was portrayed as a participant in democratic procedures, the media declared Jackson an outsider from the beginning of his campaign. Throughout the campaign Jackson expressed frustration that the media described him as a "black" leader and yet they did not refer to Mondale, Hart, or others as "white" leaders. Jackson's *black* designation only heightened the racial image many white Americans held of Jackson's candidacy and constricted his potential appeal to other parts of the rainbow.

In the end the news media recognized that most white Americans would never vote for any black candidate for president in 1984. In large part their reports became a self-fulfilling prophecy that further guaranteed the United States was not ready to elect a black man as president. In the words of Anthony Broh, the media covered Jackson's candidacy closely, but they always treated him as "a horse of a different color." [12] Race and racism, then, were Jackson's biggest constraints in appealing to a wide range of voters.

Campaign Organizing

A second constraint on Jackson's potential to appeal to a wider range of voters was lack of sufficient campaign funds. Jackson had done no serious fundraising prior to his announcement; the campaign organization operated with little knowledge of campaign finance laws; and there had been no pretesting of fundraising procedures such as direct-mail fundraising. In the end, while Mondale spent $25 million in the nomination campaign and Hart spent approximately $14 million, Jackson spent only $6 million or approximately one-fourth the amount of the front runner.[13] The United States stands out among the world's nations in the extent to which private wealth can be converted into political influence. Although the candidate who spends the most does not always win the contest, fundraising and spending decisions inevitably affect strategies and the final outcome.[14]

Additionally, Jackson's pattern of campaign spending was not appropriately structured for winning a wide coalition. Advertising, ordinarily the largest single expenditure in a presidential campaign, ranked very low in the Jackson campaign expenditures. One consequence was a lack of control over public relations. For example, questionable media overtures to the campaign were not met with an internally initiated, independent national media campaign. Without a paid media campaign Jackson was left at the mercy of news coverage to get any message across to the rainbow.[15] Consequently his message was never clear. More important, he could never control or direct the message.

The fundraising constraint led to another constraint. Limited funding compounded by lack of preparation and inadequate distribution of staff and office resources. From its inception Jackson's presidential effort demonstrated a considerable, although understandable, lack of coordination. His campaign staff had a large number of enthusiastic but inexperienced novices. In the days immediately following Jackson's announcement of his candidacy, there were not even enough telephone lines in the Washington national headquarters for operatives desiring to establish local offices or for volunteers wishing to make contact with the national campaign.

Beginning his campaign later than any of the other candidates, Jackson had little time to gather signatures or file papers to get on many state ballots. Thus an inordinate amount of effort and time had to be spent on this matter late into the campaign season. Concomitantly, papers requesting matching funds were not filed with the Federal Election Commission until mid-January 1984. All of these technical activities consumed much of the time the campaign should have been using to promote the institutionalization of the Rainbow Coalition.

Limited resources and time constraints inhibited the campaign's ability to effectively draw other black leaders and organizations into the campaign structure. While the black church, for example, was a major source of support and black unity for the campaign, its latent potential for concrete political organizing in the context of a coalition was not developed. On the positive side, the black church provided an important reprieve from the dollar dilemma for the campaign. Black ministers across the country frequently emerged as chairmen of local Jackson organizations. They formed a self-funding network of support. Yet, black church support-building is limited to black voters. The black church was virtually helpless in building an interracial coalition in the absence of ties to a larger campaign strategy. Moreover, the church cannot be counted on as an organizational core. "The church and other nonpolitical institutions are obviously handicapped by their very nature: politics is only a subsidiary purpose for the pastors and their congregations." [16]

In sum, a major weakness of Jackson's campaign was its level of disorganization. Campaigns which seek to mobilize a coalition for economic justice unquestionably depend on identifying key issues which appeal to various groups. But awareness of citizen sympathy with the goals of one's campaign is worthless if citizens are not mobilized to vote. How well candidates organize their campaigns therefore constitutes a variable independent from substance of the issues. On this variable the Jackson campaign was seriously deficient.

Personal Leadership Characteristics

Another set of problems stemmed indirectly from the candidate's own personal propensities and style. Misunderstandings, gaffes, and blunders are dangers in any campaign, but they are particularly destructive in a nontraditional campaign. Of course, the most difficult gaffe for Jackson involved his reference to Jews as "Hymies" and New York as "Hymietown." It came just at the time that Jackson's hope of building a rainbow coalition began to have greater possibilities—i.e., in January 1984 after Jackson's return from Syria, where he negotiated the release of Navy Lt. Robert Goodman.

From the start tensions and antipathies existed between the black and Jewish communities over issues such as Israel and affirmative action. In early November 1985 a "Jews against Jackson" ad was placed in the *New York Times*, showing a picture of Jackson embracing Palestinian leader Yasir Arafat. Although the ad was condemned by organized Jewish groups, Jackson was consequently bound to have difficulty attracting Jewish voters. The reference to Hymies was followed by incendiary comments made by campaign supporter and head of the Nation of Islam, Minister Louis Farrakhan. Farrakhan's denunciation of Zionists, Israel, and Jewish organizations dashed all hopes of securing anything more than a very small minority of the Jewish vote. In addition, the controversy undoubtedly hurt Jackson's chances with other parts of the rainbow.

Both episodes touched off a firestorm in the press. The media starkly characterized the comments as anti-Semitic. It is fair to say that Jackson's remark was given far more attention by the media than similar blunders by other presidential candidates: no one thought Jimmy Carter should quit in 1976 when he used the phrase "ethnic purity," and Ronald Reagan got far less attention from his 1980 slur of Italian Americans and his unsolicited admission that he did not know the United States had race relations problems until the 1960s. Nor had anyone asked Reagan to apologize for his Ku Klux Klan endorsement in 1980. However, the media turned Jackson's disparaging comment about Jews into a devastating event in 1984 by treating it as if it were an intentional expression of a political position.

In New Hampshire, where his campaign had been drawing large, enthusiastic crowds of young people and registering many new voters, the controversy over the Hymie comment erased Jackson's possibility of gaining many rainbow votes. By some estimates it cost Jackson an additional 10 percent share of the vote in New Hampshire. (He actually received 5 percent.) By the end of the campaign, 54 percent of whites and 15 percent of blacks told JCPS/Gallup pollsters they considered Jackson prejudiced. As the primary season wore on, Jackson continued to call for a broad multiracial coalition, but he seemed to concentrate his energies on winning black votes. This ultimate reduction in the reach of campaign issues was perhaps the most important internal constraint inhibiting the attraction of rainbow votes.

Issue Development

The key issues in any campaign seeking to mobilize a coalition of the dispossessed and disadvantaged ought to be economic redistribution and fairness. Any candidate hoping to mobilize such a coalition in 1984 would have had to emphasize full employment, social security, tax fairness for working people, and similar issues. Public support for these kinds of issues remains high. Even Democrats who voted for Reagan supported activist government involvement on behalf of working people. For example, in the Fingerhut/Granados poll, conducted on election day, 75 percent of Reagan Democrats agreed that government should do more to protect ordinary Americans from banks and big corporations; and 83 percent agreed that government has a responsibility to see that every able-bodied person in the country has an opportunity to work. Protection for the ordinary man from the special interests of corporations and their political supporters and access to jobs are the likely cornerstones of any campaign for support from those historically deprived.

From the start Jackson spoke of helping the poor, creating jobs, and guaranteeing equality of opportunity, but these issues remained, as they did with the other leading Democratic contenders, without grounding in concrete programs and proposals. As the campaign progressed, Jackson's public image projected these issues less and less.

Although Jackson broke no new ground in foreign policy issues, he forced other Democrats out on such issues as disinvestment in South Africa and thus narrowed the lines of demarcation. Moreover, although Jackson won a certain measure of respect when he secured the release of Lt. Goodman, this isolated accomplishment was far outweighed by Jackson's lack of service in government, much less experience in foreign policy, and his later efforts to repeat the Goodman episode with personal visits to Nicaragua and Cuba. In these latter two instances, the media and the opposing candidates were able to portray the visits as unsophisticated toadying to Communist regimes. Finally, the foreign policy positions of Mondale, Hart, and Jackson seemed to have figured little in voters' choices. Voters did rank foreign relations third and nuclear arms control fourth on their list of issue concerns, but taken together the various economic issues that filled out the rest of the top ten slots far outnumbered them.[17] Exit polls during the primaries and on general election day suggested that the economy underlay voters' decisions far more than anything else.[18]

On domestic issues the difference between Jackson and other candidates seemed to be largely one of degree rather than kind. Aside from the dual primary and affirmative action goals and timetables, he was not significantly different from Hart and Mondale, who also had liberal domestic agendas. Like other Democrats, Jackson discussed the need to rebuild America, improve the nation's infrastructure, provide plant closing legislation, and create jobs, but he proposed no concrete plans.

As the campaign wore on, Jackson's focus appeared to narrow. While he kept arguing that the Democrats should become the party of jobs, peace, new foreign policy, corporate responsibility, inclusion of the rejected, and fairness, the issue which he chose to be the litmus test of Democratic commitment to the Rainbow Coalition was the second primary. Just before the Democratic convention, Jackson's proposals for the dispossessed appeared to contract into a focus on electoral inclusion. Thus he spoke of the poor's self-interest in "ousting their oppressor" through voting and the need to end the political disenfranchisement and underrepresentation of the poor.[19] In short, near the end of the campaign the central focus became voting rights, especially the runoff primary, rather than the kinds of economic issues which could have melded the interests of many groups.

The overall timing of Jackson's retrenchment on issues may well indicate an adaptive response to a shrinking pool of potential support. By the time the "Super Tuesday" of southern primaries came around, the campaign had to recognize the limits of its white constituency and its dependence on the old civil rights black constituency. Yet, it is unclear that the runoff primary, as an issue in itself, even attracted many black voters. For example, the Fingerhut/ Granados poll found that only 15 percent of registered black voters and 15 percent of Jackson voters considered the runoff primary as an important issue.[20] In southern states with runoff primaries, such as North Carolina, 50 percent of those who voted for Jackson answered that the "runoff primary system is fair;" only 41 percent believed it to be "unfair to voters" like themselves.[21] In sum, it would appear that the runoff primary as a lead issue was a poor choice for mobilizing black voters and a totally irrelevant choice for mobilizing the rest of the rainbow. The campaign's shrinking issues agenda, then, also limited Jackson's potential to build the rainbow.

Prospects for the Future

The Rainbow Coalition did not come to full bloom in the presidential election of 1984. The coalition's potential for development was weakened by external and internal factors. While some members of each ethnic and racial group voted for Jackson, a broadly representative number of coalition voters failed to materialize. Jackson was left without sufficient strength to make the coalition a strong bargaining bloc at the Democratic convention and a significant force in the general election. To be sure, the coalition's bargaining strength was further weakened by Democratic party rules which worked in favor of front-runners and against those who sought new leadership and a new direction. Whereas Jackson got 18.3 percent of the primary votes, he got only 10 percent of the delegates. For all its originality and all of Jackson's magnificent eloquence and dramatic flair, the Jackson campaign was mostly significant for its lack of influence on the outcome. Blacks again had to confront the fact that they were a captive constituency—essential to any Democratic hopes of winning the presidency, even more important in the close Senate and gubernatorial races, but lacking significant influence either at the nominating convention or during the fall campaign.

Despite some analysts' (and later Mondale's) claims, no data exist to show that Jackson and the rainbow hurt Walter Mondale's chances in the general election. In fact, there is much evidence to the contrary: the black vote was 5.3 percentage points higher in 1984 than it was in 1980, and for the first time blacks composed more than 10 percent of the American electorate. Jackson increased black registration and turnout and thus helped the Democratic nominee. For example, the Committee for the Study of the American Electorate found that 67 percent of all black new registrants credited the Jackson campaign with influencing them to register. The growing number of black registered voters and the higher rate of black voter turnout helped Walter Mondale. Ninety percent of black voters voted for the Democratic nominee. Moreover, according to CBS/*New York Times* exit polls, while 17 percent of voters said the Jackson campaign made them less likely to vote for the Democratic nominee, 21 percent said the Jackson campaign made them more likely to vote for the Democratic nominee. Thus, at worst, the effect of the Jackson campaign on Mondale's chances was a draw. But Reagan's overwhelming popularity with other voters made the black vote meaningless.

Events after the 1984 elections left the future role of blacks in the American two-party system very uncertain. The 1988 Jackson campaign, though numerically more successful, resolved none of the racial issues in party politics. At best, Democrats are still taking black votes for granted and Republicans are still writing off black votes. At worst, the situation for blacks could be deteriorating. Reagan administration leaders are engaging in concerted attempts to ideologically disrupt blacks and divide the nation through attacks on established civil rights policy. Whatever lingering chance may have existed for detente between Reagan and blacks has probably evaporated in the wake of continued attacks on black leadership, affirmative action, and the black poor. Ironically, many of these attacks emanate from the few blacks who have marginally penetrated the Reagan fold, such as the former chairman of the United States Commission on Civil Rights and the chairman of the Equal Employment Opportunity Commission.

Simultaneously, Democrats are abandoning the concerns of blacks and moving toward the political center to feed what some have called "the revenge of the white male." Some of the postelection decisions of the Democratic National Committee and controversies over convention rules such as the delegate threshhold and electoral laws such as the runoff primary raise questions about the role of blacks in the party's future. Additionally, liberal Democratic leaders such as Edward Kennedy joined hands with staunchly conservative Republican leaders such as Phil Gramm to pass balanced budget legislation which will undoubtedly disproportionately cut programs which benefit blacks most.

With or without a Republican taking power in the White House in 1988 (unlike in four of the five last elections), it will matter little for blacks and the poor if Democrats have become the party of conservative "Me-too-ism." An ideological realignment in an age of party dealignment would still leave the lower strata of Americans without adequate representation, and this is precisely what is possible. The elections of 1984 may have essentially ideological consequences for federal policy.

Already liberal discretionary policies have been cut back, whether filing antitrust and equal-employment opportunity suits or strictly enforcing environmental and occupational safety regulations. After eight years the Reagan administration will have appointed more than half the federal judiciary serving lifetime terms, including perhaps a majority of the Supreme Court. One should well wonder whether in 1990 such things as affirmative action goals and timetables and the *Roe v. Wade* abortion decision will still stand as the law of the land.

The budgetary consequences of a conservative policy triumph will likely fall into three broad areas: a less progressive tax system, a severely reduced welfare state, and a military establishment that gets as much as 50 percent more than presently. The most difficult part of the conservative agenda to enact would be huge cuts in middle-class social welfare programs (such as guaranteed student loans and mortgage tax deductions) because they have so many vocal and voting beneficiaries. But it would be politically possible to cut programs that disproportionately benefit blacks and the poor further. A reputed "tax break" for the very poor will add more momentum to cutting programs which presently benefit them.

What are the future prospects for black politics in this scenario? One option is to forsake a strong emphasis on presidential politics and concentrate on running more black state, local, and congressional candidates. But, given the hegemonic powers of the executive branch and the national government, it is unlikely that electing a dozen or so more black congressmen (difficult as that would be) and even numerous state and local officials could substantially alter power or policy. Still, the states and localities have historically been the source of innovative policy, so electing more blacks at these levels is clearly worth the attempt.

A second possibility is that the Jackson candidacy may have actually re-legitimized the American electoral system to such an extent that blacks will simply accept that they were beaten and a conservative agenda won fairly. Increasingly, blacks, especially middle-class blacks who vote most often, might feel that it is time to jump on the political bandwagon of conservatism to secure at least individualistic gains. Already a number of middle-class blacks have joined the conservative chorus asking, what's wrong with the black underclass, as opposed to, what's wrong with a system which fails to generate enough opportunities such as decent jobs to end underclass status for all? Their emphasis is placed on self-help, as if blacks have not historically helped themselves and as if blacks do not pay taxes and have a right to expect government to finance those programs that benefit them. Simultaneously, these voices deemphasize continuing structural inequality and the role of government intervention. That Reagan's job approval rating was rising among younger, better-educated, and more affluent blacks may be a further sign of potentially accommodationist behavior by some blacks.

A third possibility may be a growing disenchantment among blacks with two-party electoral politics. Given the lack of black influence on 1984 electoral outcomes and the rightward drift of Democrats as well as Republicans, one message blacks may well have received is that their embrace of mainstream politics got them little or nothing. This disenchantment sustains the belief among blacks that historically their most important gains have come from movement politics—direct action politics, politics in the street rather than the ballot-boxes. For example, a 1986 poll showed that six in ten blacks believe that "the only time the federal government really pays attention to black problems is when blacks resort to violent demonstrations or riots." [22]

Yet a majority of blacks said the chances of violent protests are much less now than they were five years ago.[23] Thus a related message blacks may have gotten is that the two-party system is not the only possible path in mainstream electoral politics. A third-party alternative, adopted as a compromise between direct action and continued participation in the Democratic party, is a distinct possibility. For example, a recent poll showed that 53 percent of blacks said it would be "a good idea" for a black leader like Jackson to run for president as an independent, while 37 percent said it would not be a good idea.[24] The presidential campaign of Jesse Jackson may have planted the seeds of a progressive multi-ethnic, multi-racial coalition which could ultimately support a third-party or independent candidacy.

This third option would require extensive and long-range organizing. Economic justice campaigns seeking to mobilize the historically disadvantaged can be constructed in two ways: (1) by individual candidates, so that loyalties are to that candidacy and coalition members and groups are submerged after the election; or (2) by an issue-oriented coalition which can be institutionalized. The coalition then chooses to support a particular candidate because of the candidate's agreement with the coalition's positions. Such a coalition would antedate the politician's campaign and would be expected to outlive the candidacy.

Jackson's 1984 campaign demonstrates the limitations of the first approach. Jackson, or any other candidate alone, could not bring the Rainbow Coalition to full maturity. It is the nature of coalitions that each component must find its own strength before the common cause is joined. To find its common basis for institutionalization, the coalition would have to include those leaders of various targeted groups who influence their own constituencies.

Jackson at least began to confront the issues and build a structure from which such a broad coalition could grow. While his campaign met with only the most limited success and once again demonstrated the persistence of racism in inhibiting campaigns for economic justice, the almost 800 thousand votes Jackson won from nonblack voters and the more than 2.5 million from black voters represents an initial step for coalition campaigns of economic justice. If campaigning stems from an issue-oriented, adequately organized, well-funded, and institutionalized coalition, it is likely to be well received. The potential components of a new larger coalition which Jackson identified are still in the free political marketplace. They are not being coopted by the increasingly restrictive major parties. Given the strong prospect of continued political and economic retrenchment, the response to a coalition invitation may be stronger after 1988. The Jackson campaign lost in the 1984 primaries, but the Rainbow Coalition may have only just begun.

NOTES

1. Norman Nie, Sidney Verba, and John Petrocik, *The Changing American Voter* (Cambridge: Harvard University Press, 1976). The authors summarize the sociological characteristics of "normal voters" in chapters 1 and 2.

2. In Young's successful high-status coalition strategy in his 1972 election to Congress, he appealed to whites with environmental, conservation, and good government issues. See Robert Holmes, "The Andrew Young for Congress Campaign, 1972: Some Reflections on Coalition Politics and the Struggle," paper presented at the annual meeting of the National Conference of Black Political Scientists, New Orleans, Louisiana, April 1973.

3. Jesse Jackson, quoted in Thomas E. Cavanagh and Lorn S. Foster, *Jesse Jackson's Campaign: The Primaries and Caucuses, Election '84 Report #2* (Washington, D.C.: Joint Center for Political Studies, 1984), p. 2.

4. Lorenzo Morris, L. F. Williams, and Acie Byrd, "Preliminary Review of Highlights of Rainbow Voter Participation in the Jackson Campaign" (unpublished paper, Washington, D.C., July 7, 1984).

5. Morris, Williams, and Byrd, "Preliminary Review of Highlights of Rainbow Voter Participation."

6. *Los Angeles Herald-Examiner,* November 13, 1983, A-1.

7. *Fort Lauderdale News,* May 2, 1984, A-4.

8. See Leo Bogart, *Silent at the Polls* (Cambridge: Harvard University Press, 1977), chapter 3.

9. See Thomas E. Cavanagh, *Inside Black America: The Message of the Black Vote in the 1984 Elections* (Washington, D.C.: Joint Center for Political Studies, 1985).

10. For example, in the NBC Illinois exit poll, only 46 percent of blacks and 21 percent of whites answered "yes" to the question, "Do you think the voters of this country are ready to elect a black president?"

11. Roger Wilkins, address to the Woodrow Wilson School, Princeton University, Princeton, New Jersey, October 4, 1984.

12. C. Anthony Broh, "Horse of a Different Color," paper presented at the Joint Center for Political Studies Conference on the 1984 Elections and the Future of Black Politics, Washington, D.C., April 30, 1985, p. 40.

13. Federal Election Commission, "Allocation of Primary Expenditures by State for a Presidential Candidate," October 20, 1984.

14. Michael Nelson, ed., *The Elections of 1984* (Washington, D.C.: Congressional Quarterly Press), p. 174.

15. Cavanagh and Foster, *Jesse Jackson's Campaign,* pp. 12–13.

16. Chandler Davison, *Biracial Politics* (Baton Rouge: Louisiana State University Press, 1972), p. 50.

17. David Treadwell, "National Security: The Public's Views on War and Peace," *National Journal,* October 20, 1984, p. 2006.

18. Hedrick Smith, "The Economy: Still the Key for Reagan," *New York Times,* November 7, 1984.

19. Jesse Jackson, "The Keys to a Democratic Victory in 1984," speech before the

Thirteenth Annual National Convention of Operation PUSH, Inc., Washington, D.C., June 7, 1984.

20. Fingerhut/Granados Opinion Research, "Major Findings of National Voter Survey on the 1984 Presidential Election and the Future of the Democratic Party" (Washington, D.C., November 8, 1984).

21. CBS/*New York Times,* North Carolina exit poll.

22. ABC/*Washington Post* poll, January 1986.

23. Ibid.

24. Ibid.

Notes on Contributors

LUCIUS J. BARKER, Edna Gellhorn Professor of Public Affairs and professor of political science at Washington University, is the author of *Civil Liberties and the Constitution*, 4th ed. (1982), *Black Americans and the Political System* (1980), *Freedom, Courts, Politics: Studies in Civil Liberties* (1972), and *Our Time Has Come: A Delegate's Diary of Jesse Jackson's 1984 Presidential Campaign* (1987).

RONALD W. WALTERS is professor of political science at Howard University. He is the author of numerous articles and scholarly monographs.

WILLIAM CROTTY is professor of political science at Northwestern University. He is the author of *American Political Parties in Decline*, 2nd ed. (1984), *Party Reform* (1983), and coauthor of *Presidential Primaries and Nominations* (1985).

JOSEPH P. McCORMICK II is a member of the Department of Political Science at Howard University, where he teaches courses in American politics and public policy. His research interests are in the areas of public policy formulation and black electoral behavior.

ROBERT C. SMITH is a member of the Department of Political Science at Howard University, where he teaches courses in black Politics. His research interests are in the areas of black political behavior, political leadership, and urban politics.

CURTINA MORELAND-YOUNG is the director of the Master of Public Policy and Administration Program at Jackson State University. She received her B.A. degree from Fisk University and her M.A. and Ph.D. from the University of Illinois at Champaign-Urbana. She has published widely and one of her areas of interest is the impact of minority and interest groups on the foreign policy process.

ROBERT G. NEWBY is presently an associate professor of sociology at Central Michigan University, on leave from Wayne State University. Professor Newby was a Jackson delegate to the 1984 national convention from Michigan's Sixth Congressional District. His research interests focus upon issues of race and class and social change.

ALVIN THORNTON is associate professor of political science at Howard University. He served as a member of the Democratic party 1984 Platform Committee and was director of issues for the Maryland Jackson for President Committee in 1984.

FREDERICK HUTCHINSON is a tax analyst with the Center on Budget and Policy Priorities in Washington, D.C. He was a member of the Maryland Jackson for President Committee in 1984.

JOHN F. ZIPP is an associate professor in the Department of Sociology and an assistant scientist at the Urban Research Center, both at the University of Wisconsin-Milwaukee. His two main research interests are electoral behavior and economic development.

LORENZO MORRIS teaches political science at Howard University. He is the author of several books, including *Elusive Equality: The Status of Black Americans in Higher Education* (1979). His most recent articles include analyses of development, education policy, and political parties. He has just completed the forthcoming volume, *The Social and Political Implications of the 1984 Jesse Jackson Campaign*. He taught previously at the Massachusetts Institute of Technology.

LINDA F. WILLIAMS is associate director of research at the Joint Center for Political Studies. She has published widely on electoral behavior and black politics. She has taught political science at Howard University and Cornell University. She, and her coauthor as well, received their doctorates from the University of Chicago.

Index